A World Without Cages

This book is the first collection to bring together scholars and activists working to end criminal and immigration detention. Employing an intersectional lens and an impressive variety of case studies, this book makes a compelling case to rethink what justice could mean for refugees, citizens, and everyone in between.

This book connects immigration detention and prison justice towards reimagining a newer, better future. The ten chapters probe the intersections of immigration detention with current and potential forms of citizenship, membership, belonging, and punishments. Deprivation of liberty is one of the most serious harms that someone can experience. Immigration control is a nation-building project where racial, gender, class, ableist, and other lines of discrimination filter and police access to permanent residence. Employing a kaleidoscope of interdisciplinary backgrounds, the contributors bring this focus to bear on case studies spanning North America, Europe, and Asia. In conversation with social movements challenging police brutality, the contributors are thinking through the implications of de-funding the police, overhauling the 'criminal justice' system, eradicating prisons (penal abolitionism), and ending all forms of containment (carceral abolitionism). Neither the prison nor the detention centre is an inevitable feature of our social lives. This book collectively argues that abolishing detention could pave the way for new visions of justice to emerge.

The chapters in this book were originally published as a special issue of *Citizenship Studies*.

Sharry Aiken is Associate Professor at Queen's University's Faculty of Law and affiliated with the Queen's Cultural Studies Program, Kingston, Canada. She is a past president of the Canadian Council for Refugees, Co-Editor of the *PKI Global Justice Journal*, and former Editor-in-Chief of the journal *Refuge*.

Stephanie J. Silverman is a researcher, consultant, educator, editor, and scholar. She received her DPhil from the University of Oxford (2013) as a commonwealth scholar, and served as the SSHRC Bora Laskin National Fellow in Human Rights (2015–2016), on faculty at the University of Toronto for six years, and at the Immigration and Refugee Board of Canada.

A World Without Cages

Bridging Immigration and Prison Justice

Edited by

Sharry Aiken and Stephanie J. Silverman

Routledge
Taylor & Francis Group
LONDON AND NEW YORK

First published 2022
by Routledge
4 Park Square, Milton Park, Abingdon, Oxon, OX14 4RN

and by Routledge
605 Third Avenue, New York, NY 10158

Routledge is an imprint of the Taylor & Francis Group, an informa business

British Library Cataloguing-in-Publication Data
A catalogue record for this book is available from the British Library

ISBN13: 978-1-032-19789-0 (hbk)
ISBN13: 978-1-032-19790-6 (pbk)
ISBN13: 978-1-003-26086-8 (ebk)

DOI: 10.4324/9781003260868

Typeset in Minion Pro
by codeMantra

Publisher's Note
The publisher accepts responsibility for any inconsistencies that may have arisen during the conversion of this book from journal articles to book chapters, namely the inclusion of journal terminology.

Disclaimer
Every effort has been made to contact copyright holders for their permission to reprint material in this book. The publishers would be grateful to hear from any copyright holder who is not here acknowledged and will undertake to rectify any errors or omissions in future editions of this book.

Contents

Citation Information

The chapters in this book were originally published in *Citizenship Studies*, volume 25, issue 2 (2021). When citing this material, please use the original page numbering for each article, as follows:

Introduction
Decarceral Futures: Bridging Immigration and Prison Justice towards an Abolitionist Future
Sharry Aiken and Stephanie J. Silverman
Citizenship Studies, volume 25, issue 2 (2021) pp. 141–161

Chapter 1
Mutual aid as abolitionist praxis
Simone Weil Davis and Rachel Fayter
Citizenship Studies, volume 25, issue 2 (2021) pp. 162–165

Chapter 2
States and human immobilization: bridging the conceptual separation of slavery, immigration controls, and mass incarceration
Nandita Sharma
Citizenship Studies, volume 25, issue 2 (2021) pp. 166–187

Chapter 3
Crisis, capital accumulation, and the 'Crimmigration' fix in the aftermath of the global slump
Jessica Evans
Citizenship Studies, volume 25, issue 2 (2021) pp. 188–202

Chapter 4
Held at the gates of Europe: barriers to abolishing immigration detention in Turkey
Esra S. Kaytaz
Citizenship Studies, volume 25, issue 2 (2021) pp. 203–223

Chapter 5
Substituting immigration detention centres with 'open prisons' in Indonesia: alternatives to detention as the continuum of unfreedom
Antje Missbach
Citizenship Studies, volume 25, issue 2 (2021) pp. 224–237

Chapter 6

ICE comes to Tennessee: violence work and abolition in the Appalachian South
Michelle Brown
Citizenship Studies, volume 25, issue 2 (2021) pp. 238–252

Chapter 7

Migrant justice as reproductive justice: birthright citizenship and the politics of immigration detention for pregnant women in Canada
Salina Abji and Lindsay Larios
Citizenship Studies, volume 25, issue 2 (2021) pp. 253–272

Chapter 8

Immigration status and policing in Canada: current problems, activist strategies and abolitionist visions
David Moffette
Citizenship Studies, volume 25, issue 2 (2021) pp. 273–291

Chapter 9

Curated hostilities and the story of Abdoul Abdi: relational securitization in the settler colonial racial state
Nisha Nath
Citizenship Studies, volume 25, issue 2 (2021) pp. 292–315

Notes on Contributors

Salina Abji is Sociologist and Research Consultant based in Toronto. She holds a PhD in Sociology from the University of Toronto, Canada. Her SSHRC-funded postdoctoral fellowship at Carleton University, Ottawa, Canada, focused on migrant activism in response to immigration detention in Canada using a feminist intersectional framework. She has published research on borders, migrant justice, and gender-based violence in Citizenship Studies, Signs, Social Politics, and Studies in Social Justice.

Sharry Aiken is Associate Professor at Queen's University's Faculty of Law and affiliated with the Queen's Cultural Studies Program, Kingston, Canada. She is a past president of the Canadian Council for Refugees, co-editor of the *PKI Global Justice Journal*, and former Editor-in-Chief of the journal *Refuge*.

Michelle Brown is Professor of Sociology at the University of Tennessee, Knoxville, USA, with loved ones living inside and working for the prison state. She is the author of *The Culture of Punishment*, and the co-editor of *The Routledge International Handbook of Visual Criminology*; *The Oxford Encyclopedia of Crime, Media and Popular Culture*; and the *Palgrave MacMillan Studies in Crime, Media and Culture* book series.

Simone Weil Davis is Associate Director of Ethics, Society & Law at Trinity College at the University of Toronto, Canada. Simone was cofounder and first coordinator of Canada's Walls to Bridges program, and is a member of the Walls to Bridges Collective. Her current research considers emotions and embodied experience in learning spaces in and beyond the academy, as a confrontation with racism and the possibilities of anti-racism in education.

Jessica Evans is Assistant Professor in the Department of Sociology at Ryerson University, Toronto, Canada. Her research explores the political economy of prisons with a particular focus on the relationship between prisons, national identity, and capitalism in the settler colony.

Rachel Fayter is PhD student in the Department of Criminology at the University of Ottawa, Canada. While incarcerated at Grand Valley Institution for Women, Rachel engaged in the Walls to Bridges (W2B) prison education program and has been active in the alumni collective since 2014. Since her return to the community, Rachel has been advocating for prisoner rights and social justice-oriented policy changes, through publications, panel discussions, public education, and media interviews.

Esra S. Kaytaz is Research Fellow at the Centre for Trust, Peace and Social Relations at Coventry University, UK. Her research interests include immigration detention, migration journeys, and migrant decision-making.

Lindsay Larios is an interdisciplinary critical policy researcher and an assistant professor of social work at the University of Manitoba. She studies citizenship and immigration in the Canadian context, in particular, as it intersects with family and reproductive politics and policies. Her most recent work focuses on the politics of pregnancy and childbirth and precarious migration as an issue of reproductive justice.

Antje Missbach is Senior Research Fellow at the Arnold Bergstraesser Institute in Freiburg, Germany. Her research interests include refugee governance and politics of sanctuary; socio-legal dimensions of forced migration in Southeast Asia; trafficking in persons, human smuggling, and related transnational crimes in the Asia-Pacific region; diaspora politics and long-distance nationalism; as well as contemporary political, social, and cultural trends in Indonesia.

David Moffette is Associate professor in the Department of Criminology at the University of Ottawa, Canada. He studies questions related to the intersections between criminal law and immigration law, borders and bordering practices, policing, nationalism, and racism.

Nisha Nath (she/they) is Assistant Professor of Equity Studies in the Master of Arts – Interdisciplinary Studies Program at Athabasca University, Canada. In addition to working on relational securitization, she is also working on a SSHRC-funded study with Dr. Willow Allen (University of Victoria, Canada) on the settler colonial socialization of public sector workers in Canada.

Nandita Sharma is Professor of the Sociology Department at the University of Hawai'i at Manoa, USA. She is the author of *Home Economics: Nationalism and the Making of 'Migrant Workers' in Canada* (2006) and *Home Rule: National Sovereignty and the Separation of Natives and Migrants* (2020).

Stephanie J. Silverman is a researcher, consultant, educator, editor, and scholar. She received her DPhil from the University of Oxford (2013), UK, as a commonwealth scholar, and also served as the SSHRC Bora Laskin National Fellow in Human Rights (2015-2016), on faculty at the University of Toronto, Canada, for six years, and at the Immigration and Refugee Board of Canada.

Introduction – decarceral futures: bridging immigration and prison justice towards an abolitionist future

Sharry Aiken and Stephanie J. Silverman

ABSTRACT

This book focuses on what a standpoint of carceral abolitionism brings to citizenship studies, with immigration detention as the key case study. The ten contributions probe the intersections of detention with current and potential forms of citizenship. The contributions collectively emphasize what citizenship studies also documents: similar to how the prison is a site of social control, immigration control is a nation-building site where access to permanent status and citizenship is closely filtered along racial, gender, class, ableist, and other lines of discrimination. Employing a plurality of case studies spanning North America, Europe, and Asia, and coming to the subject from a spectrum of interdisciplinary backgrounds, all contributors nonetheless foreground the recognition that deprivation of liberty is one of the most serious harms that someone can experience. Like the activists protesting police brutality around the world, the special issue contributors are thinking across the spectrum of de-funding policing, overhauling the 'criminal justice' system, eradicating prisons (penal abolitionism), and doing away with all forms of containment (carceral abolitionism). The collective findings reaffirm that neither the prison nor the detention centre is inevitable in the modern, democratic order. Abolishing all forms of immigration detention would open the door for the emergence of new visions of justice.

This edited book seeks to initiate a robust conversation about what carceral abolitionism could bring to citizenship studies, with immigration detention as the key case study. This book provides an opportunity to probe the intersections of detention with current and potential forms of citizenship, and with the new visions of immigration justice that would emerge with the elimination of detention. The contributors approach the topic from a plurality of standpoints and disciplinary backgrounds. Like the activists protesting police, military, and anti-woman brutality around the world, the contributors are thinking across the spectrum of de-funding policing, overhauling the 'criminal justice' system, eradicating prisons (penal abolitionism), and doing away with all forms of containment (carceral abolitionism). Collectively, we suggest that neither the prison nor the detention centre is inevitable in the modern, democratic order. Rather, we argue that they are premised on the recognition that deprivation of liberty is one of the most serious harms that can be inflicted on a person.

These conversations are urgent. The public, politicians, and policymakers intermittently direct attention to the space in the Venn diagram where immigration overlaps with crime rates, even where studies suggest negative relationships between immigration and crime (on North America, see, for example, Davies and Fagan 2012; Ferraro 2016; Jung 2020; Miles and Cox 2014). This attention is acute during an 'emergency', such as an economic recession and a global pandemic. Targeting both border-crossers and long-term residents with legal or irregular status, the global surveillance, policing, and detention apparatus impedes residents from becoming citizens.

The *possibility* of being detained distinguishes residents from citizens. It imputes dangerousness to racialized or otherwise marginalized communities (Kaytaz and Silverman 2019; Nath this book). It stands in the way of equality and dignity for a social class of people characterized by 'legal nonexistence' (Reiter and Coutin 2017) who are inside the territory but outside its legal protections (Hernández 2008, 45; see also De Genova, 2002; Evans this book; Garcia Hernández 2013, 2019; Longazel, Berman, and Fleury-Steiner 2016; Moffette this book; Gill et al. 2018; Sharma this book).

Following Angela Y. Davis, the penal abolitionists' focus is not solely on 'a negative process of tearing down,' but rather one of collectively 're-imagining institutions, ideas, and strategies, and creating new institutions ... that render prisons obsolete' (Davis 2005, 65 quoted in McDowell and Fernandez 2018, 377). Prison and carceral abolitionists call for the redistribution of resources to meet humans' needs for adequate health, education, housing, and jobs while simultaneously rejecting the norms of racial capitalist society. Thinkers from the prison abolition collective Critical Resistance see the three converging aspects to the project as dismantle, change, and build. Abolitionist reforms can be understood as multi-fronted efforts to reject carceral expansion and free all prisoners; to historicize, challenge, and reject a powerful, discriminatory habitus that traces directly to chattel slavery; and to co-create a more equitable world valuing the opinions, experiences, and ideas for progress of those most harmed by the current system (see, e.g., Ben-Moshe 2018; Richie 2012; Rodríguez 2019; Sudbury 2004, 2008; Wilson Gilmore 2014).

A detention-free world is possible and would move us closer to achieving immigration justice. This proposal may initially appear radical, and indeed, there are some aspects to the idea of eliminating detention that are startling. But while detention-abolition may seem novel or even inconceivable to some readers, other readers will recognize long-standing carceral abolitionist theories. Given the catastrophic, ongoing harms of the COVID-19 pandemic, climate change, white supremacy, and the ensuing economic recession, now is the time to redirect our collective resources to a new vision of racial and immigration justice.

This Introduction is organized in five sections: the first explains how an intersectional and settler colonial framework opens up new terrain in the study of citizenship and the carceral state; the second provides an overview of how detention functions, and what this means for citizenship studies; the third section focuses on how prisoners' narratives illuminate the incalculable costs of the carceral state; the fourth section analyses how reforms fail to bring justice for immigrants; and the final section offers an orientation to the papers that follow. As scholars based in Ontario, Canada, we draw on local studies and Canada-focused publications, reflecting our rootedness in localized forms of community, solidarity, and resistance. Likewise, the scope is predominantly North American (e.g. Abji and Larios, Brown, Evans, Moffette, and Nath) with some scholars taking a global, supranational, or transnational view (Kaytaz, Missbach, Sharma).

Acknowledging and applying a framework of intersectionality and settler colonialism

Black feminist legal scholar Kimberlé Williams Crenshaw (1991, 1245) offers the term 'intersectionality' to capture 'the need to account for multiple grounds of identity when considering how the social world is constructed.' An intersectional framework can connect groups and causes without dominating or occluding important differences. Intersectional frameworks create spaces to negotiate 'tensions between assertions of multiple [identities] and the ongoing necessity of group politics' (Crenshaw 1991, 1296). Like penal abolitionism, intersectionality is at once a theory and a praxis. An intersectional commitment focuses on how laws, policies, regulations, and practices understand and discipline racialized and immigrant bodies and identities. An intersectional methodology indicates how immigration control and citizenship allocation mechanisms are experienced differentially across axes of identities, particularly during the neoliberal epoch (e.g. Aiken 2007; Balaguera 2018; Bassel 2010; Hill Collins and Bilge 2016; Sheth 2014; Yuval-Davis 2007).

Following Patrick Wolfe's (1999) framework, settler colonialism is not a historic event or occurrence but a condition of structural violence shaping race, gender, class, and sexual formations (see, also, Bhungalia 2018; Glenn 2015). Under the banners of nationhood and law, settler colonialism works with racial capitalism to legitimate and unjustly apportion access to land, property, human rights, and citizenship (Nichols 2014, 437; see, also, Dobchuk-Land 2017; Evans this book; Gutiérrez Nájera and Maldonado 2017; Gutiérrez Rodríguez 2018; Nash this book; Stasiulus and Yuval-Davis 1995; Tuck and Yang 2012). Since 'colonial projects simultaneously structure, race, class and sexual relations between colonists and the colonized', the settler colonial framework both complements and deepens intersectional methodologies or standpoints (Glenn 2015, 55). In Canada, it is the 'settler community that shapes the nation by enacting immigration policy that selects newcomers with particular attributes, while the longer-established Aboriginal community has no say in who is selected' (Bauder 2011, 518; see, also, Bhungalia 2018; Dauvergne 2016; Nath, this book; Sharma 2006, this book). Nation- building projects instrumentalize immigrants to further oppress Indigenous peoples. Laws and policies have long cast out racialized members from the rights of citizenship (Ngai 2004).

Detention and its earlier incarnations of quarantine, residential schools, and internments played important roles of de-mobilization, arrest, isolation, stigmatization, criminalization, and banishment from the social and legal community. A methodological framework informed by intersectionality and settler colonialism can better reveal the violence embedded and perpetrated by supposedly neutral immigration and citizenship policies and programmes, such as criminal and security inadmissibility (Aiken 2001; Benslimane and Moffette 2019; Razack 2007) or the Seasonal Agricultural Workers Program in Canada (Sharma and Wright 2008; Stasiulus 2020; Walia

2013). An intersectional standpoint also forces the recognition that policing, detention, and deportation apparatuses support a settler colonial vision of citizenship and belonging in Canada.

Further, an intersectional and settler colonial analysis reveals how racism, sexism, ableism, and heteronormativity insidiously order and overlap citizenship, access to legal pathways to immigration, and carceral laws (Alexander 2012; Brown and Schept; Maynard 2017; Struthers Montford and Moore 2018; Ware, Ruzsa, and Dias 2014). Piecemeal reform efforts can only curb the harshest edges of the carceral state (Bosworth 2011; Gómez Cervantes, Menjívar, and Staples 2017; Wilson Gilmore 2007). Abuses and experiences of criminalization and stigmatization are not aberrations but part and parcel of how prisons are *supposed* to work (Lydon 2016; Ware and Dias 2014). Theorists, practitioners, and activists consistently point out how piecemeal reforms aimed at alleviating select harms of detention rarely make life better for prisoners and detainees (see, also, Abji and Larrios this book; Russell and Carlton 2013; Turnbull 2019). Reforms short of abolition consistently lead to *more* incarceration especially of racialized and other minoritized people (Davis 2016 Spade 2013).

The long shadows of immigration detention

Most democratic countries formally legislated modern powers of immigration detention in the 1970s. Yet, they only sporadically and selectively took up and deployed these powers. Detention arose in the post-Cold War context of states of immigration legalizing and legislating increasingly draconian measures to discourage the inflow and rights to residence (and potential citizenship) of foreign nationals (Loyd and Mountz 2018; Silverman 2010; Wilsher 2012; Wong 2015). States commonly claim that the intentions of detention polices are to enable removals of people with no right to remain and to fortify the border against new arrivals; interdict overseas, or contract other States or offshore border agents to intercept migrants in transit; and hold and sort newcomers while their identities and claims are determined (Silverman and Nethery 2015). Today, *all* States are implementing laws and policies to expand the grounds to detain, therefore expanding the ambit of who can be arrested and incarcerated for lack of citizenship (Anderson, Gibney, and Paoletti 2013; De Genova 2007).

Detention's manifestations range from a small number of indefinitely detained people in Canada to a peak of 55,654 individuals detained in the US in July 2019 (Transactional Records Access Clearinghouse 2020); to the incarceration of 'boat people' in offshore processing centres in Nauru and Papua New Guinea; to the European Union's frontier 'hotspots', internal security governance, and extra-territorial detention sites (Baldo 2017; Bialasiewicz 2012; Casas-Cortes, Cobarrubias, and Pickles 2016; Kaytaz this book; Missbach 2014, this issue). States are relocating detention beyond their territories and into international waters; they are enabling it through surveillance and monitoring technologies; crafting legal manoeuvres to expand the category of detainability; and 'exporting' detention policy to other jurisdictions (Nethery, Rafferty-Brown, and Taylor 2013).

Immigration detention sits under the 'umbrella' of administrative law (Silverman 2018b). Article 9 of the International Covenant on Civil and Political Rights guarantees the right to liberty and security of person, and prohibits arbitrary arrest or detention.

Detention includes any form of deprivation of liberty of person, and these broadly defined terms encompass immigration-related incarceration (Neuman 2018, 391). Officials must demonstrate due diligence in pursuing release options. Other international instruments affirm the primacy of liberty for all human beings at all times, irrespective of citizenship, nationality, or migratory status (UNHCR 2012; UN Working Group on Arbitrary Detention 2018). In Canada, Detention Guidelines confirm that 'Canadian law regards detention as an exceptional measure' (Immigration and Refugee Board of Canada 2019, 1.13). Due to their extreme vulnerability and need for care, and that law privileges their best interests, children should not be deprived of liberty, except as a measure of last resort and for the shortest appropriate period of time. Since it is administrative, many legal 'guard rails' set up for prisoners in the criminal justice system are missing from detention, including access to free telephone calls, interpreters, or even legal counsel. Courts rarely grant more rights or limit the scope of people vulnerable to detention. As Daniel Wilsher (2012, xiii) notes, courts 'have been confronted with a deeper constitutional question: what residual rights, if any, do immigrants have if the government has declared that they are not unauthorized to be members of the community?'

There is no evidence that detention centres promote safety and security in local communities or lead to lower numbers of newcomers (Leerkes and Broeders 2010; Mainwaring and Silverman 2017; Missbach 2014; Silverman 2018a; Wong 2015). Despite popular rhetoric about detention's deterrent effects, demographic evidence finds that restrictive immigration measures like detention do not stop inflows, decrease permanent settlement, or increase 'voluntary' deportations (Alden 2017; Czaika and De Haas 2013; Golash-Boza 2015; Massey and Pren 2012). It does seem, however, that draconian immigration enforcement measures are routing migrants into natural danger zones such as the deserts, the mountains, the rivers, or the seas (Amnesty International 2015; Casas-Cortes, Cobarrubias, and Pickles 2016; Kaytaz this book; Missbach this book; Reitano, Adal, and Shaw 2014; Williams and Mountz 2016). The deaths and violence in these spaces veil the complicity of border officials in deaths and suffering en route to and at the border (De Leon 2013; Nevins 2010; Medel 2017). As Tyron P. Woods (2013) reminds us, anti-Black paradigms ('prostitution, human trafficking, international drug trade, or even feminist analyses of the larger historical context of globalization') motivate prison and detention usage; delimit South-to-North migrants in pursuit of legal and social citizenship into either victims or perpetrators; and injure people in countless ways before they arrive at a prison or detention centre.

States are capitalizing on the COVID-19 pandemic to implement a dizzying array of measures aimed at halting mobilities to stop the spreading virus: some States like Canada, Iran, Spain, and the UK have responded by reducing their low-risk immigrant detainee populations while others like India, Indonesia, Libya, Malaysia, and Tunisia have seen their detention facilities become COVID-19 hotspots (Nah, Phillips, and Park 2020). It is unclear what the mid- to long-term trajectories are for a prison population susceptible to COVID-19, the arduousness of their bail conditions and other monitoring requirements, and which public authorities or local groups are accountable for their well-being (see Moffette this book, Missbach this book, for a discussion of community-based supervision).

The significance of prisoners' narratives

Both theories and forms of praxis, intersectional, settler colonial, and carceral abolitionist frameworks bring racialized women's experiences to the forefront. The injustice, discrimination, and violence from the carceral state lead to harms to reproductive justice for both migrants and citizens, including parental separation, disruptions to parenting, and lower birth weight and gestational age of Black infants (Abji and Larios: Hartry 2012; Jones and Seabrook 2017; Legewie 2019; Patler and Branic 2017). Chenelle A. Jones and colleagues (2020) explain that, in the US, women are imprisoned at alarmingly higher rates (63 per 100,000) than they were 20 years ago (54 per 100,000). In the decade leading to 2017, the number of women sentenced to state and federal prisons increased nearly 40%, compared to an 18% increase for men. Of the 105,033 women in prisons in 2019, 19,600 are Black women whose sentences ranged broadly from violent and property offenses to drug crimes. Likewise, the Correctional Investigator of Canada reports that the number of persons of Indigenous ancestry (5% of the general population) incarcerated in Canada rose from 25% of the inmate population in 2016 to 30% in 2020. Indigenous women account for an astounding 42% of the women inmate population in Canada. Indigenous people reoffend or are returned to custody at much higher levels, as high as 70% for Indigenous men in the Prairie region (Zinger 2020). What does it mean for citizenship when criminal justice inflection points are so disparately experienced?

Prisoners' narratives indicate that, both migrants and other prisoners have innovated ways to create community, and subvert 'unfreedom' (Sharma this book; Arriola and Raymond 2017; Guenther 2015; James 2013). Victoria Law (2012) explains how the roots of the 1974 'August Rebellion' by women imprisoned at New York's Bedford Hills maximum-security prison lay in the women forming peer education groups, clandestinely arranging ways for children to visit mothers in distant prisons, and raising public awareness about their lived experiences. Likewise, Bridget Anderson, Nandita Sharma, and Cynthia Wright argue that migrants have always rejected or refused borders, and that no recorded 'set of border controls has ever worked to fully contain people's desire and need to move' (Anderson, Sharma, and Wright 2012, 82).

Over-crowding and abysmal conditions facilitate the spread of disease and viruses (Jeovany 2018; Leung et al. 2019; Trovall 2019). Prisoners and staff are at high risk of COVID-19 infections (Amnesty International 2020; Hazlewood 2020; Jackson 2020a; Kratz et al. 2020; Weill-Greenberg 2020; World Health Organization Regional Office for Europe 2020). Journalists report transfers amongst facilities are spreading the virus (Jackson 2020b). Coronavirus infection fears spurred a declining rate of detentions in Canada (Browne 2020), underlining questions about why alternatives are not routinely explored more rigorously in that jurisdiction.

Narratives and lived experiences also illustrate how the harms of the prison and the detention centre compound the trauma that many prisoners suffered before incarceration. Guards consistently perpetrate sexual and other forms of abuse towards prisoners, leading to long-lasting trauma (e.g. Conley 2019; Current and Former Employees on Nauru 2015; Johnston 2013; Stelloh 2019). It is not just the act of removing people from their lives to isolate them in prison but the daily operationalization of that incarceration that cause pain. Self-harming, suicides, and post-release deaths of prisoners are recorded across every jurisdiction with reliable data requirements (e.g. Abji 2020; Abu-Hayyeh and Webber 2015; ACLU of Texas 2014; Fleay and Briskman 2013).

Reforms are not enough

Prisoners' narratives and scholarship demonstrate that State practices of caging people can never 'get better' (Abji and Larios this book; Gerard and Pickering 2012; Gilson 2016; Gómez Cervantes, Menjívar, and Staples 2017; Nyers 2006; Pétin 2016; Piché and Major 2015). Michel Foucault (1977) argued persuasively that the prison's disciplinary techniques emanate out into public sociolegal institutions. Likewise, the Movement for Black Lives', *A Vision for Black Lives: Policy Demands for Black Power, Freedom, and Justice* (*Vision*) calls for an end to the war on Black people in the US; abolishing the school-to-prison pipeline; de-militarizing the police; 'an end to all jails, detention centers, youth facilities and prisons as we know them'; an end to mass surveillance and to privatization of police and prisons; and 'an [e]nd to [a]ll [d]eportations, [i]mmigrant [d]etention, and Immigration and Custom Enforcement [r]aids' (Akbar 2018, 430). As Crenshaw (2012, 1423–1424) argues and we can apply to our discussions of immigrant justice, siphoning out a certain vulnerability normalizes the structural harms in categorizing bodies (see, also, Gilson 2016; Ocen 2013). As Eric A. Stanley puts it, 'the only prison that would be responsive to gender is one that ceases to exist' (Stanley, Spade and Queer Justice 2012, 122).

Here we provide a few recent examples of what we see as failed reforms. These programmes and practices illustrate why alternative detention arrangements risk normalizing imprisonment of non-citizens and undercutting the struggle for freedom and human rights for all. In the US, in 2011, the Obama Administration created detention 'pods' for transgender womxn and for gay-identifying men in far-flung locations. The transfers to the pods separated the detainees from their legal, kinship, and health care networks, and detainees reported misgendering, stigma, and abusive treatment from the staff (Carson and Diaz 2015, 15–16; Dart 2017; Human Rights Watch 2016; Rosales Arriola 2016; on the politics of transferring detainees around a system, see Gill 2016; Moinester 2018). Activist Jorge Gutiérrez argued,

> You know where the best place for our queer and trans brothers and sisters is? It's with their communities. In detention, no matter where, we are harassed, we are made fun of, we are threatened, we are misgendered. We are denied medical access. If you complain about this, they put you in solitary confinement and say it's for your 'safety'—and that is punishment. I believe that is torture. Trans women who have been detained verify this.
>
> (Shah 2019, 185)

In Canada, the Liberalgovernment is piloting the five-year National Immigration Detention Framework at a financial cost of 138 CAD million to 'transform' the detention system; by subcontracting supervisory responsibilities to the Salvation Army and the John Howard Society and by introducing electronic tagging through remotely controlled ankle bracelets, however, the Framework imports new and worrying institutions and mechanisms from preventive and criminal justice settings into immigration (Silverman 2018c). In the UK, a strong activist movement to abolish child detention became riven with conflict when a respected charity accepted the government's contract to operate a 'better' detention centre for families, thus undercutting the movement's goal to end the practice (Silverman 2016; Tyler et al. 2014). There are also recent reports of makeshift detention centres disguised as refugee camps *inside* Britain, located within disused and unsanitary military barracks in Kent (Grierson 2021). The European Union has proposed a number of 'Alternatives' that are filtered through a human rights discourse but amount to detention by another name; these proposals are marked by their characteristics of 'externalization' beyond European borders and refractions of remade but recognizable colonial governance strategies (see Lemberg-Pedersen (2019) on 'regional disembarkation platforms'; Silverman (2018a) and Tazzioli and Garelli (2020) on the 'hotspot' approach; and Kaytaz and Missbach, both in this book, on the roles played by Turkey and Indonesia in containing would-be refugees from seeking protection through onward movements, respectively). The proliferation of new technologies, including the use of bail-determination algorithms at the US-Mexico border and AI-powered lie-detectors at border checkpoints in Europe, is characterized as twenty-first-century 'reforms' but impinges on the human rights of migrants in unregulated and increasingly opaque spaces (Molnar 2019). Moving to the international level, Julia Morris (2017) argues that not only has the global detention rights movement shifted its position from wholesale abolition to a much more modest goal of improving detention standards through legislative and regulatory reforms; but this shift has licensed the expansion not only of private firms looking to offer 'solutions' but of an entire capital investment market for shopping by governments.

An intersectional, abolitionist, and settler colonial lens allows us to see how detention reforms are premised not on freedom but on privileging one identity as more worthy of better treatment. In so doing, such a focus on reforms but not abolition 'anchors and reproduces geopolitical, raced, classed, and gendered borders, while simultaneously distinguishing between citizens and groups with fewer or no rights' (Mountz et al. 2013, 531). A growing body of international research confirms that while greater consideration should be given to non-custodial monitoring, no 'Alternative' is a 'durable solution' to displacement (Bloomfield 2016; Marouf 2017; Missbach 2017; Ohtani and Phelps 2016; Silverman 2013).

Decarceral futures

This collection emerged from a two-day workshop, 'De-Carceral Futures: Bridging Prison and Immigration Justice' in May 2019. The contributors seek to take account of the State's multi-scalar permutations of punishment, penality, and hardships across law, policy, and frontline practices (e.g. Beckett and Murakawa 2012; Gill et al. 2018). Such an expansive understanding better captures the 'pains of immigrant imprisonment' (Longazel, Berman, and Fleury-Steiner 2016) and the damage incarceration causes to belonging, membership, kinship, and citizenship. Racial violence permeates liberal democracies both as a notion and an action, leading communities to unconsciously adopt a notion of 'safety … predicated on banishment, mass criminalization, [and] policing' (McDowell and Fernandez 2018, 386). The prefigurative vision reimagines immigration justice along axes of equality, redistribution, and true community safety. Local movements such as Sanctuary Cities and mutual aid societies redistribute and democratize access to power, wealth, and resources, including when the police are called and who can go to school freely (Abji 2013; Abji and Larrios this book; Bauder 2016; Brown this book; Jeffries and Ridgley 2020; McLeod 2019; Moffette this book). We highlight below the central themes of each book chapter.

In 'Mutual Aid as Abolitionist Praxis,' Walls to Bridges Collective (W2BC) members Simone Weil Davis and Rachel Fayter focus on the carceral abolitionist avenue of mutual aid, or how people coordinate to help one another, as a constructive response to the directly oppositional and divisive goals of incarceration and detention. As they state, '[c]aremongering' is a human trait; it is also an abolitionist building block (Chopra 2020). It is a collective deepening of webs of relationship that are neither defined nor "managed" by carceral or capitalist structures.' Caremongering is vital and prevailing in the current social climate, as Davis and Fayter explain:

> [s]ince the militarization of the US-Mexico border, Covid, and the 2020 uprising against anti-Black racism, both existing and emergent networks of mutual aid are becoming more intentional, being coordinated into larger networks of care, refined and guided by those from marginalized communities.
>
> (p. 163)

Their contribution follows this spirit of community-building and provokes academics to rethink categorization and ways of being in community.

Nandita Sharma's article, 'States and Human Immobilization: Bridging the Conceptual Separation of Slavery, Immigration Controls, and Mass Incarceration,' examines the long history of immigration controls and mass incarceration. She traces a history from the British Empire's restrictive regulation of movement by 'coolie labourers' on sugar plantations, to the post-slavery abolition era in the US, during which the 1875 Page Act, Jim Crow laws, and Black Codes sought to continue immobilizing and criminalizing Black people in America long after slavery was outlawed. Sharma notes:

> [t]ogether, immigration and carceral controls have created groups of people denied access to the mythical institutions of liberal democracy: liberty, freedom (especially of their labour power), and equality ... through their placement in state categories of "criminal" and "migrant," both of which legislate the denial of rights.

Sharma demonstrates that, 'from the start, [immigration and carceral controls] have been racist [and] have organized and enforced the immobility of those who are hegemonically regarded as "not belonging" to the "nation"' (p. 184). Sharma argues that analysing the links between slavery and immigration controls, on the one hand, and the links between the incarceration of subordinated citizens and those classified by States as 'migrants,' on the other, strengthens contemporary social justice struggles for No Borders. Indeed, in view of this history, Sharma makes a compelling case that prison abolition and No

Borders spring from the same well of undoing and ultimately ending State controls on human mobility.

In 'Crisis, Capital Accumulation and the "Crimmigration" Fix in the Aftermath of the Global Slump,' Jessica Evans employs a political economy lens to examine the growing Canadian reliance on Public Private Partnerships in immigration controls, criminalization of immigrants, and prison expansion. Following the financial recession of 2007/2008, 'carceral expansion in Canada must be situated within a broader set of state-led attempts to restore and regulate capital accumulation in a post-recession climate'. Evans states:

> the detained and their potential freedom are assessed on the basis of how effectively they can defer from the state the costs of their own reproduction. One's ability to do so, in a settler colonial context like Canada, of course, has and continues to be coded by race, gender, and disability ... [W]omen, indigenous peoples, migrants of colour, and populations with a disability or psychiatric diagnosis are disproportionately those who make up the growing numbers of people caged by Canada's carceral infrastructure.
>
> (p. 199)

Evans' methodology, case study, and research findings traversing both political economy and detention studies deepen our collective understanding of the influence of private actors and capital in propelling the imprisonment of citizens and migrants.

In 'Held at the gates of Europe: Barriers to abolishing immigration detention in Turkey,' Esra S. Kaytaz addresses how Turkey's power dynamic with the European Union shapes Turkish practices and architecture of immigration detention, and a wider conceptualization of 'transit migration.' Kaytaz describes how '[the] "European refugee crisis of 2015" ... re-ignited public and policy discourse on transit migration due to fears of large numbers of migrants arriving in Europe' (p. 208). Since the European Union and Turkey pre-emptively identified migrants as criminals, their migration constituted 'a perceived threat in Europe.' Kaytaz observes:

> [c]entral to the operation of transit migration is ... "premature labelling" which ... assumes that people are illegal immigrants – either trafficked or smuggled – before they have even entered the territory of the state passing judgement of them ... [I]t is within this juridico-political space of premature labelling that migrants become detainable ... and deportable ... Therefore, transit migration is central to the analysis of immigration detention in Turkey and for understanding the barriers to abolishing it.

Kaytaz is simultaneously acknowledging how Turkey is instrumentalizing migrants and their desires to live in Europe, while also offering new evidence querying the relevance of the 'transit migration' framework.

In 'Substituting immigration detention centres with "open prisons" in Indonesia: Alternatives to detention as the continuum of unfreedom,' Antje Missbach reveals that the shift away from detaining in Indonesia has not actually abolished immigration containment but has realized its continuance through subtler carceral forms. Missbach emphasizes,

> it is often wrongly assumed that alternatives to detention are the opposite of the detention regime. This is not the case ... they serve the very same purpose of containing asylum seekers and refugees, albeit in a larger area than in a tiny detention cell.
>
> (p. 225)

Since migration and integration into Indonesian society remain restricted, this larger area is an 'open prison'. The State continues to use law and policy to deprive asylum-seekers of their rights and access to basic material means of survival (p. 232). As Missbach explains,

> [p]roviding less carceral and more humane forms of detention is an improvement, but [it] does not necessarily contribute to abolishing restrictive migration dogma or to ending containment policies ... Rather, because people living in alternatives to detention are far from enjoying the same rights as citizens, they prolong their unfreedom.
>
> (p. 230)

Michelle Brown's article, 'ICE Comes to Tennessee: Violence Work and Abolition in the Appalachian South,' returns us to the micro-level through an in-depth case study of a workplace raid at a meatpacking plant in a small town in Eastern Tennessee. This raid led to the arrests and detentions of 97 undocumented workers from Mexico and Guatemala. Brown explains that '[a] new form of "legal violence" has taken shape,' in the South,

> where the threat and reality of detention and deportation make family separation a normalized component of daily life across institutions for many who cross borders ... instrumental in the creation of "a climate of terror" ... against a geographic backdrop of shifting racial compositions of urban and rural counties that have become new destinations for largely Latinx immigrants.
>
> (p. 243)

Despite this violence, Brown explains how a 'politics of refusal grounded in belonging and the freedom of mobility' (p. 247) offers hope of transformative justice – the 'improvised local, temporal practice of freedom' by all community members (p. 248).

In 'Migrant Justice as Reproductive Justice: Birthright Citizenship and the Politics of Immigration Detention for Pregnant Women in Canada,' Salina Abji and Lindsay Larios also take on a case study to explore how Canadian immigration, detention, and citizenship practices operate as nation-building sites. By telling the story of Glory Anawa and her son, Alpha, they reveal how the Canadian government's denial of basic reproductive rights reinforces structural violence against unwanted, pregnant women without citizenship status: '[a]t their foundation, reproductive rights are a core component of substantive citizenship: to have autonomy over one's reproductive choices as well as access to the basic necessities required for parenting are fundamental pre-conditions for full participation in public life' (p. 256). Abji and Larios explain how tropes that are 'heightened through right-wing attacks on immigrant women's supposed "birth tourism",' and that portray 'women of colour as "bad mothers" and "welfare queens" ... and their children as "anchor babies"' demonstrate how 'racialized and poor women's reproductive choices have been used as battlegrounds in the shaping of (white) national identity and nation-building projects' (p. 254, p. 262). Pushing even further, dominant immigration controls converging with reproductive controls reveal the inherent inequality of birthright or lottery-winning citizenship. Abji and Larios therefore call for 'an abolitionist alternative to birthright citizenship ... that guarantees rights on the basis of one's status as a *person* rather than one's birthright in an unequal world' (p. 257).

David Moffette focuses on the connection between the Canada Border Services Agency and local police in 'Immigration Status and Policing in Canada: Current Problems, Activist Strategies, and Abolitionist Visions.' Police enforcement contributes to immigration detention practices, both in Canada and in most other States where 'crimmigration' has taken hold and intertwined these previously distinct realms of criminal and immigration justice. Moffette uses a unique mixed methodology of Access to Information (ATI) and Freedom of Information (FOI) requests, transcripts of a Coroner's inquest and personal narratives. His research reveals that municipal police forces in Toronto, Montreal, and Vancouver are actively collaborating with the Canadian border agents. Thus, Moffette argues that police abolition must be incorporated into immigration detention abolition, and carceral abolitionism overall: '[i]mmigration policing is often the first link in the chain leading to detention and deportation ... [making] it a key site ... to fight immigration detention and state-sanctioned coercive control over the movement of people' (p. 284). He proposes alternatives to policing and community activism strategies that can contribute to a broad 'culture of non-cooperation with immigration enforcement' in 'the spirit of police and border abolition' (p. 284). A broad sociolegal shift is therefore in the collective struggle to fight carceral social structures.

In 'Curated Hostilities and the Story of Abdoul Abdi: Relational Securitization in the Settler Colonial Racial State,' Nisha Nath documents the experiences of Abdoul Abdi. Mr. Abdi came to Canada as a child refugee seeking protection welfare services took him from his family and placed him in foster care at a young age. After incurring some criminal convictions, Mr. Abdi faced deportation to Somalia as a young adult. After a campaign led by Black Lives Matter TO, and a series of Federal Court of Canada rulings, Mr. Abdi's removal order was dropped. Nath highlights the extremely dire consequence for Mr. Abdi being that no one at the local Department of Community Services applied for his Canadian citizenship while he was in their care. To understand the 'relational' webs of interconnections entrapping Mr. Abdi, Nath situates his experiences in the contexts of Canadian immigration, detention, and deportation infrastructures; racialized hierarchies; and white settler colonial futurities. Nath argues:

> I take up Abdoul's story as a way to understand the organizing logic of the white settler colonial state, wherein the context of anti-Blackness that produces the Nova Scotia Home for Colored Children, is one where the state has a reliant interest in settler colonialism, and where securing the borders and asserting state sovereignty reinscribe the same. These processes are not separate enactments of the state, but ... rely on each other; they are relational.
> (p. 293)

Like the Movement for Black Lives' *Vision*, Nath demonstrates how 'intersecting and functionally interacting institutions' such as 'child welfare,' 'policing,' 'immigration,' and 'structures of power [such as] anti-Blackness, border imperialism, and settler colonialism' all 'work[ed] together to curate the hostilities' which Abdi faced (p. 293).

We are making strides towards what Mariame Kaba calls the 'horizon of abolition' (Berger, Kaba and Stein 2017). Many contributors – including Nath, Abji and Larios, and Brown – draw on close studies of seemingly individual or small-scale resistance to point to broader trends of solidarity and resistance between citizens and migrants. The contributors emphasize what citizenship studies has been documenting: just as the prison is a site of social control, immigration control is a nation-building site where access to permanent status and citizenship is closely filtered along racial, gender, class, ableist, and other lines. Insecure citizenship can lead to a number of predictable and unforeseen detention and deportation pathways. Yet, Brown, Davis and Fayter, and Sharma all indicate how a praxis of community based on mutual respect, aid, and a right to mobility is already coming into being. Likewise, Moffette and Nath highlight how, in Canada, citizens and migrants are challenging injustices by contesting unlawful and immoral arrests, detentions, and deportation orders through promoting sanctuary communities, mutual aid caretaking, and a culture of non-collaboration. With a rich and layered tapestry of voice and perspective, we all understand that decarceral futures are crucial *and* possible.

Acknowledgements

The authors would like to thank the Social Sciences and Humanities Research Council (SSHRC) of Canada, Queen's University (Faculty of Law, Cultural Studies Program & Department of Philosophy), the Walls to Bridges Collective, and the John W. Graham Library at Trinity College for their support of the May 2019 *De-Carceral Futures* workshop. Special thanks are owed to workshop co-convener Lisa Guenther, project assistant Ozlem Atar, and editorial assistant Olivia Isajev. The authors would like to thank the May 2019 *De-Carceral Futures* workshop participants as well as Simone Weil Davis, Engin Isin, Esra S. Kaytaz, Daniel J. Lowinsky, Antje Missbach, Falak Mujtaba, and Nandita Sharma for comments on earlier drafts.

Disclosure statement

No potential conflict of interest was reported by the authors.

References

Abji, S. 2013. "Post-nationalism Re-considered: A Case Study of the 'No One Is Illegal' Movement in Canada." *Citizenship Studies* 17 (3–4): 322–338. doi:10.1080/13621025.2012.707001.

Abji, S. 2020. "Punishing Survivors and Criminalizing Survivorship: A Feminist Intersectional Approach to Migrant Justice in the Crimmigration System." *Studies in Social Justice* 14 (1): 67–89. doi:10.26522/ssj.v2020i14.2158.

Abu-Hayyeh, R., and F. Webber. 2015. "Unwanted, Unnoticed: An Audit of 160 Asylum and Immigration-Related Deaths in Europe." *European Research Programme of the Institute of Race Relations Briefing No 10*. Accessed 07 April 2017. http://www.irr.org.uk/news/deaths-of-europes-unwanted-and-unnoticed-migrants-exposed.

ACLU of Texas. 2014. "Warehoused and Forgotten: Immigrants Trapped In Our Shadow Private Prison System." Accessed 09 January 2015. https://www.aclu.org/sites/default/files/assets/060614-aclu-car-reportonline.pdf

Aiken, S. J. 2001. "Of Gods and Monsters: National Security and Canadian Refugee Policy." *Revue québécoise de droit international* 14 (2): 1–51.

Aiken, S. J. 2007. "From Slavery to Expulsion: Racism, Canadian Immigration Law, and the Unfulfilled Promise of Modern Constitutionalism." In *Interrogating Race and Racism*, edited by V. Agnew, 55–111. Toronto: University of Toronto Press.

Akbar, A. A. 2018. "Toward a Radical Imagination of Law." *New York University Law Review* 3: 405–479.

Alden, E. 2017. "Is Border Enforcement Effective? What We Know and What It Means." *Journal on Migration and Human Security* 5 (2): 481–490. doi:10.1177/233150241700500213.

Alexander, M. 2012. *The New Jim Crow: Mass Incarceration in the Age of Colorblindness*. New York City: New Press.

Amnesty International. 2015. *Europe's Gatekeeper: Unlawful Detention and Deportation of Refugees from Turkey*. London: Amnesty International.

Amnesty International. 2020. USA: '*We Are Adrift, About to Sink*': *The Looming COVID-19 Disaster in United States Detention Facilities*. Accessed 07 April 2020. https://www.amnesty.org/en/documents/amr51/2095/2020/en/

Anderson, B., N. Sharma, and C. Wright. 2012. "'We are All Foreigners:' No Borders as a Practical Political Project." In *Citizenship, Migrant Activism and the Politics of Movement*, edited by P. Nyers and K. Rygiel, 73–91. New York: Routledge.

Anderson, B., M. J. Gibney, and E. Paoletti. 2013. *The Social, Political and Historical Contours of Deportation*. Berlin: Springer.

Arriola, E. R., and V. M. Raymond. 2017. "Migrants Resist Systemic Discrimination and Dehumanization in Private, for-Profit Detention Centers." *Santa Clara Journal of International Law* 15 (1): 1–42.

Balaguera, M. 2018. "Trans-migrations: Agency and Confinement at the Limits of Sovereignty." *Signs: Journal of Women in Culture and Society* 43 (3): 641–664. doi:10.1086/695302.

Baldo, S. 2017. "Border Control from Hell: How the EU's Migration Partnership Legitimizes Sudan's 'Militia State'." Enough: The Project to End Genocide and Crimes Against Humanity. https://data2.unhcr.org/en/documents/download/55954.

Bassel, L. 2010. "Intersectional Politics at the Boundaries of the Nation State." *Ethnicities* 10 (2): 155–180. doi:10.1177/1468796810361818.

Bauder, H. 2011. "Closing the immigration–Aboriginal Parallax Gap." *Geoforum* 42 (5): 517–519. doi:10.1016/j.geoforum.2011.03.007.

Bauder, H. 2016. "Possibilities of Urban Belonging." *Antipode* 48 (2): 252–271. doi:10.1111/anti.12174.

Beckett, K., and N. Murakawa. 2012. "Mapping the Shadow Carceral State: Toward an Institutionally Capacious Approach to Punishment." *Theoretical Criminology* 16 (2): 221–244. doi:10.1177/1362480612442113.

Ben-Moshe, L. 2018. "Dis-epistemologies of Abolition." *Critical Criminology* 26 (3): 341–355. doi:10.1007/s10612-018-9403-1.

Benslimane, S., and D. Moffette. 2019. "The Double Punishment of Criminal Inadmissibility for Immigrants." *Journal of Prisoners on Prisons* 28: 1–22.

Berger, D., M. Kaba, and D. Stein. 2017. "What Abolitionists Do.„ *Jacobin Magazine*. https://www.jacobinmag.com/2017/08/prison-abolition-reform-mass-incarceration

Bhungalia, L. 2018. "Governing Banishment: Settler Colonialism, Territory, and Life in an Economy of Death." In *Handbook on the Geographies of Power*, edited by M. Coleman and J. Agnew, 313–331. London: Edward Elgar Publishing.

Bialasiewicz, L. 2012. "Off-shoring and Out-sourcing the Borders of EUrope: Libya and EU Border Work in the Mediterranean." *Geopolitics* 17 (4): 843–866. doi:10.1080/ 14650045.2012.660579.

Bloomberg, A. 2020. "Immigrant Detention and Removal are Not Essential." *The Jurist*. Accessed 12 April 2020. https://www.jurist.org/commentary/2020/04/immigrant-detention-and-removal-are-not-essential
Bloomfield, A. 2016. "Alternatives to Detention at a Crossroads: Humanisation or Criminalisation?" *Refugee Survey Quarterly* 35 (1): 29–46. doi:10.1093/rsq/hdv018.
Bosworth, M. 2011. "Penal Moderation in the United States?" *Criminology & Public Policy* 10 (2): 335–343. doi:10.1111/j.1745-9133.2011.00711.x.
Browne, R. 2020. "The Number of Detainees Held in Canada's Immigration Holding Centres Is Declining amid COVID-19 Fears." *Global News*. Accessed 07 April 2020. https://globalnews.ca/news/6774564/coronavirus-immigration-detainees/
Carson, B., and E. Diaz. 2015. *Payoff: How Congress Ensures Private Prison Profit with an Immigrant Detention Quota*. USA: Grassroots Leadership.
Casas-Cortes, M., S. Cobarrubias, and J. Pickles. 2016. "'Good Neighbours Make Good Fences': Seahorse Operations, Border Externalization and Extra-territoriality." *European Urban and Regional Studies* 23 (3): 231–251. doi:10.1177/0969776414541136.
Chopra, G. 2020. "'Read First' Post," Caremongering-TO. Community.Response.COVID19/permalink/2661130287455762/
Conley, J. 2019. "Only the Tip of the Iceberg': Outrage over Border Abuses Grows amid Reports of Sexual Assault and Retaliation by CBP Agents." *Common Dreams*. Accessed 10 August 2019. https://www.commondreams.org/news/2019/07/10/only-tip-iceberg-outrage-over-border-abuses-grows-amid-reports-sexual-assault-and
Crenshaw, K. W. 1991. "Mapping the Margins: Intersectionality, Identity Politics, and Violence against Women of Color." *Stanford Law Review* 43 (6): 1241–1299. doi:10.2307/1229039.
Crenshaw, K. W. 2012. "From Private Violence to Mass Incarceration: Thinking Intersectionally about Women, Race, and Social Control." *UCLA Law Review* 59: 1418–1472.
Current and Former Employees on Nauru. 2015. "An Open Letter to the Australian People". Accessed 08 April 2015. http://static.guim.co.uk/ni/1428385386778/Nauru-staff-letter-of- conce.pdf
Czaika, M., and H. De Haas. 2013. "The Effectiveness of Immigration Policies." *Population and Development Review* 39 (3): 487–508. doi:10.1111/j.1728-4457.2013.00613.x.
Dart, T. 2017. "New Detention Center's Transgender Unit in Texas Raises Concerns over Intentions." *The Guardian*. Accessed 07 February 2017. https://www.theguardian.com/us- news/2017/feb/06/texas-immigration-detention-center-transgender-unit-prairieland
Dauvergne, C. 2016. *The New Politics of Immigration and the End of Settler Societies*. Cambridge: Cambridge University Press.
Davies, G., and J. Fagan. 2012. "Crime and Enforcement in Immigrant Neighborhoods: Evidence from New York City." *The Annals of the American Academy of Political and Social Science* 641 (1): 99–124. doi:10.1177/0002716212438938.
Davis, A. 2016. *Freedom Is a Constant Struggle: Ferguson, Palestine, and the Foundations of a Movement*. Chicago: Haymarket Books.
Davis, A. Y. 2005. *Abolition Democracy: Beyond Empire, Prisons, and Torture*. New York: Seven Stories Press.
De Genova, N. P. 2002. "Migrant 'Illegality' and Deportability in Everyday Life." *Annual Review of Anthropology* 31 (1):419–447.
De Genova, N. P. 2007. "The Production of Culprits: From Deportability to Detainability in the Aftermath of "Homeland Security." *Citizenship Studies* 11 (5):421–448.
De Leon, J. 2013. *The Land of Open Graves: Living and Dying on the Migrant Trail*. Berkeley: University of California Press.
Dobchuk-Land, B. 2017. "Resisting 'Progressive' Carceral Expansion: Lessons for Abolitionists from Anti-colonial Resistance." *Contemporary Justice Review* 20 (4): 404–418.

Ferraro, V. 2016. "Immigration and Crime in the New Destinations, 2000-2007: A Test of the Disorganizing Effect of Migration." *Journal of Quantitative Criminology* 32 (1): 23–45. doi:10.1007/s10940-015-9252-y.

Fleay, C., and L. Briskman. 2013. "Hidden Men: Bearing Witness to Mandatory Detention in Australia." *Refugee Survey Quarterly* 32 (3): 112–129. doi:10.1093/rsq/hdt010.

Foucault, M. 1977. *Discipline and Punish: The Birth of the Prison*. New York: Vintage Books.

Garcia Hernández, C. C. 2013. "Creating Crimmigration." *Brighman Young University Law Review* 6:1457–1515.

García Hernández, C. C. 2019. "Migrating to Prison: Immigration in the Era of Mass Incarceration." *DeCarceral Futures Conference Presentation*. Kingston, Ontario: Queens University Faculty of Law.

Gerard, A., and S. Pickering. 2012. "The Crime and Punishment of Somali Women's Extra-Legal Arrival in Malta." *The British Journal of Criminology* 52 (3): 514–533. doi:10.1093/bjc/azr094.

Gill, N. 2016. *Nothing Personal? Geographies of Governing and Activism in the British Asylum System*. London: Wiley-Blackwell.

Gill, N., D. Conlon, D. Moran, and A. Burridge. 2018. "Carceral Circuitry: New Directions in Carceral Geography." *Progress in Human Geography* 42: 183–204. doi:10.1177/0309132516671823.

Gilson, E. 2016. "The Perils and Privileges of Vulnerability: Intersectionality, Relationality, and the Injustices of the U.S. Prison Nation." *philoSOPHIA* 6 (1): 43–59. doi:10.1353/phi.2016.0011.

Glenn, E. N. 2015. "Settler Colonialism as Structure: A Framework for Comparative Studies of U.S. Race and Gender Formation." *Sociology of Race and Ethnicity* 1 (1): 52–72. doi:10.1177/2332649214560440.

Golash-Boza, T. M. 2015. *Deported: Immigrant Policing, Disposable Labor, and Global Capitalism*. New York: New York University Press.

Gómez Cervantes, A., C. Menjívar, and W. G. Staples. 2017. "'Humane' Immigration Enforcement and Latina Immigrants in the Detention Complex." *Feminist Criminology* 12 (3): 269–292. doi:10.1177/1557085117699069.

Grierson, J. 2021. "Asylum Seekers on Hunger Strike over Conditions at Kent Barracks Site." Last Modified 12 January. Accessed 29 January. https://www.theguardian.com/uk-news/2021/jan/12/ asylum-seekers-on-hunger-strike-over-conditions-at-kent-barracks-site.

Guenther, L. 2015. "Political Action at the End of the World: Hannah Arendt and the California Prison Hunger Strikes." *Canadian Journal of Human Rights* 4 (1):33–56.

Gutiérrez Nájera, L., and K. Maldonado. 2017. "Transnational Settler Colonial Formations and Global Capital: A Consideration of Indigenous Mexican Migrants." *American Quarterly* 69: 04.

Gutiérrez Rodríguez, E. 2018. "The Coloniality of Migration and the 'Refugee Crisis': On the Asylum-Migration Nexus, the Transatlantic White European Settler Colonialism-Migration and Racial Capitalism." *Refuge* 34 (1): 16–28. doi:10.7202/1050851ar.

Hartry, A. S. 2012. "Gendering Crimmigration: The Intersection of Gender, Immigration, and the Criminal Justice System." *Berkeley Journal of Gender, Law & Justice* 27 (1): 1–27.

Hazlewood, J. 2020. "5 Inmates Test Positive for COVID-19 at Grand Valley Institution." *CBC News*. Accessed 04 April 2020. https://www.cbc.ca/news/canada/kitchener-waterloo/inmates- guard-test-positive-covid-19-1.5522394

Hernández, D. 2008. "Pursuant to Deportation: Latinos and Immigrant Detention." *Latino Studies* 6: 35–63. doi:10.1057/lst.2008.2.

Hill Collins, P., and S. Bilge. 2016. *Intersectionality*. Cambridge: Polity Press.

Human Rights Watch. 2016. *Do You See How Much I'm Suffering Here?" Abuse against Transgender Women in US Immigration Detention*. New York City: Human Rights Watch.

Immigration and Refugee Board of Canada. 2019. *Chairperson Guideline 2: Detention*. Accessed 31 January 2021. https://irb-cisr.gc.ca/en/legal-policy/policies/Pages/GuideDir02.aspx

Jackson, H. 2020a. "2 Inmates at Maximum-security Prison Test Positive for COVID-19: Officials." *Global News*. Accessed 07 April 2020. https://globalnews.ca/news/6751336/coronavirus-inmates-test-positive/

Jackson, M. 2020b. "U.S. Immigration Officials Spread Coronavirus with Detainee Transfers." *Reuters*. Accessed 19 July 2020. https://theunionjournal.com/u_s-immigration-officials-spread-coronavirus-with-detainee-transfers-by-reuters/

James, A. 2013. *Upper Bunkies Unite: And Other Thoughts on the Politics of Mass Incarceration*. Santa Cruz: Goode Book Press.

Jeffries, F., and J. Ridgley. 2020. "Building the Sanctuary City from the Ground Up: Abolitionist Solidarity and Transformative Reform." *Citizenship Studies* 24 (4): 548–567. doi:10.1080/13621025.2020.1755177.

Jeovany. 2018. "Immigrant Voice: The Injustices of Quarantine." *Open Letter Published by the Migrant Center For Human Rights*. Accessed 04 April 2020. https://mailchi.mp/3bf1c2b539e0/xiwj23mikl

Johnston, A. 2013. "Italy Probes Treatment of Lampedusa Migrants 'Forced to Strip'". *BBC News Online* Accessed 20 December 2013. http://www.bbc.co.uk/news/world-europe-25423032?

Jones, C. A., and R. L. Seabrook. 2017. "The New Jane Crow: Mass Incarceration and the Denied Maternity of Black Women." *Race, Ethnicity and Law Sociology of Crime, Law and Deviance* 22: 135–154.

Jones, C.A., M. Ortiz, and K. Renner. 2020. "Depression, Perceived Discrimination, and Racial Barrier Awareness as Predictors of Offending for Black Women." *Journal of Ethnicity in Criminal Justice* 18 (1): 1–18.

Jung, M. 2020. "Immigration and Crime in Canadian Cities: A 35-Year Study." *Canadian Journal of Criminology and Criminal Justice* 62 (1): 71–97. doi:10.3138/cjccj.2019-0015.

Kaytaz, E. S., and S. J. Silverman. 2019. "Profiling Risk at the Canadian Border." *9th Annual Canadian Association of Refugee and Forced Migration Studies Conference*. Toronto: York University.

Kratz, N., C. Diaz, J. Ross, J. Merlin, and L. Davies. 2020. "Open Letter to ICE from Medical Professionals Urging the Release of Individuals in Immigration Detention Given the Risk of COVID-19." Accessed 20 April 2020. https://docs.google.com/forms/d/e/ 1FAIpQLScB1YLk-MHzdJ2ahcxx25NRRqEnlRTk_xA6Q6cJTfZXUQV-Dg/viewform?fbclid=IwAR02eh8VMxG4iqv9p6JdD9OejZMVU_npHxxVJ_rQTwmxSbr-L5s7qWKvdQ0

Law, V. 2012. *Resistance Behind Bars: The Struggles of Incarcerated Women*. Oakland, CA: PM Press.

Leerkes, A., and D. Broeders. 2010. "A Case of Mixed Motives?: Formal and Informal Functions of Administrative Immigration Detention." *British Journal of Criminology* 50 (5): 830–850. doi:10.1093/bjc/azq035.

Legewie, J. 2019. "Police Violence and the Health of Black Infants." *Science Advances* 5 (12): eaax7894. doi:10.1126/sciadv.aax7894.

Lemberg-Pedersen, M. 2019. "Manufacturing Displacement. Externalization and Postcoloniality in European Migration Control." *Global Affairs* 5 (3): 247–271. doi:10.1080/23340460.2019.1683463.

Leung, J., D. Elson, K. Sanders, M. Marin, G. Leos, B. Cloud, R. J. McNall, C. J. Hickman, and M. Marlow. 2019. "Notes from the Field: Mumps in Detention Facilities that House Detained Migrants - United States, September 2018-August 2019." *MMWR. Morbidity and Mortality Weekly Report* 68 (34): 749–750. doi:10.15585/mmwr.mm6834a4.

Longazel, J., J. Berman, and B. Fleury-Steiner. 2016. "The Pains of Immigrant Imprisonment." *Sociology Compass* 10 (11): 989–998. doi:10.1111/soc4.12434.

Loyd, J. M., and A. Mountz. 2018. *Boats, Borders, and Bases: Race, the Cold War, and the Rise of Migration Detention in the United States*. Berkeley: University of California Press.

Lydon, J. M. 2016. "Once There Was No Prison Rape: Ending Sexual Violence as Strategy for Prison Abolition." *philoSOPHIA* 6: 61–71. doi:10.1353/phi.2016.0014.

Mainwaring, C., and S. J. Silverman. 2017. "Detention-as-Spectacle." *International Political Sociology* 11: 21–38.
Marouf, F. E. 2017. "Alternatives to Immigration Detention." *Cardozo Law Review* 38 (6): 2141–2192.
Massey, D. S., and K. A. Pren. 2012. "Unintended Consequences of US Immigration Policy: Explaining the Post-1965 Surge from Latin America." *Population and Development Review* 38 (1): 1–29. doi:10.1111/j.1728-4457.2012.00470.x.
Maynard, R. 2017. *Policing Black Lives: State Violence in Canada from Slavery to the Present.* Black Point, Nova Scotia and Winnipeg, Manitoba: Fernwood Publishing.
McDowell, M. G., and L. A. Fernandez. 2018. "'Disband, Disempower, and Disarm': Amplifying the Theory and Practice of Police Abolition." *Critical Criminology* 26 (3): 373–391. doi:10.1007/s10612-018-9400-4.
McLeod, A. M. 2019. "Abolitionist Imaginings of Immigration Justice". *DeCarceral Futures Conference Presentation*. Kingston, Ontario: Queens University Faculty of Law.
Medel, C. 2017. "Abolitionist Care in the Militarized Borderlands." *The South Atlantic Quarterly* 116 (4): 873–883. doi:10.1215/00382876-4235084.
Miles, T. J., and A. B. Cox. 2014. "Does Immigration Enforcement Reduce Crime? Evidence from Secure Communities." *The Journal of Law and Economics* 57 (4): 937–973. doi:10.1086/ 680935.
Missbach, A. 2014. "Doors and Fences: Controlling Indonesia's Porous Borders and Policing Asylum Seekers." *Singapore Journal of Tropical Geography* 35 (2): 228–244. doi:10.1111/ sjtg.12059.
Missbach, A. 2017. "Accommodating Asylum Seekers and Refugees in Indonesia: From Immigration Detention to Containment in "Alternatives to Detention"." *Refuge: Canada's Journal on Refugees* 33 (2): 32–44. doi:10.7202/1043061ar.
Moinester, M. 2018. "Beyond the Border and into the Heartland: Spatial Patterning of U.S. Immigration Detention." *Demography*. Advanced Access Online:1–47.
Molnar, P. 2019. "Technology on the Margins, AI and Global Migration Management from a Human Rights Perspective." *Cambridge International Law Journal* 8 (2): 305–330. doi:10.4337/cilj.2019.02.07.
Morris, J. 2017. "Power, Capital, and Immigration Detention Rights: Making Networked Markets in Global Detention Governance at UNHCR." *Global Networks* 17 (3): 400–422. doi:10.1111/glob.12124.
Mountz, A., K. Coddington, R. T. Catania, and J. Loyd. 2013. "Conceptualizing Detention: Mobility, Containment, Bordering, and Exclusion." *Progress in Human Geography* 37 (4): 522–541. doi:10.1177/0309132512460903.
Nah, A., M. Phillips, and M. Y. Park, Edited by. 2020. *COVID-19 Impacts on Immigration Detention: Global Responses*. Sydney: International Detention Coalition, HADRI/Western Sydney University.
Nethery, A., B. Rafferty-Brown, and S. Taylor. 2013. "Exporting Detention: Australia-funded Immigration Detention in Indonesia." *Journal of Refugee Studies* 26 (1): 88–109. doi:10.1093/ jrs/fes027.
Neuman, G. L. 2018. "Detention as a Last Resort: The Implications of General Comment No. 35." In *Protecting the Migrant Child (Edward Elgar), Forthcoming*, edited by M. Crock and L. Benson. 381–395. Cheltenham: Edward Elgar.
Nevins, J. 2010. *Operation Gatekeeper and Beyond: The War on Illegals and the Remaking of the U.S.-Mexico Boundary*. London: Routledge.
Ngai, M. M. 2004. *Impossible Subjects: Illegal Aliens and the Making of Modern America*. Oxford: Princeton University Press.
Nichols, R. 2014. "The Colonialism of Incarceration." *Radical Philosophy Review* 17 (2):435–455.
Nyers, P. 2006. *Rethinking Refugees: Beyond States of Emergency*. New York: Routledge.

Ocen, P. A. 2013. "Unshackling Intersectionality." *Du Bois Review: Social Science Research on Race* 10 (2): 471–483. doi:10.1017/S1742058X13000295.

Ohtani, E., and J. Phelps. 2016. "Without Detention: Opportunities for Alternatives." Last Modified September. Accessed 16 October. http://detentionaction.org.uk/wordpress/wp- content/uploads/2016/09/Without-Detention.pdf.

Patler, C., and N. Branic. 2017. "Patterns of Family Visitation during Immigration Detention." *RSF: The Russell Sage Foundation Journal of the Social Sciences* 3 (4): 18–36.

Pétin, J. 2016. "Exploring the Role of Vulnerability in Immigration Detention." *Refugee Survey Quarterly* 35 (1): 91–108. doi:10.1093/rsq/hdv017.

Piché, J., and K. Major. 2015. "Prisoner Writing In/on Solitary Confinement: Contributions from the *Journal of Prisoners on Prisons*, 1988–2013." *Canadian Journal of Human Rights* 4: 01.

Razack, S. 2007. *Casting Out: The Eviction of Muslims from Western Law and Politics*. Toronto: University of Toronto Press.

Reitano, T., L. Adal, and M. Shaw. 2014. "Smuggled Futures: The Dangerous Path of the Migrant from Africa to Europe." Geneva: Global Initiative against Transnational Organized Crime.

Reiter, K., and S. B. Coutin. 2017. "Crossing Borders and Criminalizing Identity: The Disintegrated Subjects of Administrative Sanctions." *Law & Society Review* 51 (3): 567–601. doi:10.1111/lasr.12281.

Richie, B. E. 2012. *Arrested Justice: Black Women, Violence, and America's Prison Nation*. New York: NYU Press.

Rodríguez, D. 2019. "Mass Incarceration' Is a Useless Term: Race, Domestic War, and the Long Carceral Half-Century." In *DeCarceral Futures Workshop Presentation*, edited by S. Aiken and S. J. Silverman. Kingston, Ontario: Queens University Faculty of Law.

Rosales Arriola, E. 2016. "Queer, Undocumented, and Sitting in an Immigration Detention Center: A Post-*Obergefell* Reflection." *UMKC Law Review* 84 (3): 617–638.

Russell, E., and B. Carlton. 2013. "Pathways, Race and Gender Responsive Reform: Through an Abolitionist Lens." *Theoretical Criminology* 17 (4): 474–492. doi:10.1177/1362480613497777.

Shah, N. 2019. "Putting One's Body on the Line." *GLQ: A Journal of Lesbian and Gay Studies* 25 (1): 183–187. doi:10.1215/10642684-7275446.

Sharma, N. 2006. *Home Economics: Nationalism and the Making of 'Migrant Workers' in Canada*. Toronto: University of Toronto Press.

Sharma, N., and C. Wright. 2008. "Decolonizing Resistance, Challenging Colonial States." *Social Justice* 35 (3 (113)): 120–138.

Sheth, F. A. 2014. "Interstitiality: Making Space for Migration, Diaspora, and Racial Complexity." *Hypatia* 29 (1): 75–93. doi:10.1111/hypa.12075.

Silverman, S. J. 2010. "Immigration Detention in America: A History of Its Expansion and A Study of Its Significance." In *COMPAS Working Paper No 10 – 80*, edited by A. Rogers, 1–33. Oxford: Centre on Migration, Policy, and Society.

Silverman, S. J. 2013. "Questions over Alternatives to Detention Programmes." *Forced Migration Review* 44 (Detention, Alternatives to Detention, and Deportation): 59–60.

Silverman, S. J., and A. Nethery. 2015. "Understanding Immigration Detention and Its Human Impact." In *Immigration Detention: The Journey of a Policy and Its Human Impact*, edited by A. Nethery and S. J. Silverman, 1–12. London: Routledge.

Silverman, S. J. 2016. "Imposter-Children' in the UK Refugee Status Determination Process." *Refuge: Canada's Journal on Refugees* 32 (3): 30–39. doi:10.25071/1920-7336.40371.

Silverman, S. J. 2018a. "The EU's Hotspot Approach: Questionable Motivations and Unreachable Goals." Last Modified 17 April. Accessed 29 April. https://www.e-ir.info/2018/04/17/the-eus- hotspot-approach-questionable-motivations-and-unreachable-goals/.

Silverman, S. J. 2018b. "Under the Umbrella of Administrative Law: Immigration Detention and the Challenges of Producing Just Immigration Law." *APA Newsletter on Hispanic/Latino Issues in Philosophy* 17 (3): 9–12.

Silverman, S. J. 2018c. "Electronically Monitoring Migrants Treats Them like Criminals." Last Modified 25 January. Accessed 05 May. https://theconversation.com/electronically-monitoring-migrants-treats-them-like-criminals-90521.

Spade, D. 2013. "Intersectional Resistance and Law Reform." *Signs: Journal of Women in Culture and Society* 38 (4): 1031–1055. doi:10.1086/669574.

Stanley, E. A., D. Spade, and Q. Justice. 2012. "Queering Prison Abolition, Now?" *American Quarterly* 64 (1): 115–127. doi:10.1353/aq.2012.0003.

Stasiulis, D. 2020. "Elimi(Nation): Canada's "Post-settler" Embrace of Disposable Migrant Labour." *Studies in Social Justice* 14 (1): 22–54. doi:10.26522/ssj.v2020i14.2251.

Stasiulis, D., and N. Yuval-Davis, edited by. 1995. *Unsettling Settler Societies: Articulations of Gender, Race, Ethnicity and Class.* London: SAGE Publications.

Stelloh, T. 2019. "Transgender, Gay Migrants Allegedly Suffer 'Rampant' Abuse at New Mexico ICE Facility". *NBC News.* Accessed 29 March 2019 https://www.nbcnews.com/news/us-news/transgender-gay-migrants-allegedly-suffer-rampant-abuse-new-mexico-ice-n987286.

Struthers Montford, K., and D. Moore. 2018. "The Prison as Reserve: Governmentality, Phenomenology, and Indigenizing the Prison (Studies)." *New Criminal Law Review* 21 (4): 640–663. doi:10.1525/nclr.2018.21.4.640.

Sudbury, J. 2004. "A World without Prisons: Resisting Militarism, Globalized Punishment, and Empire." *Social Justice* 31 (1/2): 9–30.

Sudbury, J. 2008. "Maroon Abolitionists: Black Gender- Oppressed Activists in the Anti- Prison Movement in the US and Canada." *Eridians: Feminism, Race, Transnationalism* 9 (1): 1-29.

Tazzioli, M., and G. Garelli. 2020. "Containment beyond Detention: The Hotspot System and Disrupted Migration Movements across Europe." *Environment and Planning D: Society and Space.* Advanced Access Online. doi:10.1177/0263775818759335.

Transactional Records Access Clearinghouse (TRAC). 2020. "Immigration and Customs Enforcement Detention - ICE Data Snapshots, up to July 2019." Accessed 15 January. https://trac.syr.edu/phptools/immigration/detention/

Trovall, E. 2019. "More Than 400 Mumps Cases Confirmed in Texas Immigrant Facilities." In *Houston Public Media.* https://www.houstonpublicmedia.org/articles/news/politics/immigration/2019/07/29/340973/more-than-400-mumps-cases-confirmed-in-texas-immigrant- facilities/

Tuck, E., and K. W. Yang. 2012. "Decolonization Is Not a Metaphor." *Decolonization: Indigeneity, Education & Society* 1 (1): 1–40.

Turnbull, S. 2019. "Vulnerability, Immigration Detention, and (Penal) Reform." *DeCarceral Futures Conference Presentation.* Kingston, Ontario: Queens University Faculty of Law.

Tyler, I., N. Gill, D. Conlon, and C. Oeppen. 2014. "The Business of Child Detention: Charitable Co-option, Migrant Advocacy and Activist Outrage." *Race & Class* 56 (1): 03–21. doi:10.1177/0306396814531690.

UN Working Group on Arbitrary Detention. 2018. *Revised Deliberation No. 5 On Deprivation of Liberty of Migrants.* Accessed 31 January 2021. https://www.refworld.org/docid/5a903b514.html

UNHCR. 2012. *Guidelines on the Applicable Criteria and Standards Relating to the Detention of Asylum-Seekers and Alternatives to Detention.* Accessed 31 January 2021. https://www.unhcr.org/publications/legal/505b10ee9/unhcr-detention-guidelines.html

Walia, H. 2013. *Undoing Border Imperialism.* California: AK Press.

Ware, S. J. R., and G. Dias. 2014. "It Can't Be Fixed because It's Not Broken: Racism and Disability in the Prison Industrial Complex." In *Disability Incarcerated: Imprisonment and Disability in the United States and Canada*, edited by L. Ben-Moshe, C. Chapman, and A. C. Carey, 163–184. New York: Palgrave Macmillan US.

Weill-Greenberg, E. 2020. "Prisoners in Illinois Describe Dire Conditions amid Coronavirus Outbreak." *The Appeal*. Accessed 12 April 2020. https://theappeal.org/illinois-stateville-prison-conditions-coronavirus-covid-19/

Williams, K., and A. Mountz. 2016. "Rising Tide: Analyzing the Relationship between Externalization and Migrant Deaths and Boat Losses." In *Externalizing Migration Management*, edited by R. Zaiotti, 31–49. London: Routledge.

Wilsher, D. 2012. *Immigration Detention: Law, History, Politics*. Cambridge: Cambridge University Press.

Wilson Gilmore, R. 2007. *Golden Gulag: Prisons, Surplus, Crisis, and Opposition in Globalizing California*. Berkeley: University of California Press.

Wilson Gilmore, R. 2014. "Forward." In *The Struggle Within: Prisons, Political Prisoners, and Mass Movements in the United States*, edited by D. Berger. Oakland: PM Press, pp vii–xi.

Wolfe, P. 1999. *Settler Colonialism and the Transformation of Anthropology: The Politics and Poetics of an Ethnographic Event*. London: Cassell.

Wong, T. K. 2015. *Rights, Deportation, and Detention in the Age of Immigration Control*. Palo Alto: Stanford University Press.

Woods, T. P. 2013. "Surrogate Selves: Notes on Anti-trafficking and Anti-blackness." *Social Identities* 19 (1): 120–134. doi:10.1080/13504630.2012.753348.

World Health Organization Regional Office for Europe. 2020. "Interim Guidance: Preparedness, Prevention and Control of COVID-19 in Prisons and Other Places of Detention."

Yuval-Davis, N. 2007. "Intersectionality, Citizenship and Contemporary Politics of Belonging." *Critical Review of International Social and Political Philosophy* 10 (4): 561–574. doi:10.1080/13698230701660220.

Zinger, I. 2020. "Indigenous People in Federal Custody Surpasses 30% Correctional Investigator Issues Statement and Challenge". *Office of the Correctional Investigator*. Accessed 02 March 2020. https://www.oci-bec.gc.ca/cnt/comm/press/press20200121-eng.aspx

Mutual aid as abolitionist praxis

Simone Weil Davis and Rachel Fayter

ABSTRACT
Prisons, jails, and detention facilities, by definition, are designed to isolate and separate people from their communities. To challenge and upend carcerality requires not just dismantlement, but radical revisioning, a *building* – of flourishing, free and caring communities. Collectively developed responses and resources for people and ecosystems, led by those with lived experience of oppression, are the foundation for a world without prisons.

Prisons, jails, and detention facilities, by definition, are designed to isolate and separate people from their communities. With increasing rates of incarceration and migrant detention, especially among women and racialized communities (Roberts 2017; United Nations (UN) General Assembly 2010; Zinger 2019), large numbers of people are being torn from their families, forced to leave their life and everything they know behind. People in prison or on parole, the undocumented, and those in immigrant detention share experiences of dislocation, disenfranchisement, racism, violence and dehumanization. Often, they are confined in the same facility. In this bluntest of ways, the 'problems' of prison and of immigrant detention converge.

But it may be prison abolitionist 'solutions' that matter most in this convergence. To challenge and upend carcerality requires not just dismantlement, but radical revisioning, a *building* – of flourishing, free and caring communities (Davis 2003). Collectively developed responses and resources for people and ecosystems, led by those with lived experience of oppression, are the foundation for a world without prisons.

Mutual aid makes it possible both to survive the present – solidarity as resistance – and to imagine and build 'decarceral futures' (Aiken and Silverman 2019; Spade 2020; Kaba and Spade 2020). Particularly when seeking help from state and official sources is a dead end and an active harm, people organize to help each other. Perhaps there is no refugee camp, no migrant community, no institution of confinement, no group of survivors, no low-income neighborhood where people of color live, where that isn't the case.

In prisons and migrant detention facilities, mutual aid is a way of life and survival. Extensive research has shown that mutual aid or peer-support is very beneficial for criminalized people (Maruna and LeBel 2003; Pollack 2008; Sheehan, McIvor, and Trotter 2011), yet the oppressive carceral system typically does not support it. In carceral settings, relationships are highly structured and controlled (Pollack 2007), while solidarity and even friendship among prisoners is repressed (Anonymous Prisoner 4 2017; Fayter and Payne 2017; Law 2012; McCorkel 2003). Despite this, many people with lived experience of incarceration advocate for and support other prisoners and criminalized people, organizing resistance to the carceral state. Abolitionist praxis requires a politics built around this type of solidarity in action.

As a former prisoner who spent almost four years in prison, I (co-author Rachel Fayter) can personally attest to the importance of mutual aid. When I first arrived at a new institution, I relied on those who were there before me to learn the rules and how to navigate the system. I also quickly learned that fighting for my rights would result in being targeted by staff. In federal custody there were technically several prisoner employment positions focused on mutual-aid, such as inmate committee, grievance coordinator, and peer-support. These jobs were considered 'positions of trust' within the institution, which effectively meant that anyone who had a misconduct was not allowed to work. Some of these positions remained unfilled for years at a time, but informal mutual aid is persistent; when the sanctioned opportunities were not available prisoner support moved underground.

Engaging in 'everyday acts of resistance' (Scott 1985, 1990) prisoners often made care packages for new arrivals, with hygiene products, coffee, and stamps. We cooked for one another, lent clothing to someone who had a visit, and shared a book or music album. These acts of kindness were prohibited by the system and anyone who participated risked misconduct charges, which reduces one's chance for parole. Despite the risk, we strive to live in solidarity.

Resistance and solidarity coincide in mutual aid (Medina 2013). This convergence drove our own opening workshop at the 2019 *Decarceral Futures* conference. Walls to Bridges courses bring together incarcerated and non-incarcerated students as classmates (wallstobridges.ca). W2B learning circles are founded on the idea that we need each other's shared knowledges *and* our incommensurabilities (Gaztambide-Fernández 2012). Examining the hierarchical and oppressive power relations that structure institutions of punishment as well as education, students forge, test, challenge and strengthen other ways of relating. To teach, learn and unlearn together: education as mutual aid.

Since the militarization of the US-Mexico border, Covid and the 2020 uprising against anti-Black racism, both existing and emergent networks of mutual aid are becoming more intentional, being coordinated into larger networks of care, refined and guided by those from marginalized communities.

'Caremongering' is a human trait; it is also an abolitionist building block (Chopra 2020). It is a collective deepening of webs of relationship that are neither defined nor 'managed' by carceral or capitalist structures. Perhaps these long-established relational structures, coordinated networks of collective care, provide the grounds for an alternative conceptualization of 'citizenship' (Abu El-Haj 2009), one based not on papers or the nation-state, but on situated engagement in mutual aid.

Disclosure statement

No potential conflict of interest was reported by the authors.

References

Abu El-Haj, T. R. A. 2009. "Becoming Citizens in an Era of Globalization and Transnational Migration: Re-imagining Citizenship as Critical Practice." *Theory into Practice* 48 (4): 274–282. doi:10.1080/00405840903192714.

Aiken, S., and S. J. Silverman. 2019. "Introduction to DeCarceral Futures." *DeCarceral Futures Conference Presentation*. Kingston, Ontario: Queens University Faculty of Law.

Anonymous Prisoner 4. 2017. "Dispatches from Federally Sentenced Women: Fraser Valley Institution." *Journal of Prisoners on Prisons* 26 (1&2): 49–54.

Chopra, G. 2020. "'Read First' Post." *Caremongering-TO*. www.facebook.com/groups/TO.Community.Response.COVID19/permalink/2661130287455762/

Davis, A. Y. 2003. "Abolitionist Alternatives." In *Are Prisons Obsolete?*, edited by Greg Ruggiero, 105–115. NY: Seven Stories Press.

Fayter, R., and S. Payne. 2017. "The Impact of the Conservative Punishment Agenda on Federally Sentenced Women and Priorities for Social Change." *Journal of Prisoners on Prisons* 26 (1&2): 10–30.

Gaztambide-Fernández, R. A. 2012. "Decolonization and the Pedagogy of Solidarity." *Decolonization: Indigeneity, Education and Society* 1 (1): 41–67.

Kaba, M., and D. Spade. 2020. "Interviewees: 'Solidarity Not Charity': Mutual Aid and How to Organize in the Age of Coronavirus," *Democracy Now*! Accessed 21 March 2020. www.democracynow.org/2020/3/20/coronavirus_community_response_mutual_aid

Law, V. 2012. *Resistance behind Bars: The Struggles of Incarcerated Women*. 2nd ed. Oakland, CA: PM Press.

Maruna, S., and T. LeBel. 2003. "Welcome Home? Examining the 'Re-entry Court' Concept from a Strengths-based Perspective." *Western Criminology Review* 4: 91–107.

McCorkel, J. A. 2003. "Embodied Surveillance and the Gendering of Punishment." *Journal of Contemporary Ethnography* 32 (1): 41–76. doi:10.1177/0891241602238938.

Medina, J. 2013. *The Epistemology of Resistance: Gender and Racial Oppression, Epistemic Injustice, and Resistant Imaginations*. New York: Oxford University Press.

Pollack, S. 2007. "'I'm Just Not Good in Relationships:' Victimization Discourses and the Gendered Regulation of Criminalized Women." *Feminist Criminology* 2: 158–174. doi:10.1177/1557085106297521.

Pollack, S. 2008. *Locked In, Locked Out: Imprisoning Women in the Shrinking and Punitive Welfare State*. Ottawa, ON: Faculty of Social Work, Wilfrid Laurier University. Accessed 15 June 2020. https://www.academia.edu/6375218/Locked_In_Locked_Out_Imprisoning_Women_in_the_Shrinking_and_Punitive_Welfare_State

Roberts, A. 2017. *Gendered States of Punishment and Welfare: Feminist Political Economy, Primitive Accumulation and the Law*. New York: Routledge.

Scott, J. C. 1985. *Weapons of the Weak: Everyday Forms of Peasant Resistance*. New Haven: Yale University Press.

Scott, J. C. 1990. *Domination and the Arts of Resistance: Hidden Transcripts*. New Haven: Yale University Press.

Sheehan, R., G. McIvor, and C. Trotter. 2011. "Who Cares? Fostering Networks and Relationships in Prison and Beyond." In *Working with Women Offenders in the Community*, edited by Sheehan, R., G. McIvor, and C. Trotter, 268–287. . Cullompton: Willan Publishing.

Spade, D. 2020. "The Big Door Brigade." *website*. Accessed 6 June 2020. www.bigdoorbrigade.com

United Nations (UN) General Assembly. 2010. *The United Nations Rules for the Treatment of Women Prisoners and Non-custodial Measures for Women Offenders (The Bangkok Rules)*. Accessed 21 February 2020. https://www.un.org/en/ecosoc/docs/2010/res%202010-16.pdf

Zinger, I. 2019. *Annual Report from the Office of the Correctional Investigator: 2018-2019*. Ottawa: Correctional Investigator of Canada.

States and human immobilization: bridging the conceptual separation of slavery, immigration controls, and mass incarceration

Nandita Sharma

ABSTRACT

Immigration controls and incarceration both comprise state efforts to limit people's freedom of movement. Usually analyzed separately, both are part of the legacy of slavery. In this paper, I examine the British Empire's first implementation of immigration controls against 'coolie labour' from its colony of British India following the abolition of slavery in 1835. I also examine the implementation of methods of control and discipline enacted against formerly enslaved people in the United States following its abolition of slavery in 1865. Just ten years after abolition, the U.S. also passed its first immigration controls, the 1875 Page Act. I argue that both immigration controls and mass incarceration were state methods aimed at weakening people's position in the capitalist labour market and, more generally, to weaken people's ability to realize social justice. Together, immigration and carceral controls created racialized and gendered categories of people denied access to the mythical institutions of liberal democracy: liberty, fellowship, and equality. Both also strengthened nationalism(s) through the production of a U.S. 'nation' secured against 'criminals' and 'foreigners.' By making connections between immigration controls and mass incarceration, I argue, we can more clearly recognize that the success of prison abolition and No Borders movements are, together, integral parts of the unfinished project to realize liberty.

Introduction

Immigration controls and incarceration are both state-enforced ways to limit people's mobility. With few exceptions, they have normally been analyzed separately. I try to bring the two sets of literature on these topics together to show how each is a legacy of slavery and the political struggles to end it. In the absence of the enormous power that the institution of slavery gave slave owners, the state, and in important ways, to free-waged workers, new technologies of discipline, punishment, and labour control were implemented. These technologies focused on methods of containment that continue to shape our contemporary world. I focus on the state technologies of mass criminalization/incarceration and immigration controls in the United States to try and demonstrate this link.

Slavery was abolished in the U.S. in 1865, following a deadly civil war in which the 'evil institution' defined which side of the battle line between the Northern States (the Union) and the Southern states (the Confederacy) one was on. Immediately after the end of slavery, carceral methods of control and discipline were enacted against formerly enslaved people to weaken their demands for justice as well as their position in the labour market. Just ten years after abolition, the U.S. also passed its first immigration controls with the 1875 Page Act. It was designed to limit the entry into the U.S. of two main biopolitical groupings: 'Chinese coolies' and women deemed by state inspectors to be 'prostitutes.'

Together, immigration and carceral controls created racialized and gendered categories of people denied access to the mythical institutions of liberal democracy: liberty, fellowship, and equality. However, former slaves and people now regulated by immigration controls were governed by different arenas of laws. Consequently, the people subjected to these laws also came to be seen (and sometimes to see themselves) as unconnected or even antagonistic to one another. Their separation augmented the strength of nation-states – and of nationalisms – to subjugate people categorized either as Black or as Migrants. In particular, the state was able to impose unfree labour relations upon both groups. I argue that contemporary social justice struggles against state efforts at limiting people's freedom of movement will be strengthened by analyzing the links between the incarceration of subordinated national citizens and the refusal to grant citizenship to Migrants. Understanding how both sets of state practices have a crucial genealogy in the *politics* of abolishing slavery will better allow us to see how both prison abolition and No Borders work are part of the unfinished project to realize liberty.

As events in the United States cannot be studied in isolation from those taking place within the world system of which it is a part, it is important to examine the first efforts to implement immigration controls: those of the British imperial-state starting in 1835 as it transitioned from reliance on the institution of slavery to the institution of 'coolieism' to secure labour for investors across its Empire. This new method of limiting people's freedom of movement was politically important in the nationalization of state sovereignty, as, I argue occurred in the United States, in 1875 with the passing of its own first immigration controls.

Thus, in what follows, I first examine the link between the end of slavery and the beginning of immigration controls. To do so, I discuss how the British Empire broke with imperial forms of allowing relative freedom to enter imperial territory by imposing immigration controls on those of its subjects moving between British India to British Mauritius as contract indentured 'coolie' labour in the 1830s. It did so because of concerns by Mauritian sugar plantation owners that the end of slave labour relations in the Empire would jeopardize not only their profits but also their ability to control and discipline both the newly freed work force of both former slaves and the newly recruited 'coolie' labourers. The link between the abolition of slavery and the use of immigration controls to discipline workers through new methods of immobilization continued to render workers' labour unfree in the British Empire set the terms for how subsequent states responded to the end of slavery in their territories.

I then discuss how the abolition of slavery in the United States in 1865 was met with new forms of politically weakening and cheapening the labour power of freed slaves as well as creating a new state category of people – Migrants – whose mobility into the U.S., along with their mobility within the labour market, would be controlled by immigration regulations and restrictions. Black people in the U.S. faced new limits to their freedom, including racialized Jim Crow laws preventing them from exercising their civil rights, employers' practices of imposing practices of 'sharecropping,' and, later, the massive expansion of the prison system that, in part, worked to contain the radical Black political movements of the 1960s and 1970s. While the recruitment of 'coolie labour' was nowhere near as extensive in the United States as it was throughout the British Empire, nonetheless, the figure of the 'coolie' was centrally featured in the first immigration controls in the U.S.

I conclude by trying to make some conceptual and political links between movements addressing mass incarceration and evermore restrictive immigration controls. By showing that one of the reasons that incarceration and immigration controls are seen as separate processes is because the call for the 'freedom to move' has come to be narrowly associated with the ability to cross national borders, i.e. to 'migrate.' By refusing to conflate 'movement' solely with 'migration' – something nation-states and nationalists both attempt to do – and instead see that many 'national citizens' also call for the ability to move at will (e.g. move out of prison), we are better able to make the connections between calls for prison abolition and for No Borders. Both, I argue, are concerned with mobility rights.

States and mobility controls

I begin with an examination of the first immigration controls imposed on workers recruited through the 'coolie' labour system from the colony of British India to the British colony of Mauritius in 1835. In retrospect, it is evident that these first controls augured a world-historical shift in the ways imperial-states limited people's mobility. Despite the assumption within much of citizenship and migration studies that immigration controls have been a key feature of state sovereignty since the 1648 Treaty of Westphalia, which enshrined the doctrine of territorial sovereignty, it was not until the end of slavery in the British Empire that restricting people's entry into imperial territories was regarded as something states should do.

Until this time, imperial-states were generally preoccupied with ensuring that people did not leave their territories. Indeed, restricting people's freedom of movement out of imperial territories was the *sine qua non* of the project of civilization ('civilization' itself being an effect of state power according to Scott 2009). This was no easy task. Many would-be imperial subjects, keen on making an escape, practiced what James Scott (2009) nicely terms, 'the art of not being governed' and carved out non-state spaces for themselves where, when, and for as long they could. In contrast to the seventeenth century Hobbesian story of sovereignty, in which states were purportedly created by people protecting them from the violent chaos of an 'uncivilized' (i.e. stateless) life, in actuality, keeping people subjected to the state's power was the main purpose of trying to prevent their movement. Keeping people within the state's territories was crucial to keeping them subjected to state power.

This is not to say that imperial states were uninterested in people's movements into their territories. Quite the contrary. Imperial states facilitated people's movements into their territories on a massive scale and usually through force (Mongia 2007). The imperial state moved workers as slaves, indentured servants, debtors, criminals, and, starting later in the nineteenth century, as free waged workers. These state-organized movements was a structural element of European imperialism (Potts 1990, 204). Moving workers into imperial territories was crucial for the profitability of imperial enterprises, particularly where colonialism led to the death of large numbers of people categorized as the 'natives' of the colonies, often as a result of the harsh working and living conditions imposed by their enslavement (Reséndez 2016). In addition, the high death rate of people moved from Africa, Europe and, later, Asia into imperial territories meant that continuous recruitment of new workers proved to be necessary.

The Atlantic slave trade was particularly crucial to the success of European imperialism. In the mid-fifteenth century, Portugal started enslaving and moving people from the West coast of the African continent to Portugal and, soon thereafter, to its colonies in the New World, the Atlantic archipelagos, and Asia. The Spanish Empire followed suit in the early-sixteenth century. The British Empire, the first to impose capitalist social relations on its subjects, became the largest slave-trading empire as the Atlantic slave trade peaked in the 1760s and until the trade was abolished in 1807. The slave trade was the richest part of Britain's trade in the eighteenth century when slightly more than half of all people enslaved and transported from Africa to the Americas each year were carried on slave ships ultimately protected by the British navy

The end of the 'evil trade,' indeed the world-historical shift that came with the political delegitimization of slavery, was no doubt the result of the centuries-long and countless acts of rebellion of the enslaved. Later, many others joined them in an organized social movement to abolish slavery, some of them from the City of London – the seat of the British empire – where abolitionist efforts began in the late-eighteenth century (Hochschild 2005; Linebaugh and Rediker 2000). With its 25 March 1807 *Abolition of the Slave Trade Act*, the British Empire formally stopped facilitating the movement of enslaved people from Africa to its imperial territories.

Yet, because of the heavy reliance of both plantation owners and the imperial treasury on the wealth produced by slave labour, the British Empire maintained the institution of slavery for several decades afterward. It was not until Britain's *Slavery Abolition Act* of 1833 went into effect starting in 1834 that slave labour relations themselves ended. Indeed, some British imperial territories kept slavery in place for several years afterwards. The decades-long gap between the end of the slave trade (1807) and the end of slave labour relations (1834–1843), was due to the unresolved worries of planters and the British state that freed slaves would not succumb to new controls on their mobility and their labour. The issue thus became one of recruiting workers to replace them. In the political context of the successes of the slavery abolition movement, the central issue was one of rights. The question was what, if any, rights would the workers recruited to replace enslaved workers have? In this there was no uniform answer.

One answer lay in the dramatic increase of workers recruited from Europe to the colonies. Until the abolition of the slave trade in 1807, the number of Africans throughout the Americas had outstripped the combined total of Europeans by a ratio of 3, 4, or even 5:1. Between 1492 and 1820, approximately ten to fifteen million Africans were forcibly brought to the 'New World' and only two million or so people from Europe. Most of these workers went to what became known as the White Settler colonies of the United States, Canada, Australia, and New Zealand where the ratio of Whites to non-

Whites was reversed earlier on. (Steinfeld 1991). While many of these workers were held in some kind of bondage to their employers (or Masters in the parlance of the day), by the early nineteenth century, workers arriving from Europe were less and less likely to be employed in unfree employment relations.[1] Moreover, a racialized division of labour and a differential pay scale between workers racialized as White and those racialized into various categories of non-Whites was already well in place by the mid- to late-17th century, especially in what came to be the White Settler colonies. Politically, however, because this racialized division of labour was part of the overall effort to co-opt workers made White into supporting the imperial project, the 'wages of whiteness' had become significantly higher than those of non-white workers (Roediger 1999). As such, the increase in workers from Europe did not end the search for a profitable labour recruitment system to replace slavery.

The abolition of slavery and the beginning of the 'coolie' trade

The 'coolie' system – the recruitment of workers, mostly men and mostly from the colony of British India or British-controlled China to work in conditions of contracted indentured servitude – met this demand from states and investors.[2] From approximately 1830 to the 1920s coolieism was the dominant system through which people were moved (Potts 1990, 69). There is no definitive number on how many people were made into 'coolies' – some estimate a low of 12 million, while Potts (1990, 71) states that even 'an estimate of 37 million or more would not be entirely without foundation.' The British Empire was the main organizer of the 'coolie' trade, however, other imperial states, including the Dutch and the French, also recruited 'coolies,' often through negotiations with the British.

The century of coolieism (1830s-1920s), overlapped with Britain's 'imperial century.' Between 1815 and 1914, around ten million square miles (or 26,000,000 km^2) of territory and roughly 400 million people were added to the British Empire, much of it in Asia. Thus, by the beginning of the nineteenth century, millions of expropriated people across Asia came to have very little, if any, means of subsistence. In British India alone, there were successive famines: 1770, 1784, 1804, 1837 and 1861 in Bengal and northern India, and in 1877, 1878, 1889, 1892 and 1897 until 1900 in other parts of India. Some of these famines resulted from the insistence that farmers grow cash crops to provide the Empire with hard currency (silver at this time) in the international trading market. One of these cash crops was opium, which was grown in British India and sold in China in an effort to reverse the British imbalance of trade with China. Resistance from the Qing dynasty resulted in the Opium Wars (1839–42 and 1860–62) between the two imperial states. British victory gave it control over large parts of the Chinese empire and accelerated the insertion of its subjects into global capitalist markets. As a result, most people in British India and in British-controlled China were desperate for new livelihoods. Millions of them were recruited and exploited as 'coolie' labour in every part of the global British Empire.

Their recruitment was not the only issue however. A key question occupying investors and the imperial state was how they could best control 'coolie' labourers in the absence of slavery. Ending their free movement in the space of the British empire was their answer. Starting with 'coolies' from British India, a growing list of regulations began to govern their geographical as well as labour market mobility (Potts 1990, 68–71). Such regulations were first imposed by the British colonial government of Mauritius, an island in the Indian Ocean about 2,000 kilometres off the southeast coast of the African continent.

The Mauritius authorities effort to regulate and restrict the entry of people who, juridically, were fellow British subjects marked a shift from imperial concerns about controlling and limiting exit to new concerns about controlling and limiting entry. In retrospect, it was the beginning of the end of the regime of the right of all British subjects to unrestricted entry to imperial territory – even as, in practice, such mobility was difficult to exercise for most. Moreover, such restrictions also marked the start of ideas of a fragmented imperial space, one marked by racism in regards to people's mobility across it (Mongia 2018). Such ideas worked alongside growing nativism in some British colonies, especially the so-called White Settler colonies, to foment a growing nationalism heavily informed by ideas of 'race.'

Sugar plantations on British Mauritius were incredibly profitable to planters and the imperial treasury. The impending abolition of slave labour relations on Mauritius in 1835 was therefore of deep concern to both groups. In the absence of laws permitting slavery, they worried that freed slaves and newly recruited workers from British India would refuse to work under the harsh working conditions prevalent on plantations. Planters and the colonial government sought new ways to immobilize both groups of workers and keep them labouring on the plantations. Freed slaves were immobilized through the 'apprenticeship' system. Throughout the British Empire, freed slaves older than six years old were legally bound to their employers and made to work for another three to five years as 'apprentices.' Yet, given the strength of the slavery abolition movement, this could only be a temporary measure.

Thus, in 1835, the same year that slaves were formally freed and made 'apprentices,' the local British Council passed two ordinances regulating the entry of people recruited as 'coolie' labour from British India (Mongia 2007, 399). Ratified by the British Parliament in 1837, these two ordinances mandated that, first, 'coolie' workers required the permission of the colony's Governor to move and that, secondly, that would-be emigrants leaving British India as well as a newly minted Emigration Agent, were required to appear before a British India officer with a signed a contract of indenture to a planter on Mauritius, usually for an initial period of five years (renewable for further five-year terms).

Without such contracts, workers were neither permitted to leave British India nor enter British Mauritius. So central were such contracts of indenture to the operation – and normalization – of the 'coolie' labour trade that the recruited workers referred to each other as *girmit*, a creolized version of 'agreement' or contract (Mongia 2018). Contracts of indenture operated under the legal fiction that they represented an agreement between two equal parties. States enforced the terms of these contracts as far as they applied to workers' obligations under them while allowing failing to enforce those of the employers. Plantation owners were granted access to the courts and prisons to judge, punish and discipline workers accused of challenging the authority of employers or failing to fulfil their part of a contract. Employers were also granted the legal right to use corporal and other forms of punishment/abuse against 'coolies.'

Thus, after the abolition of slavery in the British Empire, new forms of imperial mobility restrictions tethered 'coolie' workers to specific employers and seriously stifled the power of these workers to demand better working and living conditions. Mr. Prosper D'Epinay, the Protector General of Mauritius, defended the right of Mauritian authorities to impose entrance restrictions on 'coolie' workers on the basis that they represented 'a measure of foresight and of internal police . . . ' without which there would be 'tumult and disorder . . . in industry' (in Mongia 2007, 401). Initially concerned about the political fallout of these new restrictions – the imperial office in London expressed two main concerns. First, they wanted to ensure that neither the new 'coolie' labour recruitment system nor the requirement to have signed contracts as a condition of moving from one part of the empire to another be viewed as a new form of slavery. Realizing the singular importance of new labour recruitment for planters, however, colonial authorities came to support the Mauritius colonial government's immigration regulations and restrictions on 'coolies.' With the joined legal mechanisms of contracts and immigration controls in place, then, approximately 25,000 indentured labourers from India were shipped to Mauritius from 1835 to 1838. This reassured planters that immigration ordinances would not prevent the recruitment of workers or harm their profits. Indeed, one enthusiastic planter, George Arbuthnot, speaking after the first cargo of 'coolie' workers was brought to Mauritius, stated that, 'their cost is not half that of a slave' (cited in Potts 1990, 63).

However, it was evident that neither the contracts required to exit British India nor the immigration controls of British Mauritius 'protected' the workers bound by them. Not only were 'coolie' workers ' . . . shipped on the same vessels that had brought the slaves they were designed to replace; some would fall to disease, die, suffer abuse, and mutiny; [and those] who survived the three month voyage would encounter coercive, confined conditions upon arrival' (Lowe 2006, 339). Slavery abolitionists forcefully argued for an end to the new trade in 'coolie' labour. Their protests centered largely on the argument that the movement of 'coolie' labourers, like those of enslaved workers, was involuntary. The later *Anti-Slavery Reporter* stated, that, 'it should be observed, that, of all the thousands who have hitherto gone to Mauritius, or other colonies, there is no proof afforded that any of them went voluntarily; but, on the contrary, decisive evidence that they were either kidnapped for that purpose, and by force put on board vessels employed in transporting them, or were obtained by the most fraudulent statements . . . ' (British And Foreign Anti-slavey Society ([2014] 1842), 47).

Such a focus valorized a particular notion of freedom, one defined by the absence of direct force. While the 'helplessness' of the labourers was foregrounded, identifying its source was avoided. The vast majority of anti-slavery campaigners paid scant attention to existing imperialist conditions in British India, precisely the conditions that might make moving preferable to staying. While some 'coolie' labourers were undoubtedly pressed into service, most were victims of the displacement resulting from British imperialism. They needed new livelihoods to replace what they had lost. Indeed, tens of millions persons across British India were on the move in search for a new means of subsistence.

Foreshadowing many contemporary 'helpers' of migrants, particularly those advocating an 'end to human trafficking,' most abolitionists concerned about the 'coolie' labour system argued that workers' 'freedom' depended on their being immobilized within British India. They argued that for their own good, would-be 'coolie' workers be prohibited from leaving. This directly contravened the survival strategies of many people who, by the millions, were on the move for their lives. After much struggle between slavery abolitionists largely based in the imperial metropole and planters and colonial officials on Mauritius, on 2 December 1842 the Governors of the East India Company ruled that the emigration of 'coolies' to Mauritius was to continue. That year, almost 35,000 'coolie' workers were shipped from India to Mauritius. To avoid further comparisons with slavery, newly minted Protectors of Emigrants were appointed at each departure point. Likewise, an office of the Protector of Immigrants was established on Mauritius. Both were portrayed as ensuring that 'coolie' workers from British India moved voluntarily and that they were freely selling their labour power. Such measures served to obfuscate how colonialism allowed for the procurement of labour as well as the *coercion* inherent in the making and reproduction of a capitalist labour force.

Approximately 366,000 indentured 'coolie' labourers from India arrived in Mauritius between 1834 and 1867. A ship transporting 'coolie' labourers arrived every few days in Mauritius and the large number of 'coolie' labourers was causing a backlog in processing. Unsurprisingly, by the mid-1850s in Mauritius, sugar production surpassed 100,000 tons a year (Allen 1999, 12). Soon thereafter, the 'coolie' trade soon expanded and became part of the global supply chain of workers for the expanding British Empire. By 1844, 'coolies' were shipped to British colonies in the West Indies, including Jamaica, Trinidad and Demerara. Eventually, 'coolie' labourers from Asia were transported throughout the British Empire and, to a lesser extent, to the French, German, Dutch, Danish, Spanish, Portuguese, Belgian and US colonies (Potts 1990, 67).

In retrospect, the regulations enacted on the 'coolie' labour trade were quite minimalist. Indeed, until the early twentieth century, the geographic mobility of all those not recruited as 'coolie' workers remained, for the most part, very much unregulated and unrestricted within the British Empire (Mongia 2007, 403). This is because the imperial state remained most interested in ensuring a stable *supply* of labourers across the empire. Nonetheless, the regulations imposed by the British on the movement of 'coolies' marked the emergence of the figure – and state category – of the Migrant. The Migrant was not simply someone who moved across space, for even at the beginning of such controls, not all people's movements were regulated or restricted. Instead, Migrants were those people whose mobility into any given administrative unit of the state was dependent on official state approval. Even though humans have moved since time immemorial, Migrants were produced out of a new regime of labor control required by investors reeling from the victory of the slavery abolitionist movement. Thus, in retrospect, the Mauritius ordinances represented a striking shift in British imperial policies regarding the governance of people's entry into imperial territories.

Indeed, the groundwork laid by the 1835 Mauritius Ordinances, particularly the idea that separate administrative units of the British Empire *could* and *ought* to be allowed to enact their own immigration controls, helped form the ideological basis for the nationalization of states and their sovereignty as well as the emergence of the legal institution of national citizenship, an institution resting on the exclusion of those people categorized as Migrants. In the next section, I demonstrate the importance of immigration controls to both the ideology of nationalism, the formation of nation-states, and the separation of people through the national binary of Citizens or Migrants.

Post-emancipation immigration controls in the United States

My focus in this section is on the first immigration controls of the United States. As 'coolie' labourers figured large in the ways the British imperial state managed the end of slavery, the regulation of the entry of 'coolies' were also significant in the first US immigration act of 1875. Passed a decade after the end of slavery in 1865, the U.S. too was concerned with ensuring a continued supply of workers in its territories. Like the British Empire, the US also developed new technologies to control freed slaves as well as novel immigration controls. However, as a former British 'White Settler' colony, both were also framed within the broader political project to assuage workers positively racialized as White.

Unlike the British Empire's desire to recruit ever greater numbers of workers through the 'coolie' labour system, the 3 March 1875 Page Act (Sect. 141, 18 Stat. 477), passed at the tail end of the period of Reconstruction, prohibited the entry of 'Chinese coolies' along with women deemed to be 'prostitutes.' Enacted ten years after the end of slavery in the US (1865) – and almost a century after the 1776 US Declaration of Independence or the ratification of its first Constitution in 1788 – the Page Act characterized coolieism as a 'relic of slavery' in an effort, largely ineffective, to prevent workers from China from entering the United States. Thus, not dissimilar to the rhetoric of coolieism as 'free labour' within the British Empire, the prohibition of 'Chinese coolies' into the US was presented as part of the its commitment against slavery.

However, it is clear that its real purposes were twofold. First, to limit labour market competition for male workers racialized as White and to hold them up as the standard bearers for the US 'nation' and, secondly, to prevent the formation of 'Chinese' families in the US. As Kerry Abrams (2005, 698) notes, enforcement of the Page Act prohibitions against 'prostitutes' resulted in the 'virtually complete exclusion of Chinese women from the United States.' Not only did the figure of the 'Chinese prostitute' have the broader effect of reproducing the heteropatriarchal wife/prostitute dichotomy within U.S. immigration (and other) laws, it also became central to the portrayal of all people from China as a 'yellow peril' endangering the emergent 'American nation' (Luibhéid 2002, 38). Thus, the Page Act also represented a new form of White nationalism in the US. organized labour. Limited largely to the membership of White men throughout the nineteenth century, it turned its ire against workers from China who were deemed to be members of an 'inferior' and 'unassimilable race.' The 1875 Page Act worked to enliven the conjoined racist/nationalist sentiment that the 'nation,' comprised of White people, needed protection against a new category of excluded people – 'immigrants.' By writing racist and sexist discrimination into immigration law, Whiteness as well as female behaviour conforming to patriarchal norms were both further enshrined as key modalities for 'national' belonging.

In contrast to the belief that immigration controls would protect Whitened workers, state legislation on citizenship and immigration produced a racialized 'split labour market' (Bonacich 1972). Placement in the new state category of 'immigrant' only constrained 'Chinese,' and, later, other immigrant workers' access to the rights and benefits that could help to raise their wages and enhance their bargaining power. In other words, immigration controls created more labour market competition, not less. This lesson was not widely learned. Demands for further immigration controls only increased as the nation-state's territorial borders quickly became the point at which the purity of 'nation' of White men and women was protected from both national labour market competition and from 'racial' contamination.

The 1882 Chinese Exclusion Act, the first to explicitly prohibit immigration on the basis of one's racialized 'nationality,' further advanced the idea of a White US 'nation.'[3] The Chinese Exclusion Act removed any reference to 'coolie' or 'forced' labor and simply prohibited the entry into the United States of all workers from China, 'skilled' as well as 'unskilled' for a period of ten years. This expanded in 1884 to include anyone from China. In 1889, the US Supreme Court's decision in *Chae Chan Ping v. US*, or the *Chinese Exclusion Case*, stated that, "the power of exclusion of foreigners being an incident of sovereignty ... cannot be granted away or restrained, thus acknowledging that the US now understood immigration controls as essential to its sovereignty. In this sense, the 1875 Page Act began the process by which the sovereignty of the US was nationalized. The 1875 Page Act marked the transition of the United States from a state which had long facilitated the entry of people into its (expanding) territories, mostly notoriously its active participation in the slave trade which it did not prohibit until 1808 (while keeping slavery in place until 1865), to a state increasingly concerned with keeping certain biopolitical groups of workers out.

Thus, when ruling against Chae's position that he was entitled to return lawfully to the US because he had first entered prior to the Chinese Exclusion Act (and held a government certificate attesting to this), the Supreme Court argued that the federal government had the right to 'preserve its independence and give security against foreign aggression and encroachment whether from the foreign nation acting in its national character or from vast hordes of its people crowding in upon us.' By arguing that the right to exclude 'aliens' from US territories stemmed from the sovereign powers defined by the 1788 Constitution, the 1889 Supreme Court ruling read the link between sovereignty and immigration controls back to the late-eighteenth century. The 100-plus year gap between the ratification of the US Constitution and the 1889 US Supreme Court ruling recognizing the nationalization of its sovereignty demonstrates the centrality of immigration controls to the national form of state power.

Successive US Immigration Acts widened restrictions on the entry of evermore groups of people and further entrenched practices that either favoured or discriminated against people through conjoined practices of racism and nationalism within immigration law. From 1919 legislation making its wartime (1918) 'exceptional' legislation targeting dissidents permanent, to a 1921 Act imposing broad limits to immigration from Europe through the use of quotas for the first time, US immigration controls increasingly limited who could lawfully enter the US. A 1924 act created the U.S. Border Patrol to enforce the growing number of immigration regulations and restrictions, including the effective bar against the entry of most Jewish people. By the end of the 1920s, the state category of 'illegal' began to be used more widely, largely against people racialized/ nationalized as 'Mexican.' Meanwhile, people with US citizenship living in territories that the US annexed from Mexico in 1848, but socially regarded as 'Mexican' continued to be denied the full rights and entitlements of US citizenship (Nevins 2010, 15). In the 1930s, the 1934 Philippine Independence Act effectively ended Filipinx immigration to the United States while mass deportations of Mexican nationals were enacted for the first time.

The initial trickle of mobility controls begun in the British Empire in the early-nineteenth century (and accelerated by the nationalization of state sovereignty of several 'independent' states across the Americas from the mid-nineteenth century), became a torrent by the end of World War One (WWI). By late-1918, some of the world's major Empires had collapsed and large parts of their territories came to be ruled by newly formed national sovereigns. In the brief period between the two world wars, further immigration controls were enacted, both by the now-shrunken number of imperial-states and the growing number of nation-states, strengthening nationalist imaginaries everywhere in the process. By the end of World War Two (WWII), national citizenship controls became a crucial part of international regimes of resource allocation and distribution, one enforced by immigration controls, ushering in what I call a Postcolonial New World Order of nationally sovereign states (Sharma 2020). All sorts of violence, symbolic and life annihilating, flowed from this as in every territory imagined as a national homeland, the negative duality of National Citizens and Migrants was enacted through citizenship and immigration laws.

In both the British Empire and the United States, immigration controls were implemented at the end of slavery. Many of the conditions of slavery – work in unfree and/or highly precarious labour conditions, racist degradation, lack of rights, normalized violence – were transferred onto those categorized as Migrants. This is not to say that Migrants were 'new slaves.' That term is bandied about far too loosely – most notoriously in the discourse of 'modern day slavery,' which works to conceal the violence of nation-states' immigration controls (Sharma 2005). Neither is it to say that only those categorized as Migrants endure such ill-treatment. Importantly, many 'citizens' do as well. It is to say however that the 'crisis' for capital and for states that the abolition of slavery brought about was resolved by a new form of immobilization previously unimaginable. The shock of immigration controls quickly wore off however, as nationalism(s) quickly made sense of limiting rights within sovereign territories on the basis of who 'really' belonged there.

End of US slavery and new modes of immobilizing black people

The United States did not follow the British imperial practice of exploiting people nominally freed from slavery as 'apprentices,' but the end of slavery in the United States did result in unceasing state efforts, particularly but not exclusively in the southern states, to immobilize Black people through other means. Two and a half centuries after slavery was written into the laws of the original colonies, slave labour relations were abolished in December 1865 with the passing of the 13th Amendment to the US Constitution. What followed was a scramble for new institutions and laws to ensure capitalists access to – and control over – the labour power of the approximately 4 million Black people who had been freed. Even as the federal government granted Black people formal U.S. citizenship, the implementation of segregationist (Jim Crow) laws, the institution of 'sharecropping' implemented with the post-Civil War subdivision of large plantations, and the massive expansion of the US (state and federal) prison system each worked to immobile Black people economically, politically, and socially.

As with the racist underpinnings of new immigration laws, these racist new institutions provided clear economic benefits to capital and the state. Each worked to cheapen and weaken the labour power of Black people. Rather than seeing these structures as simply continuing slavery under a new guise, however, I think it is best to see them as novel methods devised when it was no longer legitimate to enslave people and when the form of state power in the US was shifting from imperial methods of control to national ones. As immigration controls simultaneously privileged the 'wages of whiteness' while undermining the broader class struggle of White workers, the racist institutions of Jim Crow segregation, sharecropping, and mass incarceration created a racialized labour market that simultaneously ensured greater competition within the labour market and, thus, less power to the working class, while shoring up White nationalism with its myth of a cross-class community of White people.

All of these institutions depended on terror. Violence – and its threat – was used in no small part to quell the numerous acts of resistance, including solidarity between White workers and Black convict labourers. Each act was met with vigilantism or state-organized violence, leading to more people being imprisoned. In particular, the resurgence of White supremacist vigilantes, most notably the Klu Klux Klan, worked to contain resistance to the various forms of immobilization Black people faced. Lynchings of Black men, women and children in the Southern states peaked in the 1890s. A recent found that from 1877 to 1950, 3,959 Black people were lynched (Equal Justice Initiative 2015).

Jim Crow

Following the end of slavery, 'former slaves literally walked away from their plantations, causing panic and outrage among plantation owners' (Alexander 2012, 28). Southern states, desperate to ensure that plantations would continue to be profitable, and to amass the workforce needed to re-build war torn roads, towns, and cities, responded to this mass labour strike by passing a series of laws known as the Black Codes, for they applied only to Black people (Foner 2013). Comprised of enticement laws, contract-enforcement laws, vagrancy laws, emigrant-agent laws, and the convict-least system, tach worked to immobilize newly minted citizen-workers and to dampen their power in the labour market. As Jennifer Roback (1984, 1162) puts it, 'the laws can best be understood as attempts to enforce a labor-market cartel among white employers that could not be enforced in any other way.'

The first of these laws was passed by Mississippi, which on 22 November 1865 gave civil officers the right to hire orphaned Black children while forbidding these children to leave their place of employment. In it, White employers were curtailed from offering higher wages or better working conditions as an enticement to recruit workers employed elsewhere. Further, by criminally sanctioning workers found breaching a work contract, states gave employers tremendous power to coerce workers to continue working for them. While this goal was not always accomplished, such enticement and contract-enforcement laws significantly limited Black workers' labour market mobility. While some of these laws were struck down for violating the thirteenth amendment and the 1867 Peonage Act, nonetheless, most workers were not informed that such practices were illegal (Roback 1984, 1168). Jim Crow laws also institutionalized states' efforts to geographically immobilize recently freed Black workers. Passed to stem the out-migration of Black workers, emigrant-agent laws regulated the actions of White labour recruiters. While not entirely effective, these laws did make it more difficult for Black workers to find information about jobs outside of former confederate states (Bernstein 1997).

The core of the Black Codes comprised of vagrancy and convict-leasing laws. Nine Southern states passed vagrancy laws immediately at the end of slavery, effectively making it a crime for Black people to be out of the labour force. One such law decreed that, '"all free negroes and mulattoes over the age of eighteen" must have written proof of a job at the beginning of every year' or else be convicted as vagrants (in Alexander 2012, 28). Other practices defined and punished as vagrancy included loitering, breaking curfew, possessing weapons, and not carrying proof of employment. These laws not only worked to limit the labour market as well as geographical mobility of Black workers, but when found in violation of them, to funnel them into Southern prisons. After the abolition of slavery, the numbers of prisoners rose dramatically and prison inmates become predominantly Black. Indeed, it was with slavery's end that for the first time in U.S. history many states' held more Black prisoners than White ones. New convict-lease laws gave plantation owners and other employers access to Black people's labour at extremely low cost.

Loopholes in Reconstruction Era court rulings legalized such an outcome. The Thirteenth Amendment outlawing slavery, for example, retained an exemption for prisoners. The payoff for the lessee was evident. As Alex Lichtenstein (1996) noted in the title of his book, lessee's found that convict labour in the New South did 'twice the work of free labor.' The Southern states implementing such a system benefited as well. While allowing states to appease capital, leasing out prisoners was a significant source of their revenue. In 1898, Alabama, for example, received 73% of its revenues from convict leasing (Perkinson 2010, 105). Lessees, while legally responsible for the convict workers assigned to them by the state, treated them incredibly harshly. Death rates on the 'chain gangs' were as high as forty-five percent (Cohen 1976). The high likelihood of dying on a chain gang operated as a deadly disincentive to Black workers to refuse work or change employers.

Initially the federal government tried to overturn the Black Codes and protect freed slaves. Federal laws during the Reconstruction Era (1863–1877) included the first Civil Rights Act (1866), which granted full citizenship to Black people, the Fourteenth Amendment (1868), which provided 'equal protection of the laws' and prohibited states from denying the due process rights of any US citizen (which now included Black people), the Fifteenth Amendment (1870), which prohibited states from using racist criteria to deny citizens' from exercising their right to vote, and the Enforcement Acts, also known as the Ku Klux Klan Acts, (1870–1871), which made it a criminal offense to interfere with any citizen's civil rights and provided federal supervision of citizens' voting rights. Each of these Acts was enforced by federal troops deployed to the Southern states. One outcome was that Black people voted in large numbers. Moreover, by 1870, a minimum of fifteen percent of all elected officials in the Southern states were Black people.

Moreover, between 1865 and 1872, the federal Freedmen's Bureau provided assistance to destitute former slaves. Literacy rates also soared allowing Black people greater mobility in the capitalist labour market. And, for the first time, a public education system accessible by Black as well as poor White people was created. But it was not to last, in no small part, because Southern lawmakers discovered the large loopholes left in these protective laws. For example, the Fifteenth Amendment, while including 'race' as a prohibited criteria for voting, failed to prohibit states from putting into place other criteria to vote such as residence or education (Alexander 2012, 29–30).

With the end of Reconstruction, marked by the withdrawal of federal troops from the South in the late-1870s, ten of the eleven former Confederate states passed new constitutions or constitutional amendments effectively disenfranchising most Black people, and no small number of impoverished White people (Foner 2013). Between 1890 and 1910, a combination of poll taxes, literacy and comprehension tests, and residency and record-keeping requirements prevented them from voting. The majority US Supreme Court decision in the 1896 *Plessy v. Ferguson* case upheld the Jim Crow pretense of 'separate but equal.' The convict and vagrancy laws that Reconstruction legislation had earlier prohibited came back with a vengeance. Added to these were other laws that actively targeted Black people by selective enforcement of prohibited activities such as 'mischief' and 'insulting gestures' (Alexander 2012, 31). As intended, these changes led to the arrest of tens of thousands of Black people, many of whom were leased out as convict labour.

Sharecropping

The absence of land reform after slavery was one of the greatest problems facing freed Black people. Denied their promised 'forty acres and a mule,' most were made reliant on the capitalist labour market for their survival.[4] At the same time, without the labour of enslaved workers, Southern plantations had become unprofitable and were sub-divided into smaller landholdings. In the search for workers to replace the freed slaves, the 'coolie' labour system which had been used across the British colonies after slavery, was not fully available to the Southern states. Unlike the British, the US did not have large numbers of colonial subjects available to be transported in and indentured to planters.

In the US, the institution of sharecropping helped significantly in meeting agricultural labour shortages. Not unlike coolie-ism, sharecropping was also a system of securing labour through the means of a contract. In this case, an annual contract between a landowner and newly freed slaves who in the absence of their own means of subsistence and with few options in regards to paid labour, had few other options. Like the contracts marked by indentured 'coolie' labourers, sharecropping contracts were also heavily skewed in favour of the landowner. As sharecroppers, freed Black people were given access to the landowner's land and rudimentary housing in exchange for their heavily surveilled agricultural labour. Landowners determined which crops would be planted – mostly cash crops – while sharecroppers had to purchase their tools, seeds, and fertilizer. Sharecroppers' purchases were largely on credit from the local store, a debt which would be called in at the end of each harvest. Sharecroppers owed the landowner one-half to two-thirds of their harvest. They were further required to sell it to landowners at a price the latter dictated. Thus, at the end of each contract, sharecroppers had very little to show for their year's labour. The result was that sharecroppers experienced mal-nutrition and even deep and abiding hunger. In the worse years, sharecroppers would be indebted to the landowner and since sharecroppers were forbidden by law to leave the landowner's property until their debt was paid, the continued availability of their labour as assured.

As with other Southern efforts to subordinate Black people, poor White people were soon captured in this system too. For both Black and White sharecroppers, landowners used terror to contain any sign of resistance – including an effort to unionize sharecroppers in the 1930s. As Arthur Raper and Ira De Augustine Reid (1941) put it, the sharecropper, '. . . is at once a target subject of ridicule and vitriolic denunciation; he may even be waylaid by hooded or unhooded leaders of the community, some of whom may be public officials. If a white man persists in "causing trouble", the night riders may pay him a visit, or the officials may haul him into court; if he is a Negro, a mob may hunt him down.'

Aside from a resurgence during the Great Depression (1929–1939), sharecropping declined throughout the United States in the 1930s and 1940s, largely because industrial farming techniques such as mechanization replaced workers. Its decline resulted in a steep increase in the Great Black Northern Migration (which had begun in 1916). The percentage of Black people living in the Southern States declined precipitously as a result, from a high of 93% in the 1820s and 1830s, to 79% by 1930 and a low of 53% in the 1970s and 1980s. Millions of Black people moved to Northern cities or Western states in search of new homes and new livelihoods. In the Northern states, Black men found work in factories, usually labouring in arduous conditions and being paid less than White men doing the equivalent work (Card and Krueger 1992). Black women, in contrast, had greater difficulty securing a livelihood and were funneled towards low-paid domestic work.

Black people were not freed from the hostility of White people once they moved to the Northern states. In addition to racist discrimination in employment and housing, there was also a resurgence of organized White supremacist terror groups in the North. Against such enormous adversities, the migration of Black people from Southern to Northern states also led to the formation of significant Black neighbourhoods, most notably Harlem in New York City. These contributed to significant changes in the United States, including the development of a new, decidedly urban culture amongst Black people that would leave a legacy in both artistic movements (e.g. the New Negro Movement and the Harlem Renaissance) as well as in political organizing for civil and other rights.

Civil rights reforms and another mass incarceration

The growing strength of the Black Civil Rights movement was evident in Supreme Court rulings ordering desegregation. The 1954 ruling on Brown v. Board of Education effectively 'signaled the end of "home rule" in the South with respect to racial [sic] affairs' (Alexander 2012, 36). The Civil Rights Act of 1964 and the Voting Rights Act of 1965 prohibited racist discrimination in the law. In 1967, the Supreme Court struck down anti-miscegenation laws as a violation of the fourteenth amendment. By 1968, all forms of segregation, including those within school systems, businesses, the military, the civil services or the government had been declared unconstitutional by the US Supreme Court.

Many of the gains made by the Civil Rights Movement were severely compromised, some would even say undone, however, by the new formed 'law and order' agenda. In an effort to delegitimize their demands, activists in the Civil Rights Movement were demonized as 'lawbreakers,' even as the much reported statistical increase in crime in the 1960s was almost entirely attributable to the increase in young-adult men belonging to the 'baby boomer' generation. The infamous segregationist George Wallace captured this sentiment when exclaiming that, 'the same Supreme Court that ordered integration and encouraged civil rights legislation' was 'bending over backwards to help criminals' (in Alexander 2012, 42).

The period between the mid-1960s to the early-1970s was also the start of neo-liberal reforms in US public policy (Kolko 1988). Along with deindustrialization, the social wage – the social benefits and entitlements associated with various welfare state programs providing workers with an alternative to the capitalist wage or a supplement to it – was reduced. The power of capital was further enhanced through state sanctioned processes of privatization, deregulation, and trade liberalization. For the most subordinated parts of the working class – White and non-White – new and increasingly harsh forms of criminalization were enacted. Yet, these were not uniformly carried out. Racist practices of the police and the court served, as they had following the abolition of slavery and the end Reconstruction, to once again disproportionately incarcerate Black people. While in 1964, 63% of all state prison admissions were of White people and 35% of Black people, by 1970, the share of imprisoned Black people increased to 43%, even though they comprised only 11% of the total number of people in the US. The start of neo-liberalism in the US thus ushered in another period of mass incarceration. And, the racism that organized this system, once again, worked to drive a deeper wedge between White and non-White workers.

From less than 200,000 people in 1972 – the year President Nixon declared a 'War on Drugs' – approximately 2.3 million people in the U.S. were in jail or prison by 2016, an approximate 700% increase. Importantly, this increase occurred during a period when crime rates as well as drug use dropped (Gilmore 2007). Women are the fastest growing group of incarcerated people, however, non-White men remain the vast majority of incarcerated people (Crenshaw 2011). In 2015, Black people and Latinx people comprised 56% of all incarcerated people while, together, making up about 32% of the US population (NAACP, n.d.). The ACLU (n.d.) notes that 'one out of every three Black boys born today can expect to go to prison in his lifetime, as can one of every six Latino boys – compared to one of every 17 white boys.'

Federal and state-level policies, as well as the courts, have had much to do with this outcome. Together rulings such as the 1968 US Supreme Court ruling in *Terry v. Ohio*, which established the 'stop-and-frisk' rule, the 1991 Supreme Court ruling in *Florida v. Bostick*, which sanctioned suspicion-less police searches and sweeps, the 1996, Supreme Court ruling in *Ohio v. Robinette*, which ruled that police did not have to inform people they stopped or searched of their rights to refuse consent, to the 2001 Supreme Court ruling in *Atwater v. City of Lago Vista*, which established that police can arrest and jail motorists for minor traffic violations, even if the statutory penalty for that violation is a fine and not jail, ensured a massive rise in incarceration, one that was intensely racialized.

The 'law and order' agenda did not stop with mass incarceration. Release from prison has not always reinstated people's liberty or rights. The civil liberties of those convicted of felonies (which are not always serious crimes), for instance, are significantly diminished. Felons, for instance, are automatically excluded from the right to serve on juries. The 1988 US Anti-Drug Abuse Act 'authorized public housing authorities to evict any tenant who allows any form of drug-related criminal activity to occur on or near public housing premises' (Alexander 2012, 53). It also eliminated access to many federal benefits, including student loans, for those convicted of a drug offense. As a result of their disproportionate experience with incarceration, in 2010 one in seven Black men had lost the right to vote (Alexander 2010: 193–194). Each of these losses has resulted in the social, economic, and political immobilization of those who had been imprisoned.

However, in contrast to the mass incarceration of the post-emancipation period, today's prison-industrial complex is not defined by the capitalist profit motive, at least not in the sense that prisoners are a significant source of private profit. As Ruth Wilson Gilmore (2007) has shown, far from making significant profits for those with capital to invest, mass incarceration costs the state billions of dollars to maintain (Gilmore in Kushner 2019). As the NAACP (n.d.) notes, 'in 2012 alone, the United States spent nearly 81 USD billion on corrections.' Even as private prisons have received much attention, Gilmore (in Kushner 2019) notes that, 'ninety-two percent of people locked inside American prisons are held in publicly run, publicly funded facilities, and 99% of those in jail are in public jails. Every private prison could close tomorrow, and not a single person would go home.'

Even though private prisons are not an important factor in the rise of contemporary mass incarceration, the conjoined system of global capitalism and nation-states remains important. In the midst of a persistent crisis of legitimacy, the US nation-state uses mass incarceration as a way to create paid employment for a crucial voting bloc – people living in rural and exurban locales across the U.S. In this way, prisons act as a form of state-subsidies for employees of the Corrections Department, for the people profiting from the sale of land on which to build prisons, and for those hired to construct prisons (Gilmore 2007). Just as significantly, mass incarceration is also a way to socially manage people whose access to paid employment has been severely reduced as a result of changes in both urban and rural parts of the US (Gilmore 2007). This is true for those negatively racialized women and men who are incarcerated. It is also true for those who support the massive build-up of the prison industrial complex, as their political energy is deflected away from state policies and capitalist practices that create greater insecurity and immiseration in their lives.

Thus, while there is no straight line directly from slavery to today's mass incarceration, its legacy is evident in the use of the contemporary prison industrial complex to try and re-legitimize state and capitalist power. The social relations of capitalism after the demise of slavery as an institution continue to be harsh and markets for labour, housing, food, healthcare, finance, and more, continue to be racialized, gendered, and, since the late-nineteenth century, nationalized so that those whose US citizenship is not respected and those denied US citizenship are not only heavily disadvantaged in every area of their lives, but also face greater constraints on their geographical as well as labour market mobility.

Conclusion: making connections between outlaws and outsiders

Immigration controls and mass incarceration can both be seen as part of the legacy of slavery, or perhaps more accurately, the legacy of the incompleteness of the freedom won with the abolition of slavery. Both technologies were developed in the nineteenth century and gave states new powers to regulate both the spatial as well as labour market mobility of the people whose lives came to be governed by them. Both worked to further nationalist projects reliant on ideas of the 'national community,' which both those now categorized as Migrants or as criminals were excluded from. Bridget Anderson (2013) has argued that the system of national citizenship is certainly defined by the exclusion of migrations, however, and despite nationalist rhetoric, not all citizens are treated as equals. Citizens, Anderson argues (2013) are instead hierarchically ranked according to whether they are seen as 'good citizens,' defined as supposedly 'law-abiding and hard-working members of stable and respectable families' (2013, 28), 'tolerated citizens,' whose claims to pity allow them to be considered as 'deserving' of national membership, or 'failed citizens,' who are 'imagined as incapable of, or fail[ing] to live up to, liberal ideals' (2013, 4). People defined as 'criminals' along with 'undeserving' recipients of welfare benefits may be national citizens, but are excluded from what Anderson (2013, 2) refers to as the national 'community of value' of value, worth, and honour.

While Migrants are ultimately controlled through immigration laws that allow nation-states to determine whether they will be lawfully admitted and permitted to stay or be denied entry and/or deported, 'failed citizens,' who are not deportable, are controlled in large part through the complex web of the prison industrial complex. This is not to say, of course, that Migrants are not also captured by the system of mass incarceration. They certainly are, as the growing study of 'crimmigration' attests to (Stumpf 2006; García Hernández 2013).

Indeed, the Global Detention Project reports that the US has constructed the world's largest immigration detention system with approximately 200 facilities within the US, a growing number of which are privately operated for profit. US immigration enforcement also operates globally, as Todd Miller (2019) has recently documented. According to the U.S. Immigration and Customs Enforcement (ICE) agency (2018), in 2018, 396,448 people were booked into ICE custody: 242,778 of whom were detained by the Customs and Border Patrol agency and 153,670 by ICE's own enforcement operations. The Office of Refugee Resettlement's program for Unaccompanied Alien Children an additional held twelve thousand Migrant children across the US. Furthermore, about twenty percent of all inmates in federal prisons (which hold approximately ten percent of all prisoners in the US) were Migrants in 2019. Half of these Migrant inmates were held in segregated Criminal Alien Requirement (CAR) facilities, where they had far fewer protections than other inmates (Kaufman 2019). For instance, following the jurisprudence established by the 1889 Chae Chan Ping v. US, or the Chinese Exclusion Case, CAR prisoners do not have meaningful judicial review.

The incarceration and deportability of Migrants is thus part of the overall control that nation-states hold against non-Citizens. As discussed above, as well as in my previous work (2000; 2006), the placement of people into the state category of Migrant is also a mechanism of labour market discipline. The formal stipulations placed on people's immigration status, alongside the deep racism extant within capitalist labour markets, ensures that the political and social power of Migrant workers is severely diminished while their labour power is severely devalued. This is not dissimilar to the process by which people who have been criminalized are controlled, disciplined, and immobilized by being caged, surveilled, and denied key rights of citizenship, including mobility within housing projects and within the labour market. However, the prison industrial complex operates to not only immobilize these 'failed citizens,' it also works as a disciplinary tool to weaken the power of the entire working class. This is yet another way in which immigration controls and mass incarceration have worked in tandem historically and today.

In the British case, the transition from slavery to immigration controls is much clearer, thanks in no small part to the work of Radhika Mongia (2007; 2018). Such a direct connection between the end of slavery in the US in 1865 to the start of immigration controls in 1875 is less clear, not only due to a paucity of research, but also because unlike the British colony of Mauritius, the US neither had recourse to use of the 'coolie' system of labour recruitment on any wide scale and had a large, racist population of White people who demanded the US's first immigration controls precisely to prevent the entry of non-White workers, namely 'Chinese coolies' and 'prostitutes.' However, what is clear is that after the end of slavery, the US government (at federal and state levels) imposed other measures to limit the freedom of movement of negatively racialized people: segregation laws that limited Black people's social and economic mobility as well as their political power; immigration laws that worked not only to limit negatively racialized/gendered people from lawfully entering the US but ensured that their social, economic and political power was also severely limited (Sharma 2008). All of these measures strengthened White nationalism, which through US immigration law was formally enshrined through restrictions on the entry of those deemed non-White and, by the 1920s, as not-White-enough (e.g. people arriving from Southern and Eastern Europe).

Together, immigration and carceral controls have created groups of people denied access to the mythical institutions of liberal democracy: liberty, freedom (especially of their labour power), and equality. This is done through their placement in state categories of 'criminal' and 'migrant,' both of which legislate the denial of rights. These categories are hegemonic because of the nationalist discourses that mobilize them and that they, in turn, produce and, from the start, they have been racist. State laws – from criminal law to immigration law – have organized and enforced the immobility of those who are hegemonically regarded as 'not belonging' to the 'nation.'

However, and, over time, the people subjected to them have come to be seen as unconnected to one another and even antagonistic to one another's demands for justice. Their separation has augmented the strength of nation-states to continue to impose conditions of unfreedom on both those regarded as either 'failed citizens' or as 'migrants.' Social justice struggles for the abolition of prisons and of borders have increasingly made these connections. However, much more work is needed to understand the links between slavery and immigration controls, the links between the incarceration of subordinated citizens and those classified by states as 'migrants,' and how both prison abolition and No Borders are working to end state controls on freedom.

While No Borders movements are more often understood to be centered on the demand for freedom of movement, this, I believe, is because 'movement' has come to be conflated with 'migration.' The 'movement' of 'citizens' is presumed to always already exist. However, the prison abolitionist movement has shown us that many 'citizens,' especially working and negatively racialized ones, are also immobilized through the prison industrial complex, not only in regards to those large number who are incarcerated in the US, but also in terms of the broader political, social, and economic discipline that mass incarceration engenders. Thus, I believe it is necessary that we see both No Borders and prison abolitionist movements as understanding that freedom of movement is perhaps the 'most elementary' of all human liberties (Arendt 1968, 9). Being able to move out of one situation and into another at according to our will – to move away from violence and towards peace, to move away from exploitation and towards justice, to leave behind confinement – is perhaps 'the prototypical gesture of being free.' No Border movements demand for the freedom of mobility is therefore fundamental, I argue, to the realization of a new society that prison abolitionists also call for. Both recognize that freedom of movement for both Migrants and those who have been criminalized is a necessary precondition for the freedom of all.

Notes

1. It is estimated that more than half of all people moving from Europe to the English colonies of North America during the seventeenth and eighteenth centuries came as indentured servants (Potts 1990).
2. From 1757 until the India Act of 1858, the British East India Company had ruled much of the Indian subcontinent. Transference of authority to the British Crown in 1858 ushered in the period of British rule known as the Raj. Under the 1842 Treaty of Nanking, the British gained direct control over Hong Kong and Canton, Shanghai, Amoy, Fuzhou and Nigbo were opened up as nodes in the British-organized and controlled trade in opium.
3. People racialized as 'Asians' were also excluded from the right to naturalize until the 1940s (Haney-Lopez 1996, 44).
4. The promise of 'forty acres and a mule' was written by Union General William Tecumseh Sherman in January 1865 and approved by President Lincoln. Each freed family was to be allotted a plot of land no larger than 40 acres and lent a mule by the army on the islands and coastal regions of the state of Georgia. This order was explicitly reversed by President Andrew Johnson who succeeded Lincoln upon his assassination. Johnson ordered that any land allocated to freed Black people be re-titled to its previous White owners.

Disclosure statement

No potential conflict of interest was reported by the author.

References

Abrams, K. 2005. "Polygamy, Prostitution, and the Federalization of Immigration Law." *Columbia Law Review* 105 (3, April): 641–716.

ACLU (American Civil Liberties Union). n.d. "Mass Incarceration." Accessed 1 August 2019. https://www.aclu.org/issues/smart-justice/mass-incarceration

Alexander, M. 2012. *The New Jim Crow: Mass Incarceration in the Age of Colorblindness*. New Press.

Allen, R. B. 1999. *Slaves, Freedmen and Indentured Laborers in Colonial Mauritius*. Vol. 99. Cambridge: Cambridge University Press.

Anderson, B. 2013. *Us and Them?: The Dangerous Politics of Immigration Control*. Oxford: Oxford University Press.

Arendt, H. 1968. *Men in Dark Times*. San Diego, New York, London: Harcourt Brace and Company.

Bernstein, D. E. 1997. "Law and Economics of Post-Civil War Restrictions on Interstate Migration by African-Americans." *Texas Law Review* 76: 781–848.

Bonacich, E. 1972. "A Theory of Ethnic Antagonism: The Split Labour Market," *American Sociological Review* 37: 547–559

British And Foreign Anti-slavey Society. [2014] 1842. *Emigration from India: The Export of Coolies, and Other Labourers, to Mauritius*. New York: Cambridge University Press; London: Thomas Ward and Co.

Card, D., and A. B. Krueger. 1992. "School Quality and Black-white Relative Earnings: A Direct Assessment." *The Quarterly Journal of Economics* 107 (1): 151–200. doi:10.2307/2118326.

Cohen, W. 1976. "Negro Involuntary Servitude in the South, 1865-1940: A Preliminary Analysis." *The Journal of Southern History* 42 (1): 31–60. doi:10.2307/2205660.

Crenshaw, K. W. 2011. "From Private Violence to Mass Incarceration: Thinking Intersectionally about Women, Race, and Social Control." *UCLA Law Review* 59 (6): 1418–1472.

Equal Justice Initiative. 2015. "Lynching in America: Confronting the Legacy of Racial Terror." http://www.eji.org/files/EJILynchinginAmericaSUMMARY.pdf

Foner, E. 2013. *Forever Free: The Story of Emancipation and Reconstruction*. New York: Vintage.

Gilmore, R. W. 2007. *Golden Gulag: Prisons, Surplus, Crisis, and Opposition in Globalizing California*. Vol. 21. Univ of California Press.

Haney-Lopez, I. 1996. *White by Law: The Legal Construction of Race*. New York: New York University Press.

García Hernández, C. C. 2013. "Creating Crimmigration." *Brigham Young University Law Review* 6: 1457–1516.

Hochschild, A. 2005. Bury the Chains: Prophets and Rebels in the Fight to Free an Empire's Slaves. MA: Boston, Houghton Mifflin Harcourt

Kaufman, E. 2019. "Segregation by Citizenship." *Harvard Law Review* 132: 1379–1444.

Kolko, J. 1988. *Restructuring the World Economy*. New York: Pantheon Books.

Kushner, R. 2019. "Is Prison Necessary? Ruth Wilson Gilmore Might Change Your Mind." The New York Times. April 17. Accessed 1 March 2020. https://www.nytimes.com/2019/04/17/magazine/prison-abolition-ruth-wilson-gilmore.html

Lichtenstein, A. 1996. *Twice the Work of Free Labor: The Political Economy of Convict Labor in the New South*. London: Verso.

Linebaugh, P., and M. Rediker. 2000. *The Many-Headed Hydra: Sailors, Slaves, Commoners, and the Hidden History of the Revolutionary Atlantic*. Boston: Beacon Press.

Lowe, L. 2006. "The Intimacies of Four Continents." In Haunted by Empire: Geographies of Intimacy in North American History, Edited by Ann Laura Stoler. Durham, NC: Duke University Press.

Luibhéid, E. 2002. *Entry Denied: Controlling Sexuality at the Border*. Minneapolis: University of Minnesota Press.

Miller, T. 2019. *Empire of Borders: The Expansion of the US Border around the World*. Verso Books. London: Verso.

Mongia, R. 2018. *Indian Migration and Empire: A Colonial Genealogy of the Modern State*. Durham, NC: Duke University Press.

Mongia, R. V. 2007. "Historicizing State Sovereignty: Inequality and the Form of Equivalence." *Comparative Studies in Society and History* 49 (2): 384–411. doi:10.1017/S0010417507000539.

Nevins, J. 2010. *Operation Gatekeeper and Beyond: The War on "Illegals" and the Remaking of the US–Mexico Boundary*. NY: Routledge.

Perkinson, R. 2010. *Texas Tough: The Rise of America's Prison Empire*. New York: Metropolitan Books.

Potts, L. 1990. *The World Market for Labour Power: A History of Migration*. London: Zed Books.

Raper, A. F., and I. D. A. Reid. 1941. *Sharecroppers All*. Chapel Hill, NC: University of North Carolina Press.

Reséndez, A. 2016. *The Other Slavery: The Uncovered Story of Indian Enslavement in America*. Boston: Houghton Mifflin Harcourt.
Roback, J. 1984. "Southern Labor Law in the Jim Crow Era: Exploitative or Competitive?" *The University of Chicago Law Review* 51 (4): 1161–1192. doi:10.2307/1599563.
Roediger, D. R. 1999. *The Wages of Whiteness: Race and the Making of the American Working Class*. London: Verso.
Scott, J. C. 2009. *The Art of Not Being Governed: An Anarchist History of Upland Southeast Asia*. By New Haven: Yale University Press.
Sharma, N. 2005. "Anti-trafficking Rhetoric in the Making of Global Apartheid." *National Women's Studies Association Journal* 17 (3(Fall)): 88–112. Special Issue: States of Insecurity and the Gendered Politics of Fear.
Sharma, N. 2008. "Citizenship and the Disciplining of (Im)migrant Workers in the United States." In *Refugees, Recent Migrants and Employment: Challenging Barriers and Exploring Pathways*, edited by S. McKay, 102–120. London: Routledge.
Sharma, N. 2020. *Home Rule: National Sovereignty and the Separation of Natives and Migrants*. Durham, NC: Duke University Press.
Steinfeld, R.J. 1991. *The Invention of Free Labour: The Employment Relation in English and American Law and Culture, 1350-1870*. Chapel Hill and London: University of North Carolina
Stumpf, J. 2006. "The Crimmigration Crisis: Immigrants, Crime, and Sovereign Power." *American University Law Review* 56 (2): 367–419.
U.S. Immigration and Customs Enforcement. 2018. "Fiscal Year 2018 ICE Enforcement and Removal Operations Report." Accessed 17 April 2020. https://www.ice.gov/features/ERO-2018 (n.d.).

Crisis, capital accumulation, and the 'Crimmigration' fix in the aftermath of the global slump

Jessica Evans

ABSTRACT

In a 2006 article, legal scholar Juliet Stumpf coined the term 'crimmigration' intended to reflect the growing convergence between criminal and immigration law in the United States. To date, the robust and insightful debates that have emerged from this intervention are largely centered in legal scholarship and citizenship studies. In this article, I ask what a political economy lens can add to our discussion of crimmigration and argue that, in part, a political economy analysis allows us to parse out important nuances in national crimmigration regimes. Examining the case of settler-colonial Canada, I show how the criminalization of migration has been bound into a broader strategy of carceral expansion as a political-economic response to the financial recession of 2007/08. I argue that the specific means by which prison expansion has taken place, through Public-Private Partnerships, bears significantly on how carcerality has become entrenched in Canadian immigration policy with important implications for those organizing against the criminalization of migration.

In a 2006 article, legal scholar Juliet Stumpf coined the term 'crimmigration' intended to reflect the increasing convergence between criminal and immigration law in the United States since the late 1980s (Stumpf 2006). Stumpf's concept was critical in that it named and analyzed a set of phenomena which merged, in a two-way relationship, domestic and international law. Since its original articulation, the term crimmigration has gained a great deal of traction within the legal community, eventually branching into broader citizenship studies – indeed, the origins of the term were to explain a particular legal nexus which (re)defined the limits of inclusion into the body politic (Stumpf 2006). However, less attention has been paid to the political-economic dimensions of crimmigration – that is the political economic conditions within which the law is situated, and the political economic ends or objectives that legal norms assist in achieving. Taken in this light, it is important to understand how legal norms condition processes of capital accumulation, as well as how such changes in patterns of accumulation (and the role of carcerality therein) contribute to a reconfiguration of political subjectivity.

The need for a political-economy analysis of crimmigration is evidenced by the fact that in both popular and academic writing, crimmigration is often explained in reference to specific leaders and their political ideologies. While in the U.S. this has meant a focus on Donald

Trump, in Canada debates around crimmigration have tended to point to former Prime Minister Stephen Harper and, then-Minister of Immigration, Jason Kenney. However, ideological and political considerations only get us so far. In the U.S. it has frequently been pointed out that the Obama administration was, contrary to its popular rhetoric, responsible for a significant increase in deportations (Golash-Boza 2015; Zug 2015), while in Canada policy initiatives and investments (to be discussed in more detail below) have continued to expand the capacity to reject, detain and/or deport migrants in spite of a change of government (see, e.g. Piché 2017).

In this article, I ask what a political economy lens can add to our discussion of crimmigration. In answering this question, I advance two related arguments. First, I argue that attention to the political-economic dimensions of crimmigration allow us to parse out important nuances in national crimmigration regimes. Second, and related, I argue that attending to the political economy of crimmigration provides compelling evidence that advocacy for criminalized migrants must extend beyond an exclusive focus on migrants and challenge the criminal (in)justice system itself – that is, the analysis I advance insists on an approach grounded in prison abolition. I do this by shifting focus away from the most commonly studied spaces of crimmigration (notably the United States and Western Europe) to a country whose crimmigration regime is, only in recent years, beginning to raise concerns in the broader spectrum of political and popular discourse: settler colonial Canada (Ellis 2015; Ellis and Stam 2017; Goldring et al. 2009).

At an ideological level, it is easy to paint all movements towards the criminalization of migration with a single brush. However, important distinctions remain, one of which is the political-economic nature of the financing, ownership and operation of carceral facilities. I highlight these differences, not to affirm some imagined world of a humane, fully public approach to detention, but because these differences bear importantly on the capacities for governments to actually reduce a reliance on detention, while also speaking to the different strategies activists in the community might more successfully engage in to challenge detention. As such, there is a great need for comparative empirical work which I aim to contribute to in this article. What becomes evident, in the Canadian case, is that an opposition to migrant detention cannot simultaneously affirm the legitimacy of criminal forms of detention. The exclusion and detention of migrant bodies is fundamentally grounded in the same economic and ideological conditions which serve to legitimize and affirm the settler state, through the exclusion and detention of internal populations – disproportionately indigenous and racialized (Malakieh 2019). As such, our efforts must be abolitionist in scope.

In order to reach this conclusion, I argue that recent carceral expansion in Canada must be situated within a broader set of state-led attempts to restore and regulate capital accumulation in a post-recession climate and that both this broader need to regulate accumulation and the expansion of spaces for incarceration have become wedded to the increasing criminalization of migrants. I argue this by showing how carceral expansion since 2008 has proceeded through partnerships with the private sector, often institutionalizing long-term financial obligations to private consortia. This has had the effect of entrenching detention as a primary policy choice (Buitenhuis 2013), while also necessitating a steady and growing supply of 'bodies' to fill these spaces. In Canada, this growing 'need' has, in part, been supplied by an increasing pool of detainable migrants.

From this perspective, it becomes necessary to shift our discussion away from a simple critique of the criminalization of migrants. While the crimmigration literature has raised essential critiques about the criminalization of migration, too often that critique has found its way into a form of activism which positions immigrants and incarcerated peoples as occupying diametrically opposite moral positions. The narrative becomes one in which immigrants are 'not like them' (the criminals) whereby the rights and privileges of one group relies on defining another group as unworthy. This is dangerous ground, and also premised on patently false claims. For example, the idea that incarcerated populations occupy an inherently compromised moral ground – 'they' have committed a crime – cannot be supported by evidence. In Ontario alone, more than 70% of those occupying provincial jails are being held on remand – meaning they have not been convicted of a crime or sentenced, while remand accounts for a greater proportion of adults held in provincial/territorial jails across the country than those held under a sentence (Malakieh 2019). Furthermore, this narrative implicitly reinforces and legitimizes the criminal legal system which, contrary to its purported objectives of public safety, has historically been built upon and through the need to safeguard the privileges of dominant social factions by policing and defining as 'criminal' so-called transgressors of racial and national boundaries (Alexander 2012; Calathes 2017; Comaroff 2001; Coyle and Schept 2018; Davis 1998; Gilmore 2007; Maynard 2017).

The history of carcerality in Canada is one which is bound by settler-colonial efforts to police the limits of political subjectivity and inclusion vis a vis the need to dispossess indigenous peoples from their lands and legitimize settler sovereignty, on the one hand, and to manage a highly flexible, exploitable and deportable labor force, on the other hand (Evans 2018). The historical origins of the North West Mounted Police, for example, is tied to the enforcement of the Pass System which criminalized indigenous mobility and cultural practices in order to legitimize and enforce capitalist agricultural practices (see for example Dafnos 2014; Shantz 2016), while Heidi Kiiwetinepinesiik Stark's exceptional *Criminal Empire* (2016) has pushed this analysis further to argue that settler legality has been crafted through the construction of indigenous illegality. Furthermore, the ability to criminalize, detain, and sometimes deport racialized migrant labor in the late 19th and early 20th centuries has been a key strategy in managing tensions between flexible and 'liberal' labor market requirements and the settler states' need to define its national identity through so-called racial whiteness (Evans 2018; Goutor 2008). As such, there is no sharp boundary between the criminalization and detention of so-called domestic 'criminals' and international migrants (Kaufman and Bosworth 2013).

In the next section, I review the critical theoretical and empirical contributions of US scholars working on the political economy of carcerality – those of Ruth Wilson Gilmore and Tanya Golash-Boza. I then provide a sketch of the penal landscape in Canada, along with the changes that have occurred since the 2007–08 Recession. Following this, I examine changes to immigration policy in this same period, tracking not only the legal overlap between criminal and immigration policy, but also their political-economic interpenetration. I close by considering how the political economy of carcerality bears importantly on studies of citizenship in order to highlight future research avenues. Far from simply a distinction in how prisons are funded, the difference between state-funded, fully privatized, or partially commodified carcerality has consequences for how we define and regulate citizenship, and how we might explore potential strategies to transform such.

Crisis and carcerality: from the golden Gulag to deportation

If we are to understand the criminalization of migration in Canada, it is necessary to think beyond one of the most common approaches being used in the U.S. and much of Western Europe which draws from the 'Prison Industrial Complex' (PIC) thesis (Davis 1998; Schlosser 1998). The PIC, while incredibly important in highlighting drastic changes in the carceral landscape since the 1980s has a tendency to fetishize the role of fully privatized carceral infrastructure and service provision in explaining the rise of mass incarceration and deportation regimes (Ackerman and Furman 2013; Douglas and Saenz 2013; Luan 2018), though more nuanced variants also exist (Golash-Boza 2009; Trujillo-Pagan 2014). While privatization has certainly been important to the U.S. and some European contexts, it has limited analytical applicability in a place like Canada, where (with the exception of a brief experiment in the early 2000s) prisons and detention centers have remained public. As such, it is instructive to turn to Ruth Wilson Gilmore, whose 2007 *The Golden Gulag*, challenged the PIC thesis as one-dimensional.

Throughout the opening chapters of her study, Gilmore rigorously documents the composition of prison infrastructure in California (perhaps the site of the greatest prison-expansion throughout the final decades of the 20th Century), demonstrating that private ownership and prison labor are statistically unable to account for the extent of carceral expansion that took place throughout this period (Gilmore 2007). In contrast to a crudely functionalist account of the relationship between capital and carcerality, Gilmore advanced a nuanced, if deeply troubling, argument linking economic crisis and the re-composition of accumulation to the rise of mass incarceration. In doing so, Gilmore shifted focus from the exceptional and corrupt, to the mundane, systemic and normalized role of carcerality in the regulation of accumulation.

Briefly, Gilmore's argument is that the rise of mass incarceration and the expansion of the penal landscape in California must be understood within the context of crises of capital accumulation to which neoliberalism was the dominant response. Gilmore argues that the state during this period underwent a process of restructuring, in order to politically organize a geographical 'fix' to socioeconomic problems. For Gilmore, the transition to neoliberalism produced a series of surpluses (finance, capital, land, labor, and state capacity) which were absorbed and spatially 'fixed' in the carceral landscape. Critically, Gilmore's analysis allows us to locate shifts in carceral practice relating to political economy which does away with the simplistic choice between either for-profit or state-run. Instead, Gilmore shows how the state is itself reconstituted to play a different role in capital accumulation without resorting to a 'fire sale'-like offloading of state assets (Gilmore 2007).

This more nuanced formulation also allows us to connect political economy to citizenship studies in that this geographical 'fix' relies on a steady supply of bodies whose rights of citizenship can be suspended. Expanding and ensuring a constant supply of bodies, in turn, requires a renegotiation of the limits of the 'deserving citizen' and introduces new, often more expansive, definitions of the (internal or external) 'enemy.' As Gilmore argues, 'An entire development path has been created through the assumption that there is a perpetual enemy who must always be fought, but who can never be conquered. And that is where international militarization and domestic militarization meet – at this notion that there is the production of an enemy around which we organize everything, *everything*, not simply profit.' (Loyd 2012, 45) The bodies absorbed by this spatial fix (the prison) are not simply human, fleshy bodies – they are bodies that are thoroughly raced, classed, and gendered. Decisions to immobilize certain bodies as a spatial 'fix' to overaccumulation declares loudly and visibly who is and is not a full and deserving political subject.

In part, for Gilmore, the internal enemy was generated through the neoliberal strategy of violent union busting which would both facilitate a restoration of class power and profits, while also conveniently carving out a population who could be read as 'underserving' through the criminalization of poverty and subsequent war on drugs (Alexander 2012; Gilmore 2007; Harvey 2007). The first, and hardest hit, victims of this strategy were those in low-skilled occupations, often disproportionately black (Loyd 2012). In turn, these low-skilled, unionized jobs and black workers were increasingly replaced by precarious, temporary, sometimes undocumented, brown workers. Thus, the rise of mass incarceration was deeply wedded to a secular rise in precariously documented, 'deportable' immigrant labor (Loyd 2012). Shorn of the protections and legal obligations afforded (even if only in name) by citizenship, these workers became a crucial lever for jump-starting capital accumulation.

Picking up this thread, Tanya Golash-Boza has argued that a contraction in the, predominantly Latinx, U.S. construction sector since the Global Recession has led to a rapid and sustained expansion in efforts to detain, deport, and otherwise criminalize migrant workers who have been made redundant. Criminalization is not about 'enforcing' the border, as such, but instead expelling those already within the borders – many of whom have long been central to the economy since deindustrialization in the 1970s (Golash-Boza 2015; 2016). Crimmigration is about the absorption of these newly generated surpluses. Surplus, here, refers to migrant labor, of course, but also surpluses in state capacity and built infrastructure. Thus, for example, Congress passed a bill in 2009 mandating that immigration detention facilities must fill at minimum 34,000 beds each day, while a preoccupation with interior enforcement also served to absorb the capacities of the state, notably through the expansion of the Department of Homeland Security (Golash-Boza 2016).

Golash-Boza argues that in general, studies focusing on the criminalization of immigration fail to attend to how and why it is that immigrants subjected to the violence of the state are gendered and racialized. She further argues that this lacuna arises from the failure to contextualize these practices in the broader historical scope of global capitalism (Golash-Boza 2016). It is for this reason that Golash-Boza draws on Gilmore, who's attention to crisis, socio-economic re-composition and penality offers potentially fruitful insights. For, what is key in Gilmore's account, as well as in Golash-Boza's, is the fact that the violence of the state must be preceded by a dehumanization of the population that comprises the states' targets. Racialized and classed workers become primary objects of state efforts to release the pressures of surplus – workers who are easily constructed as 'undeserving' or 'enemy' and therefore 'legitimately' (or at the very least, regrettably) the rightful subjects of state violence.

Reframing the 'Threat' of criminality and immigration in the post-recession period

Unlike in the U.S. and much of Europe, in Canada, the majority of migrants subjected to detention and deportation via their status as 'irregular' are not undocumented migrants, per se but rather exist in a space of lapsed documentation (Ellis and Stam 2017; Goldring et al. 2009; Walia 2010). In other words, most of Canada's irregular migrants enter the country lawfully and with proper documentation, and are *made* irregular by lapses in status, failed asylum claims, and importantly, changes in policy. While such processes are of course evident in the U.S., undocumented border crossings tend to be far greater there (as well as in Continental Europe), making the Canadian situation comparatively unique (Ellis and Stam 2017). In Canada, while estimates are vague (given the very nature of irregular status), scholars have suggested that the number of migrants in Canada with irregular status is between 80,000 and 500,000 (Ellis 2015). In 2003, estimates were a fraction of this, ranging from 20,000 to 200,000 (Magalhaes et al. 2010). Given that irregular status in Canada is not dominantly designated on arrival, but instead is a complex process of *becoming*, the question we must ask is how and why are more migrants becoming irregular? To answer this question, I argue it is important to examine the ways in which criminality and illicit migration were mobilized to frame national economic recovery following the global financial crisis.

In Canada, the immediate post-recession economic recovery fell into the hands of the federal Conservatives under Prime Minister Stephen Harper (first through a minority government, and then through a majority government in 2011). A great deal of media and academic attention has focused on the Conservatives' recovery strategy centering on natural resources, transport, and western economic development to stimulate trade and job creation. The importance of these areas can be evidenced by the extraordinary growth in net expenditure each of these ministries experienced in the post-recession period. However, on this count, it is surprising that little attention has been paid to the role of penality and immigration in the recovery, given that alongside the three aforementioned, Citizenship and Immigration, and Public Safety were among the top five ministries whose net expenditure grew between 2006 and 2011 (Stoney and Krawchenko 2013). While, to be sure, an increased politicization of penal practices, including their application to the management of immigration predated the recession, the post-recession period is marked by both a qualitative and quantitative transformation of legislation, spending, and construction related to detention.

In qualitative terms, this shift is registered in the recasting of criminality and immigration in terms of economic cost-benefit and threat analyses. A report from the Collaborative Center for Justice and Safety titled *The Economics of Canadian Policing Five Years Into the Great Recession*, argued vociferously that in the post-recession period it was imperative and efficient to invest greater public (and private) monies in policing – largely to manage those rendered vulnerable, precarious, and therefore potentially troublesome, by the contraction of labor market opportunities and social welfare programs. Among the recommendations of the report were an increase in so-called targeted, 'hot-spot' policing as a 'value for money' strategy, and the increasing use of both civilian and private sector actors in the business of policing (Ruddell and Jones 2014). Public discourse on criminality, then, began to draw on debates around economic value – both in terms of the nature and cause of so-called increased criminality and the conditions by and through which increased policing should be evaluated. These recommendations were made in spite of ample statistical evidence which showed that the 'volume and seriousness of crime has been decreasing since its peak in 1991', and justified on the basis that 'police practitioners … are not convinced …. the validity of statistics related to policing and crime is a key concern' (2014, 36).

Similarly, efforts to 'crack down' on so-called illicit immigration ramped up following the recession. These efforts are most visible through the public debates and hyper criminalization of the MV Ocean Lady landing in 2009, the introduction of the bilateral Beyond the Border Action Plan (4 February 2011), the Conservative Federal Budget – Jobs Growth and Long-Term Prosperity (29 March 2012), and the introduction and Royal Assent of Bill C-31

(28 June 2012). These high profile political and popular interventions into immigration policy were also notable given their explicit connection to matters of national economic health. Whereas previous efforts to criminalize migration were largely premised on an assumption of a terrorist threat couched in the language of securitization, these new policies were increasingly justified through the fear of potential economic threat. The threat to the body politic was no longer exclusively about literal or physical violence, but was now also about the lateral threat of economic 'violence'; the unworthy or unproductive (both from abroad and from within) were cast as a threat to 'our' economic wellbeing, and thereby also, our personal economic security, health, and access to the benefits of citizenship. Indeed the Beyond the Border Action Plan argued that identifying border threats early and addressing 'irregular flows' would be necessary to ensure the free flow of 'legitimate goods and people' identified as to key to economic recovery (2011). Thus, in the post-recession period 'criminal' and immigration threats were increasingly linked to economic health, marking a shift in the crimmigration discourse.

Policy transformations of the crimmigration landscape in post-recession Canada

It is necessary to view the increased role of carcerality in immigration management in the context of broader changes to penal institutions and policies in Canada. Following a majority electoral victory in 2011, Stephen Harper's Conservatives passed the omnibus Bill C-10 (the so-called Safe Streets and Communities Act) which served to expand Canada's incarcerated population, even while crime rates had hit an all-time low (Blaze Carlson 2011; Bronskill 2011). The Act imposed mandatory minimum sentencing for a range of street-level crimes, removing the sentencing discretion of judges. The Act also eliminated conditional sentences, pardons in certain cases, and 'double credit' for time served, while imposing more serious forms of punishment on youth offenders. All of this added significantly to pressures on provincial jails and federal penitentiaries, and thus Bill C-10 was complemented by a ballooning in Correctional Services Canada budgets and federal funding for carceral expansion. For example, in the fiscal year 2005–06 Correctional Services Canada's budget totaled 1,729.9 USD million, while in fiscal year 2008–09 it was 2,231 USD million and by the end of the 2018–19 fiscal year, budgets are expected to reach about 2,629 USD million, the vast majority of which has been dedicated to custody-related costs (Correctional Services Canada). In terms of explicit commitments to new infrastructure, following the passage of Bill C-10, the Harper administration announced 2 USD billion in funding for prison expansion over 5 years, and the creation of 2,700 new 'beds' in the correctional system (Bronskill 2011). Under the Trudeau government, data collected by the No Ottawa Prison Expansion (CPEP 2017) project has found that since 2016, detention construction and renovation projects across Canada have exceeded 1,223.6 USD million (some projects have not disclosed budgets, while others are awaiting funding approval). This, despite a 4% drop in the incarceration rate of adults in provincial-territorial jails since 2014–15 (Green et al. 2017).

However, prison expansion and changes to criminal law were not the only relevant changes under the Harper administration. In 2012, similarly punitive changes were put into place by (then) Minister of Immigration and Citizenship Jason Kenney through Bill-C31 (the 'Protecting Canada's Immigration System' Act). The Act was an amendment to the IRPA and aimed to legally distinguish between the 'deserving' and 'undeserving' refugee

(Bourbeau 2018). Indeed, the name itself suggested that Canada's immigration system was under attack by, presumably, criminal, dangerous, and undeserving 'outsiders.' The Act introduced a new legal category of migrants – the 'designated foreign national' which formalized a link between 'irregularity' and 'criminality' by mandating the automatic and indefinite detention of so-called 'designated foreign nationals' or 'irregular arrivals' over the age of 16 (Ellis and Stam 2017; Moffette and Askin 2018). While narrowing down the range of acceptable asylum claims, the Ministry, under Kenney, created further barriers to status by increasing the language skills required by immigrants, instituting mandatory credential assessments of those with foreign credentials, wiping out all backlogged applications for the FSWP (dated prior to 27 February 2008), and replacing family class applications with a *temporary* 'super visa' (Government of Canada 2012a). All these measures have contributed to the complexity of immigration status and create the administrative space within which shifts into and out of 'status' become possible. This scope of precarity is further reflected by the shift in the composition of Canada's migrant population, which since 2008, has seen the volume of temporary admissions exceed permanent (Bourbeau 2018; Ellis and Stam 2017).

While a good deal of literature has, rightly, focused on carceral expansion under the Harper administration, much of this trajectory has been maintained under Prime Minister Justin Trudeau's Liberal government, despite rhetoric to the contrary. Though Trudeau committed to reviewing the impact of Harper's Safe Streets Act and investing in alternative and restorative measures of justice, federal funding in this area has continued to prioritize the construction of new beds in corrections. Meanwhile, the Trudeau government has created the new Ministry of Border Security and Organized Crime, and despite an announcement from the Minister of Public Safety, Ralph Goodale, to 'enhance alternatives to detention' (2016), funding to the tune of 138 USD million has been sunk into updating existing detention facilities in Laval, Toronto and Vancouver (Piche 2017). Such a focus on detention and deportation does not seem to be waning, either. On 10 April 2019 Trudeau announced new measures which would crackdown on the capacity of those crossing through unauthorized ports of entry to obtain a full hearing on their asylum claims (despite an overall reduction in the number of unauthorized border crossings in the last two years, which this adjustment is purported to address) (Wright 2019).

In Canada, immigrants detained for administrative purposes occupy either one of the three purpose-built immigration holding centers in Toronto, Laval, and Vancouver, or they are increasingly held in medium and maximum-security provincial jails (Ellis and Stam 2017; Walia and Tagore 2012). Reliance on provincial carceral infrastructure (rather than Immigration Holding Centers) to detain immigrants has in fact increased over the past several years, accounting for 35% of the total detainee population in 2010–2011, and 38% in 2016–2017 (Global Detention Project). As such, the increasing criminalization of migrants in Canada cannot be understood without reference to earlier tough on crime policies and carceral expansion.

Thus, at the same time that carceral infrastructure has been expanding, so too was the literal pool of bodies that could be contained by such cages. As I show in the next section, the expansion of carceral infrastructure in Canada has constituted a potent response to financial crisis, and migrant bodies play a key role in this. Firstly, carceral expansion has (as per Gilmore above) functioned to absorb and 'fix' surplus capital, mitigating problems of overaccumulation. Second, carceral expansion has allowed for the 'absorption' of bodies made redundant by productive restructuring following the crisis. In Canada,

I want to suggest that it is useful to consider how migrant laborers with precarious status might be increasingly subject to detention. Indeed, contrary to popular rhetoric, most of those with precarious status in Canada (as many as 95%) entered the country under a temporary status which has, subsequently, been lost (Ellis 2015). Such loss of status can arise for any number of reasons, but often have profound socio-economic connections. As Ellis shows, those who continue to 'make it' are rarely subject to detention and deportation; however, those who might lose employment or otherwise lack the financial resources to support themselves or their families are subject to far greater legal, political, and social scrutiny (Ellis 2015). In shifting the conditions under which migrants might obtain legal status, governments have been able to a) shed 'redundant' labor, and b) provide bodies for a growing carceral landscape, while c) minimizing direct impact on 'national' (i.e. voting) populations, thereby minimizing public outcry. In the next section, I consider more closely the role of carceral expansion as a 'fix' to crises of accumulation, to show how *expanded* and *expanding* detention have become (for the foreseeable future) a permanent policy commitment, requiring mechanisms which can ensure a ready and steady supply of detainable populations (Walia and Tagore 2012).

The political economy of canadian carceral expansion: private finance and the entrenchment of detention

It is critical to understand that the carceral expansion I have identified above has been achieved through Public-Private Partnerships (PPPs), notably through Alternative Finance Procurement (AFP) (Buitenhuis 2013). While the use of PPPs to fund and build public infrastructure in Canada is not new, its application to prisons is. Under AFP models of financing, private equity and debt, which are tied to a *specific* project, is used to finance infrastructure rather than government bonds which function as a form of generalized debt used for any number of projects (Buitenhuis 2013). When private actors are contracted to finance specific projects, they are paid a lump sum upon the completion of design/construction phases, while the remainder is paid out as monthly installments for the duration of the contract, often several decades (Buitenhuis 2013). In this way, governments are locked into long-term spending and partnerships with private actors such that these public assets (here prisons) must be continuously in use.

Since 2008, a total of five correctional facilities have been constructed through PPPs and are operational, totaling over 1 USD billion in disclosed costs and covering the Okanagan Correctional Center, Roy McMurty Youth Centre, Sorel-Tracy Detention Centre, South-West Detention Centre and Toronto South Detention Centre (P3Spectrum). At present, at least four more new or renovated facilities are being proposed through PPPs: a 170 USD million new facility in Nanaimo which will replace the Nanaimo Correctional Centre and add 36 beds; a 200 USD million penitentiary to replace Her Majesty's Penitentiary in St. John's which is slated to double existing beds; a 200-400 USD million Thunder Bay Correctional Complex which will replace the Thunder Bay Jail and Thunder Bay Correctional Centre, adding 81 beds to existing capacity, and the Ottawa Correctional Complex which will cost 500 USD million – 1 USD billion and add 140 beds to existing capacity[1] (Criminalization and Punishment Education Project 2017; P3 Spectrum).

More recently, AFP adjacent models have begun to creep into the construction and renovation of Immigrant Holding Centers. In 2015 Corbel Management Corporation was awarded a contract to build and service Toronto's IHC which runs until 2028. According to a Government News Release the contract awarded is to 'help the CBSA deliver its National Detention Program in a more effective and sustainable manner.'[2] (Government of Canada 2015) Under the contract, CBSA is to administer the center while Corbel will provide the facility, housekeeping, maintenance, and food services. Indeed, the use of AFP and value-for-money assessments to fund infrastructure, including detention facilities, has been explicitly named as a key commitment and ambition of the Ontario government (Government of Ontario 2015b). It is difficult to envision how the present Liberal government can remain on-course with its purported commitment to alternatives to detention when provincial and federal governments are locked into decade-plus commitments to maintain detention infrastructure and services.

The use of PPPs and investment in infrastructure has been (and continue to be) key components of Canada's responses to the recession. Indeed, in 2008 the federal government launched PPP Canada Inc. a Crown Corporation tasked with assessing, advising, managing, and negotiating PPPs as part of a mandate to improve the delivery of public infrastructure in Canada under the Financial Administrations Act and the Canada Business Corporations Act. While PPP Canada Inc. ceased operations in 2017, under the newly elected federal Liberals, it was quickly replaced by the Canada Infrastructure Bank whose mandates, similarly, involves working with provincial, territorial, municipal, federal, and Indigenous actors to 'seek and attract investment from private sector investors and institutional investors, in revenue-generating infrastructure projects that are in the public interest' (Canada Infrastructure Bank). Similarly, in Ontario, the use of AFP has been a cornerstone of the provincial government's Infrastructure for Jobs and Prosperity Act (Government of Ontario 2015a; McElligot 2017).

Understanding the relationship between the increasing use of PPPs and state responses to crisis as a variation on Gilmore and Golash-Boza's discussion of state activities following financial crisis may provide some illumination on the Canadian case. As Heather Whiteside has argued it is important to attend to the variety of ways that states might intervene in the economy in order to restore profitability following a crisis, in particular noting the role of PPPs. Under the PPP model, infrastructural projects and services can be used as a solve for crisis by absorbing surplus capital in two ways. First, through the partial privatization of these projects, new spaces are opened up for capital, effecting a spatial displacement which draws excess capital out of circulation (Whiteside 2012). Additionally, built infrastructure serves as a form of temporal displacement – capital from the private sector is sunk into long-term infrastructure, offsetting its reentry into circulation. Capital, in this case, is not destroyed in order to solve overaccumulation, but is instead deferred (Whiteside 2019). The state, in this scenario plays a critical role in capital accumulation (particularly in times of crisis) as they both create the conditions of possibility for surplus absorption while nevertheless retaining overall governmental responsibility and control. In retaining partial public control, the state can avoid destabilizing social contestation as PPPs tend to depoliticize the privatization of politically sensitive pieces of infrastructure (i.e. hospitals, prisons, etc.) (Buitenhuis 2013; Whiteside 2009; 2019). This is a form of asset restructuring which is an essential component of state responses to financial crisis (Ashman and Callinicos 2006).

Now, prisons are not simply a neutral piece of infrastructure – they also hold social functions to both manage and model population. Beyond opening up new spaces of accumulation, the state might also restore profitability by temporarily 'pulling existing devalued assets out of circulation.' (Whiteside 2012) This form of state involvement might also be read in terms of a spatial or temporal fix, whereby certain unprofitable or potentially troublesome factors of production are displaced from the private realm to be temporarily fixed in the public sector (Gilmore 2007; Harvey 2007). This spreads out the costs of crises so that they are absorbed by the whole of society rather than allowing capital alone to assume the burden." (Whiteside 2012, 66) In doing so, the state enables the renewal of private accumulation, absent the 'dead weight' of unproductive 'assets.'

Such observations bear importantly on the study of carcerality as a response to crisis. First, this idea of pulling 'devalued assets' out of circulation and 'spreading the costs of crisis' throughout society speaks powerfully to the ways in which those made 'idle' by labor market restructuring are 'pulled' from the realm of circulating labor in order to restore wages and employment to a level capable of quelling public anxieties. For example, in Canada, within a year of the recession (from October 2008 to October 2009), the manufacturing sector had shed 218,000 jobs, while other sectors like construction, retail, transportation, and warehousing were also badly hit, losing more jobs than any other industrial sectors in Canada (Larochelle-Cote and Gilmore 2010). These sectors, of course, also happen to be the sectors where temporary foreign workers tend to be employed, and indeed, we can also note significant changes in the realm of immigration policy and detention. Targets for permanent admission were reduced between 2008 and 2009, as were targets for all categories of economic migrants, while in 2009 stricter guidelines were imposed on Labour Market Opinion (LMO) approvals, thereby restricting approvals for low-skilled temporary migrant workers. According to Chaloff et al., drawing on figures from Human Resources Canada, authorizations of temporary migrants following an LMO dropped by 57% in 2009 and was sustained at this level until 2010 (Chaloff et al. 2012). In this same period, Canada spent 45.7 USD million on immigration detention, up 17.7% from figures reported in 2005–2006, while removals had risen from 12,363 in 2006–2007 to 13,249 in 2008–2009. Though much of this is on account of rejected asylum applications (73%) there is still a significant number (27%) that is presumably comprised of those already within Canada (Global Detention Project). While this speculation requires far greater research, I argue that, moving forward, it is important to think through migrants' pathways to detention in order to ascertain the role of labor market restructuring.

Prisons, PPPs and citizenship

While a full analysis of the relationship between PPPs, prisons, and citizenship is beyond the scope of this article, I wish to close by flagging three key relationships which warrant further consideration. As discussed above, the use of public infrastructure in the form of prisons as a 'fix' to crises of overaccumulation is a potentially explosive and contentious strategy. The success of such tactics relies on the effective construction of some bodies as 'enemy' and/or 'undeserving'; and it is those members of society with the least access to effective political voice and protection which will be most easily targeted. So, in the first instance, if carcerality as a 'fix' to overaccumulation involves pulling 'dead weight' out of circulation we need to ask what are the criteria for determining who is labeled 'dead weight'? In part, the answer to this question may lie with the second point to consider which is the particular role of PPPs in effecting a reconstitution of citizenship. Public-Private Partnerships are utilized on the basis of Value for Money assessments – in other words, they operate according to a language of 'cost savings' and 'efficiency.' In many ways, it is clear that this language governs not only the financing, construction, and operation of the service/infrastructure but also its content – this is to say that, with the prison, the detained and their potential freedom are assessed on the basis of how effectively they can defer from the state the costs of their own reproduction. One's ability to do so, in a settler-colonial context like Canada, of course, has and continues to be coded by race, gender, and disability. Unsurprisingly, then, women, indigenous peoples, migrants of color, and populations with a disability or psychiatric diagnosis are disproportionately those who make up the growing numbers of people caged by Canada's carceral infrastructure. Finally, if carcerality is a response, not to rising crime and criminality, but to broader concerns of capital accumulation, policy-makers are cognizant of the need to avoid panic and outrage amongst its voting constituents. This means those targeted by carceral practices will be groups deemed unimportant as a political constituency owing to a lack of effective political voice, advocacy, and public sympathy. Individuals occupying precarious forms of status, on these counts, can become politically salient targets for an expanding carceral infrastructure.

Conclusion

Using a political-economy analysis of crisis to understand shifts in the carceral landscape in Canada allows us to understand these changes and their longevity independent of an exclusive focus on specific political administrations. It moves us past an exceptional focus on individuals and ideologies, for example, Stephen Harper's Conservative administration, and instead points us to the very systemic and material role of carcerality in the Canadian state. Furthermore, a focus on political economy allows us to bridge abolition and immigration justice. In the analysis above, I have shown how the expansion of immigration detention, or crimmigration, has been intimately connected to the broader politics of prison expansion in Canada. Indeed, I have argued that expanding the scope of immigrant detention is firmly related to the needs of prisons under Public-Private Partnerships to continuously operate, at a maximum capacity. Expanding the scope of criminal admissibility is a volatile political strategy, and as such, moving to the 'non-citizen' as a target of detention resolves the need for detainable bodies, without necessarily stoking political outrage among voters. In Canada, where provincial prisons have long served the purpose of de facto immigration holding centers, such a fix could be accomplished with relative bureaucratic ease. The conclusion to be drawn is that it is politically infeasible and ineffective to contest the detention of immigrants on the basis of the non-criminal nature of their purported offense. Such rhetoric only strengthens the legitimacy of criminal detention itself, thereby inadvertently providing support for the very infrastructural and political conditions which make possible, perhaps even necessary, an increasing scope for the detention of individuals with precarious status. As such, it is necessary to think through the combined interests of prison abolitionists and immigrant justice activists. Such interests, I argue, must be grounded in an abolitionist framework.

Notes

1. Figures drawn from information disclosed by P3 Spectrum and Infrastructure Ontario.
2. https://www.ontario.ca/page/mandate-letter-progress-economic-development-employment-and-infrastructure#section-4

Disclosure statement

No potential conflict of interest was reported by the author.

ORCID

Jessica Evans http://orcid.org/0000-0003-2649-2560

References

Ackerman, A., and R. Furman. 2013. "The Criminalization of Immigration and the Privatization of the Immigration Detention: Implications for Justice." *Contemporary Justice Review* 16 (2): 251–263. doi:10.1080/10282580.2013.798506.

Alexander, M. 2012. *The New Jim Crow: Mass Incarceration in the Age of Colorblindness*. New York: New Press.

Ashman, S., and A. Callinicos. 2006. "Capital Accumulation and the State System: Assessing David Harvey's the New Imperialism." *Historical Materialism* 14 (4): 107–131. doi:10.1163/156920606778982572.

Blaze Carlson, K. 2011. "The Largest Expansion of Prison Building 'Since the 1930's'." *The National Post*. https://nationalpost.com/news/canada/the-largest-expansion-of-prison-building-since-the-1930s

Bourbeau, P. 2018. "Detention and Immigration: Practices, Crimmigration, and Norms." *Migration Studies* 1–17. doi:10.1093/migration/mnx069.

Bronskill, J. 2011. "Critics Say Government Throwing Prison Expansion Money Away." *The Toronto Star*. https://www.thestar.com/news/canada/2011/01/10/critics_say_harper_government_throwing_prison_expansion_money_away.html

Buitenhuis, J. 2013. "Public-Private Partnerships and Prison Expansion in Ontario: Shifts in Governance, 1995-2012." Unpublished Doctoral Dissertation. The University of Toronto.

Calathes, W. 2017. "Racial Capitalism and Punishment Philosophy and Practices: What Really Stands in the Way of Prison Abolition." *Contemporary Justice Review* 20 (4): 442–455. doi:10.1080/10282580.2017.1383774.

Government of Canada. 2015. *Contract Awarded for Toronto Immigration Holding Centre*. Ottawa.

Government of Canada. 2012a. "The Protecting Canada's Immigration System Act." https://laws-lois.justice.gc.ca/eng/annualstatutes/2012_17/page-1.html

Government of Canada. 2012b. "Jobs, Growth, and Long-Term Prosperity Economic Action Plan." *Public Works and Government Services Canada*. Ottawa.

Chaloff, J. et al. 2012. "The Impact of Economic Crisis on Migration and Labour Market Outcomes of Immigrants in OECD Countries." *Research Report*. Munich: CESifo Group.

Comaroff, J. 2001. "Symposium Introduction: Colonialism, Culture, and the Law: A Forward." *Law & Social Inquiry* 26 (2): 305–314. doi:10.1111/j.1747-4469.2001.tb00180.x.

Coyle, M., and J. Schept. 2018. "Penal Abolition Praxis." *Critical Criminology* 26: 319–323. doi:10.1007/s10612-018-9407-x.

Criminalization and Punishment Education Project. 2017. "Tracking the Politics of Criminalization and Punishment in Canada." http://tpcp-canada.blogspot.com/

Dafnos, D. 2014. "Negotiating Colonial Encounters: (Un)mapping the Policing of Indigenous Peoples' Protests in Canada." Unpublished Doctoral Dissertation submitted to the Department of Sociology, York University, Toronto, ON.

Davis, A. 1998. "Masked Racism: Reflections on the Prison Industrial Complex." *Colorlines Magazine.*

Douglas, K., and R. Saenz. 2013. "The Criminalization of Immigrants and the Immigration Industrial Complex." *Daedalus* 142 (3): 199–227. doi:10.1162/DAED_a_00228.

Ellis, B. D. 2015. "The Production of Irregular Migration in Canada." *Canadian Ethnic Studies* 47 (2): 93–112. doi:10.1353/ces.2015.0011.

Ellis, B. D., and H. J. Stam. 2017. "Cycles of Deportability: Threats, Fears, and the Agency of 'Irregular' Migrants in Canada." *Migration Studies* 1-24. doi:10.1093/migration/mnx049.

Evans, J. 2018. "Colonialism(s), Race, and the Transition to Capitalism in Canada." In *Case Studies in the Origins of Capitalism*, edited by C. Post and X. LaFrance, 191–213, London: Palgrave, Macmillan.

Gilmore, R. 2007. *Golden Gulag: Prisons, Surplus, Crisis, and Opposition in Globalizing California.* Berkley: University of California Press.

Golash-Boza, T. 2009. "The Immigration Industrial Complex: Why We Enforce Immigration Policies Destined to Fail." *Sociology Compass* 3 (2): 295–309. doi:10.1111/j.1751-9020.2008.00193.x.

Golash-Boza, T. 2015. *Deported: Immigrant Policing, Disposable Labor and Global Capitalism.* New York: New York University Press.

Golash-Boza, T. 2016. "The Parallels between Mass Incarceration and Mass Deportation: An Intersectional Analysis of State Repression." *Journal of World-System Research* 22 (3): 484–509. doi:10.5195/jwsr.2016.616.

Goldring, L., et al. 2009. "Institutionalizing Precarious Migratory Status in Canada." *Citizenship Studies* 13: 3. doi:10.1080/13621020902850643.

Goutor, D. 2008. *Guarding the Gates: The Canadian Labour Movement and Immigration, 1872-1934.* Vancouver, BC: UBC Press.

Green, et al. 2017. "Carceral Expansion in Canada's Provinces and Territories: An Opportunity for Prison Divestment and Justice Reinvestment." *NOPE Submission to the Senate Standing Committee on Human Rights.*

Harvey, D. 2007. *A Brief History of Neoliberalism.* Oxford: Oxford University Press.

Kaufman, E., and M. Bosworth. 2013. "The Prison and National Identity: Citizenship, Punishment and the Sovereign State." In *Why Prison*, edited by D. Scott, 170–188. NY: Cambridge University Press.

Kiiwetinepinesiik Stark, H. 2016. "Criminal Empire: The Making of the Savage in a Lawless Land." *Theory & Event* 19 (4).

Larochelle-Cote, S. and J. Gilmore. 2010. *Canada's Employment Downturn.* Ottawa: Statistics Canada. .

Loyd, J. 2012. *Race, Capitalist Crisis, and Abolitionist Organizing: An Interview with Ruth Wilson Gilmore, in beyond Walls and Cages: Prisons, Borders, and Global Crisis (Ed. Jenna M. Loyd, Matt Mitchelson, and Andrew Burridge)*, 42–56. London: University of Georgia Press.

Luan, L. 2018. "Profiting from Enforcement: The Role of Private Prisons in U.S. Immigration Detention." *Migration Information Source.* Migration Policy Institute.

Magalhaes, L., et al. 2010. "Undocumented Migrants in Canada: A Scope Literature Review on Health, Access to Services and Working Conditions." *Journal of Immigrant Minority Health* 12: 132–151. doi:10.1007/s10903-009-9280-5.

Malakieh, J. 2019. "Adult and Youth Correctional Statistics in Canada, 2017/2018." *Statistics Canada*, May 2. https://www150.statcan.gc.ca/n1/pub/85-002-x/2019001/article/00010-eng.htm#c-g02

Maynard, R. 2017. *Policing Black Lives: State Violence in Canada from Slavery to the Present.* Fernwood, Toronto: Fernwood.

McElligot, G. 2017. "Invested in Prisons: Prison Expansion and Community Development in Canada." *Studies in Social Justice* 11 (1): 86–112. doi:10.26522/ssj.v11i1.1246.

Moffette, D., and N. Askin. 2018. "Fighting Smuggling or Criminalizing Refugees? Regimes of Justification in and around R. V. Appulonappa." *Canadian Journal of Law and Society* 33 (1): 21–39. doi:10.1017/cls.2018.2.

Government of Ontario. 2015a. *Infrastructure for Jobs and Prosperity Act.*

Government of Ontario. 2015b. "Mandate Letter Progress: Economic Development, Employment and Infrastructure." https://www.ontario.ca/page/mandate-letter-progress-economic-development-employment-and-infrastructure

Piche, J. 2017. "The Liberals Promised Prison Reform, so Why are They Funding Prison Expansion?" *Ottawa Citizen*. https://ottawacitizen.com/opinion/columnists/piche-the-liberals-promised-prison-reform-so-why-are-they-funding-prison-expansion

Ruddell, R., and N. Jones 2014. "The Economics of Canadian Policing Five Years into the Great Recession." *Collaborative Centre for Justice and Safety*. Regina, SK.

Schlosser, E. 1998. "The Prison-Industrial Complex." *The Atlantic Monthly*.

Shantz, J. 2016. "They Have Always Been Military: On So-Called Militarized Policing in Canada." *Journal of Social Justice* 6: 1–26.

Stoney, C., and T. Krawchenko. 2013. "Crisis and Opportunism: Public and Finance Trends from Stimulus to Austerity in Canada. Alternate Routes." *A Journal of Critical Social Research* 24: 33–58.

Stumpf, J. 2006. "The Crimmigration Crisis: Immigrants, Crime, and Sovereign Power." *American University Law Review* 56 (2): 367–419. https://digitalcommons.wcl.american.edu/cgi/viewcontent.cgi?article=1274&context=aulr

Trujillo-Pagan, N. 2014. "Emphasizing the 'Complex' in the 'Immigration Industrial Complex'." *Critical Sociology* 40 (1): 29–46. doi:10.1177/0896920512469888.

Walia, H. 2010. "Transient Servitude: Mirant Labour in Canada and the Apartheid of Citizenship." *Race & Class* 52 (1): 71–84. doi:10.1177/0306396810371766.

Walia, H., and P. Tagore. 2012. *Prisoners of Passage: Immigration Detention in Canada, in beyond Walls and Cages: Prisons, Borders, and Global Crisis (Ed. Jenna M. Loyd, Matt Mitchelson, and Andrew Burridge)*, 74–90. London: University of Georgia Press.

Whiteside, H. 2009. "Canada's Health Care 'Crisis': Accumulation by Dispossession and the Neoliberal Fix." *Studies in Political Economy* 84 (1): 79–100. doi:10.1080/19187033.2009.11675047.

Whiteside, H. 2012. "Crises of Capital and the Logic of Dispossession and Repossession." *Studies in Political Economy* 89: 59–79. doi:10.1080/19187033.2012.11675001.

Whiteside, H. 2019. "Advanced Perspectives on Financialized Urban Infrastructures." *Urban Studies* 56 (7): 1477–1484. doi:10.1177/0042098019826022.

Wright, T. 2019. "Trudeau Defends Changes to Asylum Laws that Have Asylum Workers Alarmed." The Star. https://www.thestar.com/news/canada/2019/04/10/trudeau-defends-changes-to-asylum-laws-that-have-refugee-workers-alarmed.html

Zug, M. 2015. "The Mirage of Immigration Reform: The Devastating Consequences of Obamas Immigration Policy." *Kansas Law Review* 63: 953–980. https://papers.ssrn.com/sol3/papers.cfm?abstract_id=2652369

Held at the gates of Europe: barriers to abolishing immigration detention in Turkey

Esra S. Kaytaz

ABSTRACT
By examining how Turkey has strategically leveraged its immigration detention practices in its relationship to the EU, this article draws scholarly attention to the neglected international dimensions of detention policy-making. While narratives of national security bolster the justification for detention of asylum seekers and other migrants, this article focuses on additional roles that Turkey calls on detention to play in its relationship with the European Union. In particular, the article discusses 'transit migration' as a policy discourse Turkey has strategically adopted and leveraged to its advantage when dealing with the EU. As form of 'premature labelling', this discourse undermines the claims of belonging that foreign nationals labelled as transit migrants have in Turkey. Thus, it provides a narrative for justifying detention expansion. This international dimension of detention policy-making must be taken into account for future discussions around how to curb or abolish the practice at the borders of Europe and elsewhere.

Introduction

This article examines the trajectory through which immigration detention in Turkey has become a normalised practice in border management. In doing so it demonstrates that while immigration detention may be couched in narratives of national security, it serves numerous functions within Turkey's relationship with the EU. Thus, this paper draws attention to the importance of addressing the international policy dimensions of immigration detention within debates on the abolition of immigration detention.

The evolution of immigration detention in Turkey highlights the significance 'global border regimes' (Benslimane and Moffette 2019, 61) in how immigration detention becomes normalised. Detention became entrenched as a border management tool within Turkey's relationship with the EU as part of negotiations to accede to the EU and as a neighbouring state of the EU. The normalisation of immigration detention is embedded in discourses on 'transit migration'. Transit migration refers to irregular migration to Europe by migrants who have had to move through neighbouring countries to access Europe. While 'transit migration' has been extensively critiqued as an analytical concept, it is a cornerstone of Turkish asylum and migration policy. I draw on the conceptualisation of transit migration by Oelgemöller (2011) as 'premature labelling' of certain migrants by virtue of their perceived migration intentions arrival into Europe as the basis for creating 'detainable' (De Genova 2016) migrants in Turkey.

Less scholarly and public attention is devoted to immigration detention and its abolition compared to other lived experiences of asylum and migration policies in Turkey such as xenophobia and racism towards migrants and refugees, challenges of the asylum system, and deportation (e.g. Ataç et al. 2017). Nevertheless, this research supplies ample evidence of the harms of immigration detention to support an abolitionist position. The violence of immigration detention practices in Turkey have been documented since their inception (e.g. Helsinki Citizens Assembly 2007). Even with a new legislative framework issues such as rights violations in detention, including difficulties applying for international protection, inadequate material conditions and deportation persist (e.g European Council on Refugees and Exiles 2020).

In this paper I argue that on the borders of the EU, support for the abolition of detention must be sought as much within the uneven and dynamic relationships between the EU and its neighbours as within national politics on immigration and asylum. When Turkey seeks to leverage its position of a gatekeeper to Europe during political crises to obtain financial support for hosting refugees, exert influence over EU membership negotiations or obtain support for its military position in Syria, immigration detention functions as a 'spectacle of migration enforcement' directed at an international audience (Mainwaring and Silverman 2017). This international role of immigration detention is an additional barrier to its abolition.

This article begins with an overview of the history, legislative framework and practices of immigration detention in Turkey. This discussion highlights the role of Turkey's relationship with the EU in developing legislative framework and estate for detention. The second section of the paper posits that transit migration, conceptualised as a Eurocentric policy concept that externalises European border management to neighbouring nations, is essential for creating detainable migrants in Turkey. The readmission agreement and Turkish asylum regime sustain and expand on the categories of detainable migrants. In the final section of this article, I argue that barriers to immigration detention lie in the international dimension of the Turkish 'economy of detention' (De Genova 2016).

Immigration detention in Turkey

Turkey's relations with the EU, both as a candidate state and a neighbour of the EU and of the 'broader Middle East' (Kirişçi 2007, 3), have substantially shaped Turkish asylum and migration policy including its policy on immigration detention. As a candidate state, Turkey is expected to harmonise its asylum and migration policy with the *acquis communautaire*, EU Law. Some of the important issues in the negotiations with the EU that relate to migration, such as lifting of the geographical limitation of the UN Convention on the Status of Refugees[1] and policies to combat irregular migration, have significant implications for detention policy and practices in Turkey. This section discusses the emergence and significance of immigration detention within the context of Turkey's evolving relationship to the EU.

Turkey is typically described as having evolved from being primarily a migrant sending country to a transit as well as a destination country over the recent decades. In the 1980s, Turkey began receiving a steady influx of migrants from the Middle East, Europe and parts of Africa. The number of these migrants has been rising steadily since the 1990s. İçduygu (2000) identifies seven strands of migration into Turkey during the 80s and 90s. Refugees arriving in Turkey at this time included Iranians fleeing the Khomenei regime, Iraqis fleeing the first Gulf War, persecuted Bulgarian Turks, Bosnian refugees escaping the Bosnian War and Albanian refugees fleeing the Kosovo War. The breakdown of the Soviet Union ushered in trader-tourists from former Soviet bloc countries. Finally, from the early 80s onwards migrants from parts of Asia and Africa begun arriving in Turkey. Similar trends of refugee arrivals from neighbouring countries and further afield from parts of Africa, Middle-East and Asia persisted throughout the 2000s as well as migrants arriving from former Soviet Block countries. There are currently over 1.1 million migrants with resident permits living in Turkey, which is a marked increase from 179.000 foreign residents in 2005.[2]

The increase in applicants for international protection and undocumented migrants has pushed immigration and asylum up the political and public agenda. In a short period of time Turkey became the largest refugee-hosting country in the world. Syrian refugees who have been arriving in Turkey since 2011 now number approximately 3.6 million. A further 330.000 asylum seekers and refugees from countries such as Afghanistan, Iran and Iraq are registered in Turkey(UNHCR Turkey 2020). In addition, large numbers of migrants are apprehended each year on the borders of Turkey. Turkey has responded to these trends through a number of legislative and policy measures, including immigration detention, informed by its position as both a candidate state and gatekeeper to the EU.

Immigration detention is a recent phenomenon in Turkey. Until 2010, foreign nationals in Turkey were held in euphemistically titled 'Foreigners Guesthouses'. The first mention of the Foreigner Guesthouses in official Turkish documents is a regulation by the Ministry of Interior from 1983 which regulated the administration of guesthouses.[3] These were facilities often attached to local police stations and airports (Helsinki Citizens Assembly 2007). In 2010, the presence of 13 'Foreigners' Guesthouses' had been confirmed.[4] Migrants were also reported to be detained in police stations, a juvenile detention centre in Istanbul and the Istanbul Airport transit zone (Amnesty International 2009; Helsinki Citizens Assembly 2007). The 'Foreigners' Guesthouses' were renamed 'Removal Centres' in a circular in 2010,[5] which also stipulated that Foreigners' Police Departments in every city would be responsible for facilities that would hold up to 50 persons. Migrants in these facilities would be moved across Turkey in the event of overcrowding and additional centres would be built if necessary. Until 2014 detention was governed through a patchwork of legislative measures primarily constituted of administrative tools.[6] Turkish authorities disputed that foreign nationals held in guest houses were detained, contending instead that they were 'guests' (Kaytaz 2015). Beginning with the case of *Albdolkhani and Karimnia v. Turkey*[7] in 2009, the European Court of Human Rights (ECtHR) ruled in 17 cases that immigration detention in Turkey was unlawful and thus in violation of Article 5(1) of the European Convention on Human Rights (ECHR) (Ibid.) until the new legislative framework was introduced in 2014.

Turkey's relationship with the EU has directly influenced the infrastructure and legislation that governs immigration detention in Turkey today. The construction of detention facilities has featured in negotiations with EU and EU funding has been used to construct detention facilities. There are currently 28 Removal Centres in Turkey with a holding capacity of 20.000.[8] The capacity for detention has more than doubled since 2017 (DGMM 2019). Turkey's detention capacity has grown significantly over the past few years with financial and logistical support from the EU. (ECRE 2020; Kaytaz 2014, 2015; Özçürümez and Şenses 2011). The establishment of detention centres, or Removal Centres, was mentioned both in the 2003 Turkish National Plan and the 2005 Asylum and the Migration National Action Plan. Furthermore, the Twinning Project[9] (2009–2011) titled 'Support to Turkey's Capacity in Combating Illegal Migration and Establishment of Removal Centres for Illegal Migrants' provided for the construction of Removal Centres in the cities of Ankara and Erzurum with financial support from the European Commission. The project also included non-pecuniary support with developing guidelines and training. Finally, five of the six EU-funded Reception and Accommodation Centres as part of this twinning project have been repurposed as Removal Centres following the recent negotiations between Turkey and the EU.

The numbers of detainees in each Removal Centre or the total number of detainees at any given time are not publicly available. Figures on irregular migrant apprehensions by the Turkish authorities offer some clues in this regard. Over 450.000 foreign nationals with irregular status were apprehended in 2019.[10] The numbers of apprehensions have been in steady increase since 2013. The majority of the migrants apprehended in 2019 came from Afghanistan, Pakistan, Syria, Palestine and Iraq, respectively. The data provided by the DGMM does not state whether these migrants were held in Removal Centres, the length of their detention or whether these include migrants who were detained several times within the same year.

The legislative framework for immigration detention is set out by the Law on Foreigners and International Protection (henceforth, LFIP). LFIP is Turkey's first law on international protection and asylum and the backbone of the legislative framework governing migration. It was enacted in 2014 as part of the harmonisation process to ensure compliance with the EU *acquis*[11] and amended in December 2019. The law also established the Directorate General of Migration Management (DGMM) as part of the Ministry of Interior to implement migration policies and strategies.[12]

The LFIP lays down the legal grounds for detention as well as procedural safeguards. LFIP allows for the detention of applicants for international protection under exceptional circumstances on these four grounds[13]: where there is serious doubt regarding the identity and nationality the applicant has provided; at the border gates to prevent irregular entry; where it would not be possible to identify the elements the applicant's claim for international protection unless subjected to administrative detention and when the applicant poses a serious threat to public security or safety. European Council of Refugees and Exiles (ECRE) (2020, 88) found that there is 'no substantial information' on detention being ordered on these grounds. Instead, most asylum seekers appear to be detained as part of pre-removal procedures (Ibid). Pre-removal detention may be mandated[14] in case the foreign national is at risk of absconding; has breached the rules of entry into and exit from Turkey; uses false or forged documents; does not leave Turkey after the period of voluntary departure without a reasonable excuse or is deemed to be a threat to public order, public security or public health. The 2019 amendment to the law introduced alternatives to pre-removal detention such as residence at a particular address, reporting duties, counselling on return and electronic surveillance.[15]

The LFIP establishes some legal safeguards around the duration of detention. Detention should be ceased immediately if no longer deemed necessary.[16] The LFIP sets a six-month limit to detention, which can be extended for a maximum of a further six months.[17] There is a 30-day limit on the detention of applications for international protection.[18] Furthermore, the LFIP introduces a monthly review by the governorate which may take place sooner if necessary.[19] Importantly, the LFIP also states that the detainee or the legal representative will be informed of all aspects of the detention review.[20] Detainees who want to appeal the decision to detain but do not have the financial means to retain a representative or lawyer may be provided with legal aid.[21] The 2019 amendments to the LFIP have introduced alternatives to pre-removal detention such as residency requirements, financial guarantees, return counselling and electronic surveillance.[22]

While the enactment of the LFIP is seen as a positive consequence of Turkish-EU relations as Turkey's first law on asylum and international protection, there are concerns around its limitations and implementation with regard to detention and deportation procedures. The provisions in the LFIP that have been criticised include, for instance, that the 15-day limit for appealing against deportation orders is too short a time period for migrants in detention. This was reduced to seven days with the amendment in 2019. The decision of the criminal court on appeals to deportation is final, therefore cannot be challenged at a higher court. In practice, asylum seekers have been found to be held in detention longer than the 30-day limit on their detention (ECRE 2020).[23] Human rights organisations have criticised the introduction of electronic surveillance as an alternative to detention for further criminalising migrants. While the 2019 amendment to LFIP has removed the provisions for the detention of unaccompanied minors. Children continue to be detained with their families.[24]

Concerns around the implementation of LFIP centre on the lack of communication between detainees and the outside world, their inability to access legal counsel in detention and not being informed of the grounds for their detention, in violation of their rights under the LFIP (DCR and ECRE 2016; Izmir Bar Association 2017). The difficulties faced by lawyers in obtaining the power attorney is a barrier the right to effective legal remedy (Refugee Rights Turkey 2016). Notaries, for example, do not accept the documents issued to those by the Turkish Government under LFIP as 'official documents' or accept witness testimonies (Ibid.). Instead they require identity documents other than those issued by the Turkish state. Persons apprehended in airport transit zones, asylum seekers apprehended outside of their designated province of residence and Syrians under the temporary protection regime face challenges in giving power of attorney to their legal representatives (Ibid.). The lack of translators and staff with necessary language skills is a significant barrier to accessing rights detention (e.g. Human Rights Inquiry Commission of the Parliament 2012, 2014, 2017). Lawyers report facing numerous challenges when visiting their clients (e.g. ECRE 2020; Izmir Bar Association 2017). The Izmir Bar Association, for instance, reported that eight of their lawyers and an interpreter were arbitrarily detained in the Removal Centre in Izmir for two hours in May 2019.[25] Since the earliest reports on detention, there have been reports of alleged mistreatment in detention facilities (Helsinki Citizens Assembly 2007; Human Rights Watch 2008), which continue until today (Amnesty International 2019; Ataç et al. 2017).[26]

European Council of Refugees and Exiles (ECRE 2020) identify two frequently reported circumstances of unlawful detention. Firstly, asylum seekers found outside of their provinces of designated residence,also called 'satellite cities', without authorisation, may be detained for the purposes of transfer to their satellite cities.[27] Asylum seekers are required to provide the Governorate their address in the satellite city and may have reporting requirements to the police.[28] Services such as healthcare and education are accessible in the designated satellite city. Asylum seekers need authorisation from authorities to leave their cities. If they are found not to be residing at their given address or to be away from their satellite cities without authorisation, asylum seekers may face serious sanctions including withdrawal of status of temporary protection.[29] Although the LFIP does not cite being outside of the satellite city without permission as a ground for detention, asylum seekers found outside of their cities of residence have been detained for transfer to their satellite cities.[30] Secondly, applicants for international protection may be detained at facilities at airports when designated as 'inadmissible passengers'. Turkish authorities do not formally recognise this practice as a form of detention as they argue that foreign nationals may leave these areas by travelling to another country. The 2019 amendment to the LFIP[31] that allows for inadmissible passengers to be held at the gates until they can leave raises concerns regarding procedural safeguards.[32]

There have been numerous reports of deportations from detention facilities in violation of the principle of *non-refoulement* since the enactment of the LFIP, in particular following the EU-Turkey Joint action plan in 2015 and the subsequent EU-Turkey Statement of 18 March 2016. These reports state that non-Syrian returnees have been denied the opportunity to access asylum, given false or misleading information on the grounds of their detention and forced to sign return or repatriation documents (e.g. Alpes et al. 2017; Ataç et al. 2017; Izmir Bar Association 2017; Ulusoy and Battjes 2017).[33] More recently, following a declaration by the Istanbul governorate, it was reported Syrians apprehended in Istanbul on the premise of being returned to their satellite cities were forced or misled into signing so-called forms saying they were willing to return to Syria before being deported to Syria (Amnesty International 2019).[3435]

While the material conditions in Removal Centres across Turkey vary, they are consistently inadequate. The ECtHR has ruled between 2008 and 2015 that conditions of immigration detention in Turkey constituted inhuman and degrading treatment in seven cases in four Removal Centres, none of which are operational anymore.[36] More recently, reports by the Human Rights Inquiry Commission of the Parliament (2012, 2014, 2017), the Association for Human Rights and Solidarity of the Oppressed (MazlumDer 2014), the National Human Rights Institution of Turkey (2014), the Turkish Human Rights and Equality Commission (2018a, 2018b, 2018c) and European Council of Refugees and Exiles (ECRE) (2020) highlight the varied conditions of detention. These reports document overcrowding, insufficiency of nutrition, unhygienic conditions, inadequate medical care and limited recreational activities in facilities across Turkey.

Transit migration as a logic for 'detainability'

Transit migration is an enduring yet nebulous concept problematized by many migration scholars. There is no agreed definition of transit migration or who a transit migrant is. Turkey has been long identified as a country of transit migration by migration scholars (e.g. İçduygu 1995, 2000) and by policymakers (e.g. Oelgemöller 2011). Turkish authorities define Turkey as a country of 'transit migration' in official documentation (e.g. DGMM 2017). Transit migration forms a cornerstone of the logic of immigration detention in

Turkey. Firstly, it underpins policies on irregular migration. Secondly, it helps create a category of deportable migrants, asylum seekers and refugees who do not 'belong' in Turkey. In this section, I first provide an overview of the concept of transit migration arguing that transit migration is central to the creation of a category of detainable migrants through its logic of 'premature labelling' (Oelgemöller 2011). Then, I demonstrate how Turkey has adopted the notion of transit migration during the harmonization process. Finally, I argue that Turkish asylum policies expand the category of detainable migrants to include asylum seekers and refugees on its territory.

Transit migration

Transit migration emerged as a Euro-centric policy concept for describing certain migration trends in and around the EU, rather than an analytical concept for understanding migration dynamics. The concept of transit migration can be traced to the concept of 'new migration' in 1990s relating to the break-up of the USSR and 'new wars' of the post-Cold War era (Collyer, Düvell and de Hess 2012). Düvell 2006, 22) argues that the emergence of the discourse of transit migration in the 1990s 'seemed to have coincided with European efforts to negotiate specific return, deportation and readmission policies with all its non-EU neighbours.' Transit migration is intertwined with fears around irregular migration and its management (Collyer, Düvell and de Hess 2012; Düvell 2006).

At the heart of the concept of transit migration is the perceived intention of migrants to migrate to another country. UN Economic Commission for Europe (1993, 7), for instance, defines transit migration as 'migration in one country with the intention of seeking the possibility there to emigrate to another country as the country of final destination, by means that are partially, if not fully, illegal.' İçduygu (1995, 127) defines transit migration occurs when 'migrants come to a country of destination with the intention of going and staying in another country.' The DGMM defines Turkey as a country of transit migration for its 'position as a bridge to Europe' for migrants (Göç İdaresi Genel Müdürlüğü (DGMM) 2017, 95). Academic research on transit migration identifies several limitations with this approach to transit migration which centres migrant intentions in its definition. Migrants may arrive at their country without the intention to migrate and change their intentions (Papadopoulou-Kourkoula 2008). Even when migrants arrive at a country with the intention of transiting through, they may decide or be forced to settle there (e.g. Papadopoulou-Kourkoula 2008; Schapendonk 2013; Suter 2012). Intentions to migrate may continue despite living in these countries after long periods of time (e.g. Danış, Taraghi and Perouse 2009; Düvell 2012; Wissink, Düvell, and Van Eerdewijk 2013). Although the so-called European refugee crisis of 2015, when large numbers of refugees from countries such as Syria, Afghanistan, and Iraq arrived at the EU by crossing the Mediterranean or overland through Southeastern Europe, has re-ignited public and policy discourse on transit migration due to fears of large numbers of migrants arriving in Europe (Oelgemöller 2017; Phillips and Missbah 2017), research conducted into the decision-making processes of migrants on the crisis continues to problematize the notion of migrants setting out with intentions of onward movement, and to migrate to the EU (e.g Collyer, Düvell, and de Haas 2012, Crawley 2016; Crawley et al. 2017). As Oelgemöller (2017) argues this portrayal is driven by a perceived threat in Europe.

Central to the operation of transit migration is what Oelgemöller (2011, 407) terms 'premature labelling' which is 'the imposition of judico-political status from one sovereign state into the realm of another, assumes that people are illegal immigrants – either trafficked or smuggled – before they have even entered the territory of the state passing judgement of them'. In other words, transit migration is a discourse that pre-emptively illegalizes certain migrants by virtue of their perceived migration intentions or threat of undesired arrival into Europe. In this article, I argue that it is within this juridico-political space of premature labelling that migrants become detainable (De Genova 2016) and deportable (De Genova 2002). Therefore, transit migration is central to the analysis of immigration detention in Turkey and for understanding the barriers to abolishing it.

Turkey was the first country to be called 'a country of transit migration' in the aftermath of the Iranian Revolution during the Informal Consultations as part of the Intergovernmental Consultations of Asylum, Migration and Refugees (ICG) which began in 1985 (İçduygu 2005; Oelgemöller 2011). Turkey applied to accede to the EU in 1987, the same year as the Informal Consultations, and was recognised as a candidate for full membership in 1999. As a candidate state, Turkey is expected to harmonise its migration and asylum policy with the *acquis*, EU Law. Transit migration as a 'tool of governance' (Oelgemöller 2011) has been central to Turkey's immigration and asylum policies developed within the context of accession to the EU. These have included negotiations over the lifting of the geographical limitation of the 1951 UN Refugee Convention[37] (thus enabling Turkey to offer asylum to refugees coming from outside of Europe), the signing of the readmission agreement measures for combating irregular migration and trafficking, and the restructuring of the visa system in accordance with the Schengen visa regime (Kirişçi 2009; Vukašinović 2011). Turkey has also adopted the language of transit migration in its official documents. In the official justification for the LFIP provided in 2013, Turkish authorities claim that the law was necessary given Turkey's transition from being a transit country to a destination as a result of 'its increasing economic prowess and stability'. In official documentation, the Turkish migration authorities still refer to Turkey as a country of transit migration as well as a country of destination (e.g. Göç İdaresi Genel Müdürlüğü (DGMM) 2017).

Immigration detention in the harmonisation process

The harmonisation process enables standardisation of regulations and norms to ensure the eventual incorporation of candidate states within the boundaries of the EU. As such harmonisation is a process of boundary negotiation. Babül (2017) describes the harmonisation process as part of Turkey's accession to the EU 'as a pedagogical process, which revolves around the uneven yet dynamic process between the learner and learned'. Transit migration can be viewed as part of the pedagogical process on defining and managing irregular migration.

The process of harmonisation has been ongoing without the certitude that Turkey will become a member state. Negotiations with EU have been long drawn with negotiations on various chapters being stopped and started. Turkey has resisted elements of the harmonisation process that relate to its status as a country of transit migration (e.g. Baklacıoğlu 2009; Üstübici 2019; Vukašinović 2011). Negotiations in these areas of resistance have allowed Turkey to leverage its status a country of transit migration.

Thus, the mobilities of migrants that are labelled as the most problematic within the discourse of transit migration, are beneficial bargaining tools for Turkey in its negotiations with the EU.

The transit migration paradigm is a 'governance tool' (Oelgemöller 2011) directed at transit states. The transit migration paradigm shifts responsibility and blame onto the transit states to manage their borders so as to prevent unwanted migrants entering EU borders. Readmission agreements are expressions of this paradigm. The readmission agreement between EU and Turkey obliges Turkey to readmit migrants who have passed through Turkey before entering Europe irregularly. Turkey has long resisted signing the agreement for fear of becoming a 'dumping ground for Europe's unwanted migrants' (Kirişçi 2008). Scepticism on the part of Turkish authorities was informed by the fact that Turkey was the only country in the process of negotiating membership to be asked to sign a readmission agreement. The readmission agreement became especially significant in the aftermath of the Syrian humanitarian crisis. The readmission agreement was signed in 2013 with the promise of the liberalisation of the visa regime for Turks entering Europe and the re-opening of negotiations on Chapter 24 of the *acquis* on 'Justice, Freedom and Security.' It also formed the legal basis of the 1:1 scheme under the EU-Turkey Agreement of 18 March 2016, whereby all new irregular migrants crossing from Turkey to the Greek Islands would be returned to Turkey, and for every Syrian returned to Turkey, another Syrian would be resettled to the EU. Turkey unilaterally suspended the readmission agreement with the EU in July 2019, after many threats to do so, for reasons such as delays in the visa liberalisation process an insufficiency of funds.[38]

This signing and suspending of the readmission agreement is important for the purpose of this article for two reasons. Firstly, it demonstrates how the discourse on transit has become embedded in Turkish migration policy. In its reference to readmission agreements, the DGMM in its annual report claims that 'states should take responsibility for irregular migrants who use their territories as transit routes and avoid activities that may cause harm to their neighbours' (Göç İdaresi Genel Müdürlüğü (DGMM) 2017: 60, my own translation). Readmission agreements are thus described as a means through which transit states 'take responsibility for problems caused in their own territories' (Ibid.). The commitment taking responsibility for actions of irregular migrants who 'may cause harm to neighbours' (Ibid.) demonstrates that internalisation of the logic of 'premature labelling' of migrants for possible future actions they may never undertake. Secondly, the readmission agreement resulted in the detention of 1959 migrants returned from Greece while it was in place[39] and if reinstated would continue to do so.

Turkey's continued refusal to lift the geographical limitation of the 1951 UN Refugee Convention means that it offers temporary protection to approximately 3.7 million Syrian and several tens of thousands of Iraqi and Afghan asylum seekers[40] among other nationalities on its territory. The temporary protection regime further reinforces its position as a country of transit migration in three ways which expands on its function of premature labelling (Oelgemöller 2011) to intersect with international protection.

Firstly, it explicitly designates the residence asylum seekers as 'temporary'. The DGMM describes the protection system to which Syrian and non-Syrian asylum seekers are admitted to as temporary protection until there is a possibility of resettlement to a third country or a return is possible. Syrian and non-Syrian asylum seekers are treated differently. Syrians, referred to as 'guests', are admitted under the 'temporary protection regime'. The protection claims of 'non-Syrians' are assessed as 'conditional refugees'. The DGMM defines conditional refugee as 'a person who as a result of events occurring outside European countries alleges to be subject to conditions which are stated in definition of refugee and applies for international protection in Turkey until he/she is resettled to a third country.'[41] It is possible for Syrians to obtain Turkish citizenship. As of December 2019, approximately 110.000 Syrians acquired citizenship, of whom 53.000 were adults and remainder were children.[42] Naturalisation may occur under three circumstances: legal continuous residency for 5 years, marriage to a Turkish citizen and under 'exceptional circumstances'. In citizenship applications, time spent with temporary protection may not count towards fulfilling the five-year residency requirements for citizenship. Temporary protection status holders can apply for citizenship under 'exceptional circumstances procedure'. The criteria for eligibility and the decision-making for acquiring citizenship is opaque and appears to extend only to some high-skilled professionals such as doctors, engineers and teachers (ECRE 2020).[43] Therefore, citizenship is still out of the reach of many Syrian refugees. Furthermore, children of Syrian refugees born in Turkey risk becoming stateless due to discriminatory nationality laws in Syria and loss of documentation during flight.[44] Refugee and subsidiary protection are temporary by nature because surrogate protection host states offer is intended to until the persons of concern are no longer refugees by either becoming citizens of the receiving country or are able to return to their countries of nationality. The temporariness of the Turkish system, however, means that there is limited opportunity for the rights of refugees to increase as their level of attachment to the state grows as would be the case if Turkey lifted the geographical limitation of the Refugee Convention (Hathaway 2005).

Secondly, the temporary nature of protection and the lack of access to services in Turkey puts incentives for irregular onward movement in place for persons seeking permanent protection. Migration decisions are complex and informed by a number of circumstances. However, the limitations of the asylum system in Turkey have been cited as a contributing factor that informs the decisions of migrants to leave Turkey (e.g. Crawley et al. 2017; Kuschminder 20187; Öner and Genç 2015). Both Syrian (e.g. Baban, Ilcan, and Rygiel 2017) and non-Syrian refugees (Leghtas and Sullivan 2017) face many challenges in Turkey as a result of the precarity and forms of exclusion inherent in the asylum system. The situation of non-Syrians is reported to have worsened significantly after UNHCR transferred registration and status determination for non-Syrian asylum seekers to the DGMM (e.g. European Council of Refugees and Exiles (ECRE) 2020; Leghtas and Thea 2018).

Thirdly, the asylum system increases the likelihood of irregular residence of asylum seekers in two ways: through barriers accessing the system and residency requirements of the system. As irregular stay in countries bordering the EU signifies the potential to engage in irregular travel in the discourses of transit migration (Collyer, Düvell and de Hess 2012), the asylum system can be said to be expanding on the category of transit migrants through a logic of premature labelling in this third way. Non-Syrian asylum seekers have faced challenges in registering their applications for international protection after UNHCR has transferred the duties of registration to the DGMM. Afghan asylum seekers, for instance, have reported difficulties registering their asylum applications and obtaining identity cards (e.g. Leghtas and Thea 2018) and are thus 'kept as unregistered irregular migrants' (European Council of Refugees and Exiles (ECRE) 2020, 33). Large numbers of Syrian and non-Syrian asylum seekers live outside of their satellite cities, particularly in Istanbul, to access employment and services not available to them otherwise (e.g Leghtas 2019) or be closer to family members. Asylum seekers found not to be complying with residency requirements, such as leaving their satellite cities without authorisation or overstaying their 30-day permit can be said to be residing in Turkey irregularly. The International Protection Applicant Identification Card asylum seekers are issued with to prove their status in Turkey is valid only in province the document was issued. Their application for international protection may be withdrawn if they fail to comply with residency requirements as asylum seekers will be considered to have withdrawn their application for protection if not residing in their satellite cities.[45] Although the LFIP does not allow for the detention of asylum seekers for the purpose of removal to their cities of residence, it is a commonly reported practice (European Council of Refugees and Exiles (ECRE) 2020). In July 2019, for example, over 4000 registered Syrian temporary protection status holders were detained in Istanbul for the stated purpose of repatriating them to their satellite cities.[46]

Discussion: barriers to the abolition of immigration detention in Turkey

Academic research and social activism in Turkey have so far focused on issues such as xenophobia and racism towards migrants and refugees, the harms of the asylum system, and deportation (e.g. Ataç et al. 2017). Immigration detention and arguments for its abolition have received relatively less attention, although detention features in each of these aspects of Turkish immigration and asylum addressed in this literature. This relative lack of attention to detention practices reflects the normalisation of immigration detention in Turkey. I argue that the barrier to abolishing immigration detention lies in the role of immigration detention for Turkey in leveraging its position as a country of transit migration.

Understanding barriers to immigration detention requires understanding the function of immigration detention. Governments may deploy immigration detention as a tool for deterring migrants or to signal control over borders to national audiences (Silverman and Aiken, this issue). The role of immigration detention as a deterrent to migrants or a signal of control towards domestic audiences of control does not appear a significant rationale for immigration detention in Turkey. In press and government reports on the apprehension and deportation of irregular migrants on Turkey's borders, the role of immigration and the detention estate in achieving these acts is underemphasised. The legal purpose of immigration detention is to ascertain the identity of applicants for international protection and ensure deportation. While detention is a necessary step for deportation, the discrepancy between the number of apprehensions and deportations suggests that detainees are not always deported.[47] Research demonstrates that some detainees are released with deportation orders and those deported may return back to Turkey (e.g. Kaytaz 2016). As such migrants in transit contexts who are unable or unwilling to return to their countries of nationality but are also unable to leave may become 'stuck in mobility' (Hess 2012). Furthermore, while the detention estate has grown significantly recently and numbers of deportations have increased, the capacity for detention would nevertheless appear low relative to the population of irregular migrants apprehended each year.[48]

While detention in Turkey is important domestically for facilitation deportation, I argue that barriers to its abolition must also be sought in its international function , both as a part of the harmonization process and of Turkish negotiation with the EU over issues such as membership status, support for refugees and its military strategy in Syria. Drawing on Mainwaring and Silverman (2017)'s conceptualization of 'detention-as-spectacle', I argue that immigration detention in Turkey is a form a 'border spectacle' for an international audience primarily constituted of EU states. Much like Mainwaring and Silverman's (Ibid: 33) example of Malta, Turkey's detention spectacle signals 'simultaneous chaos and control' to an international audience. Turkey's repeated threats opening up its borders to allow migrants passage to Europe since 2015 exemplify such spectacles. These threats have taken place against the backdrop of increased migrant apprehensions, thus signalling 'simultaneous chaos and control' (Ibid.). In 2016, President Erdoğan threatened to open the 'border gates' in response to a temporary break to EU membership talks.[49] After the meeting between the heads of the EU states and Turkey on 29 March 2016 where the earmarking of 3 billion Euros for Turkey was announced, for instance, almost 3000 migrants who were attempting the journey to Lesvos were detained.[50] In July 2019, the same month when the readmission agreement was suspended with the EU, the Governorate of Istanbul began a mass campaign of detention and deportation of irregular migrants and Syrian refugees residing in Istanbul without authorisation, which resulted in over 16.000 detentions Removal Centres in August.[51] The DGMM boasted that Turkey has reached its highest levels of migrant apprehensions in a single year in 2019 and of a single month in September 2019 in its pursuit of combatting irregular migration.[52] The following month in October 2019, President Erdoğan again threatened to allow Syrians refugees passage to Europe in response to criticism of his plan for the 'safe zone' in Syria and perceived lack of support towards Turkey.[53]

President Erdoğan's announcement on 27 February 2020 that Turkey 'would not stop' migrants trying to reach Europe is the latest and perhaps the boldest example of the Turkish border spectacle buttressed by detention. President Erdoğan made his announcement after the Turkish Army sustained 33 fatalities during a single attack in Syria's Idlib Province as part of the 'Operation Spring Shield'. Shortly after his announcement migrants began arriving at the 'Pazarkule' border crossing between Turkey and Greece. These movements were also orchestrated by Turkish authorities who 'facilitated and encouraged the movement of asylum seekers and migrants' to the Pazarkule border crossing (Amnesty International 2020, 10). A settlement emerged around the crossing as migrants made attempts at crossing the border. Greece responded to these developments with a temporary suspension of the asylum system, practices of arbitrary detention and violent pushbacks from the border (Ibid.). Turkish authorities began dismantling the camp that emerged on the border on 19 March 2020 amid fears of the spread of Covid-19,[54] declaring the camp shut on 27 March 2020 (Ibid.; Çoban 2020). During the disbanding of the camp, migrants were taken to Istanbul and across different locations in Turkey (Ibid.). Turkish authorities orchestrated this border spectacle by mobilising migrants as pawns for political gains. Detention made this border spectacle possible by enabling authorities to exert a degree of control over the spectacle from start to end. It was reported, for instance, that some of the first migrants to arrive on the Greek border were first detained and then taken to the border.[55] After the settlement was disbanded some migrants were held in quarantine in removal centres (Çoban 2020). The Minister of Interior announced that 5.800 migrants were taken from Pazarkule to be 'housed as guests' in Removal Centres across 9 different locations.[56] Some of these migrants were issued deportation orders upon release.[57] While hundreds of migrants after being released following the 14-day quarantine period were sent to the Removal Centre in Izmir on Turkey's Aegean Coast where they were detained for two days.[58]

İşleyen (2018) argues Turkey has internalised EU borders through its asylum and migration policy. Removal Centres act as physical manifestations of these internalized borders. Transit migration creates the category 'detainable' (De Genova 2016) non-citizens through its logic of 'premature labelling' (Oelgemöller 2011). It underpins the policy and legislative framework for what De Genova (2016) refers to as the 'economy of detention': distribution of state power in selecting whom to detain and maybe deport among all the foreign nationals who could be detained or deported. This paper argues that it is in the international dimension of 'economy of detention' in Turkey that the barriers to abolish it are situated. How the Turkish authorities mobilise their powers to detain foreign nationals and choose which foreign nationals to detain is determined within Turkey's geopolitical positioning vis-à-vis Europe.

A key criticism of immigration detention, and an argument for its abolition, is that detention criminalises and punishes foreign nationals who have moral and legal claims of belonging to the countries they are detained in. As De Genova (2016, 1) argues, detention of migrants is 'incarceration on the basis of little more than their sheer existential predicament as "undesirable" non-citizens'. The categories of detainable specific national context perpetuating structural violence based on intersection of factors such as race, ethnicity, class and gender (e.g Hernández and Cuauhtémoc 2017; Griffiths 2015; Turnbull 2018). The discourse of transit migration further weakens non-citizens' moral, legal or social claims belonging to Turkey. Migrants typically thought of as being in transit who, for instance, have been immobilized through European border regimes despite intentions of onwards movement or who have revised their intentions of onward movement (e.g. Suter 2012; Schapendonk 2013) are permanently detainable. Within this paradigm such migrants are seen as having no intention or opportunity for settling in Turkey since the intention of onward movement is paramount to the definition of transit migration.

Transit migration is Euro-centric policy tool that identifies migrants on the fringes on Europe whose presence was unwanted within Europe (e.g. Collyer, Düvell and de Hess 2012; Oelgemöller 2011, 2017). In response to Syrian humanitarian crisis and persisting conflict and insecurity in its neighbouring regions, Turkey has continued to uphold the geographical limitation of the 1951 Refugee Convention. By doing so, Turkey has denied pathways to permanent residence to large numbers of refugees on its territories and erected barriers to accessing effective international protection or settlement. Thus, the category of detainable non-citizens 'in transit' has expanded to include those in the asylum system and persons who come from countries with ongoing conflict and insecurity such as Afghanistan, Iraq and Palestine who cannot access international protection in Turkey. This population is detainable in Turkey in part because they are perceived as a threat in Europe. To challenge immigration detention in Turkey it is, therefore, necessary to address the exclusionary logic of externalisation which governs multi-faceted levels of 'precarious inclusion' (Rytter and Ghandchi 2020) into Turkish society (Baban, Ilcan, and Rygiel 2017; Üstübici 2019).

Conclusion

In focusing on immigration detention in Turkey, this article sought to call attention to the international dimensions of barriers to the abolition of immigration detention. Immigration detention has become a normalized practice of border management frequently justified as a measure of national security in countries typically seen as 'destination countries'. Arguments for the abolition of immigration detention in response to the practices of immigration detention of non-citizens particularly along racial identities and harms caused detainees (Benslimane and Moffette 2019; Hernández and Cuauhtémoc 2017; Silverman and Aiken, this issue) are also relevant for Turkey. The discourse of transit migration has created a group of 'detainable' migrants by weakening their claims of belonging to Turkey. A further challenge of putting forward an agenda to abolish immigration detention in Turkey is that detention is the manifestation of internalised EU borders and accompanying restrictive rhetoric and policy practices. Turkey's ability and willingness to detain migrants unwanted within European territories has become an indispensable tool in its negotiations with the EU both as part of the formal harmonisation process as well as border spectacles directed at the EU.

Notes

1. Turkey is signatory to the 1951 Convention relating to the Status of Refugees and its 1967 Protocol but it has maintained the 'geographical limitation' clause of 1967 Protocol, which restricts its protection obligations only to individuals who become refugees 'as a result of events occurring in Europe'. Thus, asylum seekers from non-European countries are admitted to the temporary asylum procedure in Turkey but cannot get refugee status under Turkish law.
2. According to figures provided by Turkish Ministry of Interior available at: https://www.goc.gov.tr/ikamet-izinleri
3. *Regulation on Refugee Guesthouses* Regulation No.: 18,032, 29 April 1983.
4. Global Detention Project. 2010. 'Turkey Detention Profile: 2010". Available at: http://english.madde14.org/index.php?title=Global_Detention_Project_-_Turkey_Detention_Profile_(2010)http://english.madde14.org/index.php?title=Global_Detention_Project_-_Turkey_Detention_Profile_(2010)
5. The Circular on Combatting Irregular Migration (Article 2(b1)) renamed 'Foreigners' Guesthouses' as 'Removal Centres'.
6. For a discussion of the legal framework on detention prior to the LFIP, see: Helsinki Citizens Assembly (2007), Kaytaz (2014; 2015).
7. Council of Europe (2009) Abdolkhani and Karimnia v. Turkey, Appl. No. 30,471/08, European Court of Human Rights, 22 September 2009
8. Information on the location and capacity of Removal Centres is available at: https://www.goc.gov.tr/geri-gonderme-merkezleri33
9. The European Commission's Twinning System' aided EU candidate states such as Turkey as a 'Pre-Acquisition Instrument' to restructure their public institutions and to implement and enforce EU laws.
10. Statistics provided by the Ministry of Interior are available at: https://www.goc.gov.tr/duzensiz-goc-istatistikler
11. The official justification of the law is available at: https://www.goc.gov.tr/genel-gerekce18
12. Article 103
13. Article 68 (2)
14. Article 57 (2)
15. Article 57/A

16. Article 57(4)
17. Article 57(3)
18. Article 68 (5)
19. Article 57(4)
20. Article 57(6)
21. Article 57(7)
22. Article 57/A
23. See also *Joint Assessment: Proposed Amendments in the Law on Foreigners and International Protection of Turkey*. 4 December 2019. signed by multiple human rights organisations working with refugees available at: http://www.multeci.org.tr/en/haberler/english-joint-assessment-proposed-amendments-in-the-law-on-foreigners-and-international-protection-of-turkey/
24. Article 59 (1)f
25. Izmir Bar Association press statement on this incident is available at: https://www.izmirbarosu.org.tr/HaberDetay/1598/meslektaslarimizin-ugradigi-kotu-muamele-nedeniyle-harmandali-geri-gonderme-merkezinde-basin-aciklamasi-yapildi
26. Evrim Kepenek. 2019. 'Harmandalı Removal Center Told from Inside: Battery, Attempted Suicide, Illness, Death.' *BIA News Desk*. 23 July 2019. BiaAvailable at: https://bianet.org/english/women/210765-harmandali-removal-center-told-from-inside-battery-attempted-suicide-illness-death
27. This practice of assigning applicants for international protection to a city of residence can be traced back to 1950 Law on the Residence and Travel of Foreigners (Article 17). Satellite cities are defined in the 2016 Regulation on the Implementation of the Law on Foreigners and International Protection (Regulation No: No 29,656) (Article 3(hh)) as provinces where applicants for international protection reside.
28. The LFIP (Article 71(1)) states that applicants for international protection may be required to reside in a reception centre or a particular province where they may be under reporting obligations. Article 71(2) requires that applicants for international protection provide their address to the Governorate.
29. DGMM Circular 2017/10 *on Principles and Procedures for Foreigners under Temporary Protection*, 29 November 2017
30. See below for the discussion on the satellite cities system in the context of transit migration.
31. Article 7 (3)
32. *Joint Assessment: Proposed Amendments in the Law on Foreigners and International Protection of Turkey*. 4 December 2019. signed by multiple human rights organisations working with refugees available at: http://www.multeci.org.tr/en/haberler/english-joint-assessment-proposed-amendments-in-the-law-on-foreigners-and-international-protection-of-turkey/
33. Amnesty International UK. 'Press Release: Turkey: Illegal Mass Returns of Syrian Refugees Expose Fatal Flaws in EU-Turkey Deal', 31 March 2016, https://www.amnesty.org.uk/press-releases/turkey-illegal-mass-returns-syrian-refugees-expose-fatal-flaws-eu-turkey-dealOffice of the United Nations High Commissioner for Refugees. 'UNHCR Urges Immediate Safeguards to Be in Place before Any Returns Begin under EU-Turkey Deal.' News Release, 1 April 2016, http://www.unhcr.org/uk/news/briefing/2016/4/56fe31ca9/unhcr-urges-immediate-safeguards-place-returns-begin-under-eu-turkey-deal.html.
34. The DGMM disputes these claims and maintains that it has been upholding its obligations under international law in accordance with the principle of non-refoulement (Amnesty International 2019, 7).
35. For voluntary return forms see also: Gerry Simpson. 2019. ' "Repatriation" of Syrian in Turkey Needs EU Action'. 7 November 2019. *Human Rights Watch News*. Available at: https://www.hrw.org/news/2019/11/07/repatriation-syrians-turkey-needs-eu-action
36. *Tehrani and Others v. Turkey*, Applications nos. 32,940/08, 41,626/08, 43,616/08, Council of Europe: European Court of Human Rights, 13 April 2010; *Charahili v. Turkey*, Application no. 46,605/07, Council of Europe: European Court of Human Rights, 13 April 2010; *Kurkaev v. Turkey*, Application no. 10,424/05, Council of Europe: European Court of Human Rights,

19 October 2010; *Asalya v. Turkey*, Application no. 43,875/09, Council of Europe: European Court of Human Rights, 15 April 2014; *Yarashonen v. Turkey*, Application no. 72,710/11, Council of Europe: European Court of Human Rights, 24 June 2014; *Musaev v. Turkey*, Application no. 72,754/11, Council of Europe: European Court of Human Rights, October, 21 2014; *S.A. v. Turkey*, Application no. 74,535/10, Council of Europe: European Court of Human Rights, 15 December 2015.

37. Turkey is signatory to the 1951 Convention relating to the Status of Refugees and its 1967 Protocol but it has maintained the 'geographical limitation' clause, which restricts its protection obligations only to individuals who become refugees 'as a result of events occurring in Europe'. Thus, asylum seekers in Turkey coming from non-European countries are admitted to the temporary asylum procedure in Turkey but cannot get refugee status under Turkish law.
38. 'The readmission agreement with EU no longer functional Ankara says'. *Daily Sabah*. 23 July 2019. Available at: https://www.dailysabah.com/eu-affairs/2019/07/23/readmission-agreement-with-eu-no-longer-functional-ankara-says
39. https://www.goc.gov.tr/geri-alim
40. I use the term asylum seeker here to refer to anyone who has sought or attempted to seek asylum in Turkey in order to avoid the confusion between the different protection categories offered by the Turkish state.
41. https://en.goc.gov.tr/conditional-refugee
42. See for instance: https://multeciler.org.tr/turkiyedeki-suriyeli-sayisi/
43. See press briefing by Turkish Minister of Interior Süleyman Soylu on 2 August 2019 available at: https://www.hurriyetdailynews.com/turkey-granted-citizenship-to-over-92-000-syrians-145480
44. Institute on Statelessness and Inclusion and European Network on Statelessness. 2020. *Joint Submission to the Human Rights Council at the 35th Session of the Universal Periodic Review*. (Third Cycle, January 2020) Available at: https://www.statelessness.eu/sites/www.statelessness.eu/files/attachments/resources/ENS-ISI_UPR%20Submission%20Turkey.pdf
45. LFIP Article 77(1)(ç)
46. 'Turkey: Mass Detention Following Istanbul Push for Return of Refugees to "Satellite Cities"' 30 August 2019. Available at: https://www.ecre.org/turkey-mass-detention-following-istanbul-push-for-return-of-refugees-to-satellite-cities/
47. The DGMM reports that as of October 2019, 72.029 foreign nationals were deported in 2019. (https://www.goc.gov.tr/duzensiz-gocle-mucadele-araliksiz-devam-ediyor). The number of foreign nationals apprehended in Turkey as of December 2019 is 448.938 (https://www.goc.gov.tr/duzensiz-goc-istatistikler).
48. The capacity for detention is reported to be 20.000 (https://www.goc.gov.tr/geri-gonderme-merkezleri33), which is well below the numbers of the foreign nationals that are apprehended which number more than 400.000 in 2019 (https://www.goc.gov.tr/duzensiz-goc-istatistikler).
49. Caroline Mortimer, 'President Erdogan: I will open gates for migrants to enter Europe if EU blocks membership talks', *The Independent*, 25 November 2019, Available at:https://www.independent.co.uk/news/world/europe/president-erdogan-turkey-eu-membership-migrants-refugees-europe-warning-a7438316.html
50. Doğan News Agency. '2,933 migrants detained in four days in Turkey's West', *Hürriyet Daily News*, 14 December 2015 http://www.hurriyetdailynews.com/Default.aspx?pageID=238&nID=92074&NewsCatID=341; Özkan, Yusuf and Ali Çelikkan, 'Parayı görünce düğmeye basıldı', *Cumhuriyet*, 2 December 2015, http://www.cumhuriyet.com.tr/haber/turkiye/439281/Parayi_gorunce_dugmeye_basildi.html
51. '16-bin-423-multeci-istanbuldan-gonderildi' *Gazere Duvar*. Available at: https://www.gazeteduvar.com.tr/turkiye/2019/08/27/16-bin-423-multeci-istanbuldan-gonderildi/
52. 'Düzensiz Göçle Mücadele Aralıksız Devam Ediyor'. *DGMM*. 15 October 2019. Available at: https://www.goc.gov.tr/duzensiz-gocle-mucadele-araliksiz-devam-ediyor
53. Chris Baynes, 'Turkey's Erdogan threatens to send millions of refugees to Europe unless it backs Syria 'safe zone', *The Independent*, 26 October 2019. Available at: https://www.

independent.co.uk/news/world/europe/erdogan-syria-turkey-refugees-safe-zone-kurds-trump-europe-borders-a9172311.html

54. Hikmet Adal 'Refugees at Turkey-Greece Border Being Sent to Istanbul Esenler Bus Terminal' *Bianet*. 20 March 2020. Available at: http://bianet.org/english/migration/221670-refugees-at-turkey-greece-border-being-sent-to-istanbul-esenler-bus-terminal
55. 'Geri Gönderme Merkezinde Zorla Sınıra Götürülüyoruz Çığlığı' *Müteci Net*. 4 March 2020 Available at: http://multeci.net/2020/03/geri-gonderme-merkezinde-zorla-sinira-goturuluyoruz-cigligi/?fbclid=IwAR36nKG-DZXlCCEplpcnJWcta_cWWBJq_4E1isiUcxbJYf8xdo68vm4F4kM
56. 'Çadırlar yakıldı, Pazarkule boşaltıldı: Yunanistan sınırındaki mülteciler sessiz sedasız illere götürüldü'. *Sendika.Org*. 28 March 2020. Available at: https://sendika63.org/2020/03/cadirlar-yakildi-pazarkule-bosaltildi-yunanistan-sinirindaki-multeciler-sessiz-sedasiz-illere-goturuldu-581,793/
57. Burcu Karakaş 'Bir göçememe hikâyesi: "Her yere gidiyoruz, bir yere yetişemiyoruz"', *DW*, April, 23, 2020. Available at:https://www.dw.com/tr/bir-göçememe-hikâyesi-her-yere-gidiyoruz-bir-yere-yetişemiyoruz/a-53221085
58. 'Karantina sonrası İzmir'e getirilen mülteciler kaldıkları illere yollandı.'*Müteci Medyası*, 14 April 2020.https://multecimedyasi.org/2020/04/14/kamplardan-izmire-getirilen-multeciler-gemiye-bindirecegiz-diye-kandirdilar/

Acknowledgement

I would like to thank the Special Issue guest editors Dr Stephanie Silverman and Prof Sharry Aiken for the opportunity to contribute to this Special Issue and for their feedback. I would also like to thank the two anonymous reviewers for their comments. All errors are my own.

Disclosure statement

No potential conflict of interest was reported by the author.

References

Alpes, M. J., S. Tunaboylu, O. Ulusoy, and S. Hassan. 2017. "Post-deportation Risks under the EU-Turkey Statement: What Happens after Readmission to Turkey?" Migration Policy Centre. Policy Brief. Issue 2017/30. November.

Amnesty International. 2009. "Stranded: Refugees in Turkey Denied Protection." EUR 44/001/2009. London: Amnesty International.

Amnesty International. 2019. "Sent to a War Zone: Turkey's Illegal Deportations of Syrian Refugees." EUR 44/1102/2019. London: Amnesty International.

Amnesty International. 2020. "Caught in a Political Game: Asylum-Seekers and Migrants on the Greece/Turkey Border Pay the Price for Europe's Failures." EUR 01/2077/2020. London: Amnesty International.

Ataç, I., G. Heck, S. Hess, Z. Kaşlı, P. Ratfisch, C. Soykan, and B. Yılmaz. 2017. "Contested B/Orders. Turkey's Changing Migration Regime. An Introduction." *Movements. Journal for Critical Migration and Border Regime Studies* 3 (2): 9–21.

Baban, F., S. Ilcan, and K. Rygiel. 2017. "Syrian Refugees in Turkey: Pathways to Precarity, Differential Inclusion, and Negotiated Citizenship Rights." *Journal of Ethnic and Migration Studies* 43 (1): 41–57. doi:10.1080/1369183X.2016.1192996.

Babül, E. M. 2017. *Bureaucratic Intimacies Translating Human Rights in Turkey, Stanford Studies in Middle Eastern and Islamic Societies and Cultures*. Stanford: Stanford University Press.

Baklacıoğlu, N. Ö. 2009. "Building "Fortress" Turkey: Europeanisation of Asylum Policy in Turkey." *The Romanian Journal of European Studies*, no. 7–8/2009: 103–118.

Benslimane, S., and D. Moffette. 2019. "Continuing the Dialogue on the Canadian Carceral State the Double Punishment of Criminal Inadmissibility for Immigrants." *Journal of Prisoners on Prisons* 28 (1): 44–65.

Çoban, F. 2020. "Türkiye-Yunanistan Sınırında Neler Oldu?" GöÇ Araştırmaları Derneği, https://www.gocarastirmalaridernegi.org/attachments/article/160/turkiye-yunanistan-sinirinda-neler-oldu.pdf

Collyer, M. 2010. "Stranded Migrants and the Fragmented Journey." *Journal of Refugee Studies* 23 (3): 273–293. doi:10.1093/jrs/feq026.

Collyer, M., F. Düvell, and H. de Haas. 2012. "Critical Approaches to Transit Migration." *Population, Space and Place* 18 (4): 407–414. doi:10.1002/psp.630.

Crawley, H. 2016. "Managing The Unmanageable? Understanding Europe's Response To The Migration 'Crisis'." *Human Geography* 2 (9): 13–23. doi:10.1177/194277861600900202.

Crawley, H., F. Düvell, K. Jones, S. McMachon, and N. Sigona. 2017. *Unravelling Europe's 'Migration Crisis': Journeys over Land and Sea*. Bristol: Policy Press.

Danış, D. A., C. Taraghi and J. Pérouse. 2009 "Integration in Limbo. Iraqi, Afghan, Maghrebi and Iranian Migrants in Istanbul", In *Land of Diverse Migrations. Challenges of Emigration and Immigration in Turkey*, edited by A. İÇduygu & K. KirişÇi. 443–636. Istanbul: Bilgi University Press.

De Genova, N. 2016. "Detention, Deportation, and Waiting: Toward a Theory of Migrant Detainability." *Global Detention Project Working Paper* No. 18. November. Geneva: Global Detention Project.

De Genova, N. P. 2002. "Migrant "Illegality" and Deportability in Everyday Life." *Annual Review of Anthropology* 31 (1): 419–447. doi:10.1146/annurev.anthro.31.040402.085432.

Dutch Council for Refugees (DCR), and European Council of Refugees and Exiles (ECRE). 2016. "The DCR/ECRE Desk Research on Application of a Safe Third Country and a First Country of Asylum Concepts to Turkey." https://www.asylumlawdatabase.eu/sites/www.asylumlawdatabase.eu/files/aldfiles/turkeynote%20final%20edited%20DCR%20ECRE.pdf

Düvell, F. 2012. "Transit Migration: A Blurred and Politicised Concept." *Population, Space and Place* 18 (4): 415–427. doi:10.1002/psp.631.

Düvell, F. 2006. Crossing the Fringes of Europe: Transit Migration in the EU's Neighbourhood. Working Paper WP-06-33. Oxford: COMPAS. https://www.compas.ox.ac.uk/wp-content/uploads/WP-2006-033-Düvell_Fringe_Migration.pdf

European Council of Refugees and Exiles (ECRE). 2020. "Asylum Information Database (AIDA), Country Report: Turkey (2019 Update)." https://www.asylumineurope.org/reports/country/turkey

Göç İdaresi Genel Müdürlüğü (DGMM). 2019. 2018 *Yılı Faaliyet Raporu*. Ankara: Göç İdaresi Genel Müdürlüğü. https://www.goc.gov.tr/2018-faaliyet-raporu

Göç İdaresi Genel Müdürlüğü (DGMM). 2017. "Stratejik Plan 2017-2021." https://www.goc.gov.tr/stratejik-planlar

Griffiths, M. 2015. ""Here, Man Is Nothing!": Gender and Policy in an Asylum Context." *Men and Masculinities* 18 (4): 468–488. doi:10.1177/1097184X15575111.

Hathaway, J. 2005. *The Rights of Refugees under International Law*. Cambridge: Cambridge University Press.

Helsinki Citizens Assembly (HCA). 2007. *Unwelcome Guests: The Detention of Refugees in Turkey's "Foreigner's Guesthouses*. Istanbul: Helsinki Citizens' Assembly.

Hernández, G., and C. Cuauhtémoc. 2017. "Abolishing Immigration Prisons." *Boston University Law Review* 97 (1): 245–300.

Hess, S. 2012. "De-naturalising Transit Migration. Theory and Methods of an Ethnographic Regime Analysis." *Population, Space and Place* 18 (4): 428–440. doi:10.1002/psp.632.
İçduygu, A. 1995. *Transit Migration in Turkey.* Geneva: IOM.
İçduygu, A. 2000. "The Politics of International Migratory Regimes: Transit Migration Flows in Turkey." *International Social Science Journal* 52 (165): 357–368. doi:10.1111/1468-2451.00265.
İçduygu, A. 2005. "Transit Migration in Turkey: Trends, Patterns and Issues." Technical Report, [Migration Policy Centre], [CARIM-South], CARIM Research Report, 2005/04
Human Rights Watch. 2008. *Stuck in a Revolving Door: Iraqis and Other Asylum Seekers and Migrants at the Greece/Turkey Entrance to the European Union.* Washington DC: Human Rights Watch.
İşleyen, B. 2018. "Transit Mobility Governance in Turkey." *Political Geography* 62: 23–32. doi:10.1016/j.polgeo.2017.09.017.
Izmir Bar Association. 2017. "İzmir Geri Gönderme Merkezlerinde Adalete Erişim Hakkı ÇerÇevesinde Yaşanan Sorunlar Raporu." July. http://bit.ly/2Dyc87X
Kaytaz, E. S. 2014. "Immigration Detention in Turkey." In *The EU, Migration and the Politics of Administrative Detention*, edited by M. Ceccorulli and N. Labanca, 169–186. New York, Oxford: Routledge.
Kaytaz, E. S. 2015. "At the Border of 'Fortress Europe': Immigration Detention in Turkey." In *Immigration Detention: The migration of a policy and its human impact*, edited by S. J. Silverman and A. Nethery, 59–68. Oxford, New York: Routledge.
Kaytaz, E. S. (2016). "Afghan Journeys to Turkey: Narratives of Immobility." *Travel and Transformation Geopolitics* 21(2): 284–302. https://doi:10.1080/14650045.2016.1151874
Kirişçi, K. 2007. "Border Management and EU-Turkish Relations: Convergence or Deadlock." *Euro-Mediterranean Consortium for Applied Research on International Migration (CARIM) Research Reports (CARIM-RR 2007/03).* San Domenico di Fiesole (FI): Robert Schuman Centre for Advanced Studies, European University Institute.
Kirişçi, K. 2008. "Managing Irregular Migration in Turkey: A Political-Bureaucratic Perspective." *Euro-Mediterranean Consortium for Applied Research on International Migration (CARIM) Analytic and Synthetic Notes [CARIM-AS 2008/61].* San Domenicao Di Fiesole: European University Institute, Robert Schuman Centre for Advanced Studies.
Kirişçi, K. 2009. "Harmonisation of Migration Policy and Turkey's Security Challenges." *Discussion Paper Series 2019/01.* Istanbul: Centre of Economics and Foreign Policy Studies (EDAM).
Kuschminder, K. 2018. "Afghan Refugee Journeys: Onwards Migration Decision-Making in Greece and Turkey." *Journal of Refugee Studies* 31 (4): 566–587. . doi:10.1093/jrs/fex043.
Leghtas, I. 2019. *Insecure Future: Deportations and Lack of Legal Work for Refugees in Turkey.* Washington DC: Refugees International.
Leghtas, I., and D. Sullivan. 2017. *'Except God, We Have No One': Lack of Durable Solutions for non-Syrian Refugees in Turkey.* Washington DC: Refugees International.
Leghtas, I., and J. Thea. 2018. *"You Cannot Exist in This Place:" Lack of Registration Denies Afghan Refugee Protection in Turkey.* Washington DC: Refugees International.
Mainwaring, C., and S. J. Silverman. 2017. "Detention-as-Spectacle." *International Political Sociology* 11 (1): 21–38. doi:10.1093/ips/olw016.
MazlumDer. 2014. "Adana Mülteci Kabul Barinma Ve Geri Gönderme Merkezi Gözlem Raporu." http://adana.mazlumder.org/tr/main/yayinlar/yurt-ici-raporlar/3/adana-multeci-kabul-barinma-ve-geri-gonderme-/1189
Oelgemöller, C. 2011. "'Transit' and 'Suspension': Migration Management or the Metamorphosis of Asylum-Seekers into 'Illegal' Immigrants." *Journal of Ethnic and Migration Studies* 37 (3): 407–424. doi:10.1080/1369183X.2011.526782.
Oelgemöller, C. 2017. "The Illegal, the Missing: An Evaluation of Conceptual Inventions." *Millennium* 46 (1): 24–40. doi:10.1177/0305829817708812.
Özçürümez, S., and N. Şenses. 2011. "Europeanization and Turkey: Studying Irregular Migration Policy." *Journal of Balkan and near Eastern Studies* 13 (2): 233–248. doi:10.1080/19448953.2011.578867.
Öner, A. Ş., and D. Genç. 2015. "Vulnerability Leading to Mobility: Syrians' Exodus from Turkey." *Migration Letters* 12 (3): 251–262. doi:10.33182/ml.v12i3.278.

Papadopoulou-Kourkoula, A. 2008. *Transit Migration: The Missing Link between Emigration and Settlement, Migration, Minorities, and Citizenship*. Basingstoke: Palgrave Macmillan.
Phillips, M., and A. Missbah. 2017. "Introduction." *International Journal of Migration and Border Studies* 3 (2/3): 113–120.
Piché, J., and M. Larsen. 2010. "The Moving Targets of Penal Abolitionism: ICOPA, Past, Present and Future." *Contemporary Justice Review* 13 (4): 391–410. doi:10.1080/10282580.2010.517964.
Refugee Rights Turkey. 2016. *Barriers to the Right to Effective Legal Remedy: The Problem Faced by Refugees in Turkey in Granting Power of Attorney*. Istanbul: Refugee Rights Turkey.
Rytter, M., and N. Ghandchi. 2020. "Workers for Free: Precarious Inclusion and Extended Uncertainty among Afghan Refugees in Denmark." In *Digesting Difference: Migrant Incorporation and Mutual Belonging in Europe*, edited by K. McKowen and J. Bourneman, 185–207. Palgrave Macmillan. https://doi.org/10.1007/978-3-030-49598-5_9
Schapendonk, J. 2013. "From Transit Migrants to Trading Migrants: Development Opportunities for Nigerians in the Transnational Trade Sector of Istanbul." *Sustainability* 5 (7): 2856–2873. doi:10.3390/su5072856.
Suter, B. 2012. "Social Networks in Transit: Experiences of Nigerian Migrants in Istanbul." *Journal of Immigrant & Refugee Studies* 10 (2): 204–222. doi:10.1080/15562948.2012.674327.
Türkiye Büyük Millet Meclisi İnsan Hakları Komisyonu (Human Rights Inquiry Commission of the Parliament). 2012. *Edirne, Istanbul Ve Kırklareli Illerinde Bulunan Geri Gönderme Merkezleri Hakkında Inceleme Raporu*. Ankara: Türkiye Büyük Millet Meclisi İnsan Hakları Komisyonu
Türkiye Büyük Millet Meclisi İnsan Hakları Komisyonu (Human Rights Inquiry Commission of the Parliament). 2014. *Ege Kıyılarında (İzmir-Aydın) Gerçekleşen Yasa Dışı Göç Hakkında İnceleme Raporu*. Ankara: Türkiye Büyük Millet Meclisi İnsan Hakları Komisyonu
Türkiye Büyük Millet Meclisi İnsan Hakları Komisyonu (Human Rights Inquiry Commission of the Parliament). 2017. *İzmir Ve Aydin İllerİnde Bulunan Gerİ Gönderme Merkezleri İncelemesi Raporu*. Ankara: Türkiye Büyük Millet Meclisi İnsan Hakları Komisyonu
Türkiye İnsan Hakları Kurumu (National Human Rights Institution of Turkey). 2014. *İstanbul Geri Gönderme Merkezi Raporu*. Ankara: Türkiye İnsan Hakları Kurumu
Türkiye İnsan Haklari ve Eşitlik Kurumu (TIHEK) (Turkish Human Rights and Equality Commission).2018a. "Kayseri Geri Gönderme Merkezi Ziyareti." Report No: 2018/14. November. https://bit.ly/2HLRi62
Türkiye İnsan Haklari ve Eşitlik Kurumu (TIHEK) (Turkish Human Rights and Equality Commission). 2018b. "Erzurum Geri Gönderme Merkezi Ziyareti." Report No 2018/16. December. https://bit.ly/2UJjyKd
Türkiye İnsan Haklari ve Eşitlik Kurumu (TIHEK) (Turkish Human Rights and Equality Commission). 2018c. "İzmir Harmandalı Geri Gönderme Merkezi Ziyareti." Report No: 2018/18. December. https://bit.ly/2UOmJj
Turnbull, S. 2018. "Immigration Detention and the Racialized Governance of Illegality in the United Kingdom." *Social Justice* 44 (1): 142.
Ulusoy, O., and H. Battjes. 2017. "Situation of Readmitted Migrants and Refugees from Greece to Turkey under the EU-Turkey Statement." Migration Law Series. University of Amsterdam, Faculty of Law. https://rechten.vu.nl/en/Images/UlusoyBattjes_Migration_Law_Series_No_15_tcm248-861076.pdf
UNECE. 1993. "Migration Bulletin."No.3, November. http://www.unece.org/fileadmin/DAM/pau/_docs/pau/PAU_1993_Publ_IntMigrBull3.pdf
Üstübici, A. 2019. "The Impact of Externalized Migration Governance on Turkey: Technocratic Migration Governance and the Production of Differentiated Legal Status." *Comparative Migration Studies* 7 (1): 46. doi:10.1186/s40878-019-0159-x.
UNHCR Turkey. 2020. "UNHCR Turkey Operational Update February 2020." https://www.unhcr.org/tr/wp-content/uploads/sites/14/2020/03/UNHCR-Turkey-Operational-Update-February-2020.pdf
Vukašinović, J. 2011. "Illegal Migration in Turkey-EU Relations: An Issue of Political Bargaining or Political Cooperation?" *European Perspectives', Journal on European Perspectives of the Western Balkans* 3 (2(5)): 144–166.

Wissink, M., F. Düvell, and A. Van Eerdewijk. 2013. "Dynamic Migration Intentions and the Impact of Socio-Institutional Environments: A Transit Migration Hub in Turkey." *Journal of Ethnic and Migration Studies* 39 (7): 1087–1105. doi:10.1080/1369183X.2013.778026.

Substituting immigration detention centres with 'open prisons' in Indonesia: alternatives to detention as the continuum of unfreedom

Antje Missbach

ABSTRACT

This paper sets out how Indonesia has shifted away from arbitrary and indefinite immigration detention towards so-called alternatives to detention. This shift has been fuelled by the Australian government's cuts to funding the International Organization for Migration (IOM), which was responsible for the costs of immigration detention until 2018. Although the abolition of immigration detention in Indonesia has been praised as a success, it would be wrong to say that alternatives to detention are without any carceral purposes. While their conditions are more humane overall than those in detention centres, alternatives to detention also serve containment purposes and perpetuate a 'continuum of unfreedom', albeit in more subtle ways. More importantly, the decarceration policies have fostered a new hierarchy of refugee deservingness that discriminates against recently arrived asylum seekers. Establishing alternatives to detention has created additional problems that reach beyond the detention/abolitionist dichotomy. The categorical non-integration into the local community and ongoing restrictions on basic rights show that current alternatives to detention, though better than immigration detention, still leave ample room for improvement in decarceration policies in Indonesia and beyond.

Introduction

While many democratic countries, including the United States and Australia, are opting for more restrictive detention measures in order to immobilise asylum seekers in the midst of the so-called global refugee crisis (Moran, Gill, and Conlon 2013; Rung 2020), in 2018 Indonesia opted to relax its carceral migration management of refugees and asylum seekers[1]. Over the preceding decade, the Indonesian government had faced stern international criticism for detaining asylum seekers and refugees, including unaccompanied children. Not only were asylum seekers incarcerated in immigration detention centres indefinitely, but there was no accountability in these state-owned institutions for the human rights violations that took place within them (UNHCR 2016). Several asylum seekers have died in detention as a result of violence, negligence, and suicide (Amnesty International 2012; Missbach and Sinanu 2013). International protest was fuelled not only by reports that detailed the overcrowded conditions, poor services, and frequent violence among detainees and between detainees and guards, but also by the arbitrary and indefinite terms of detention (Human Rights Watch 2013). Against claims by Indonesian state officials that asylum seekers were put into detention centres primarily for administrative or even humanitarian purposes, immigration detention clearly served as punishment. Asylum seekers and refugees were incarcerated in prison-like conditions without any chance of defending themselves in court. Arbitrary detention functioned as a means of deterrence for other asylum seekers considering coming to Indonesia (Missbach 2016).

Despite Indonesia's inclination to detain, it is fair to acknowledge that the limited capacity of the Indonesian immigration detention system meant that not all asylum seekers and refugees were detained all of the time. In 2016, for example, roughly a third of all asylum seekers and refugees in Indonesia were kept in immigration detention centres, with their maintenance covered by generous Australian government funding of the International Organisation for Migration (IOM) in Indonesia.[2] Another third was accommodated in so-called alternatives to detention or 'community shelters', which are also financed by Australian contributions to the IOM in Indonesia. As will be explained below in more detail, alternatives to detention were available only to those who had been detained (and thus punished) first. The remaining third lived independently in self-funded accommodation, usually overpriced rentals in the cities and peri-urban locations.

In 2018, the Indonesian government decided to cease using immigration detention centres for accommodating asylum seekers and refugees.[3] As of January 2020, out of 13,626 persons registered with the United Nations refugee agency (UNHCR) in Jakarta, only ten persons remained in immigration detention, while the approximately more than 4,000 people formerly detained have all been transferred to alternatives to detention. Together with the previous inhabitants of alternatives to detention, in 2020 there were approximately 8,000 refugees and asylum seekers accommodated in community shelters receiving monthly financial and material support from the IOM. There they enjoy greater mobility and can mingle with the Indonesian host society to a certain extent; they can also attend schools and other educational services. While the establishment of alternatives to detention has been praised as a great success (UNHCR 2019), because, overall, they offer more humane living conditions, this article argues that the recent policies do not go far enough and have done little to provide a durable solution for refugees.

As will be explained in more detail throughout this article, this shift in Indonesia's migration management of refugees and asylum seekers from incarceration to decarceration is the result of two main developments. While international non-governmental organisations, such as the International Detention Coalition, had lobbied the Indonesian government for years and thus initiated the rethinking of migration management options and promoted an openness to test alternatives to detention, it was the loss of Australian government funding that ended the incarceration of asylum seekers and refugees in Indonesian detention centres. Once the Australian government cut its funding of IOM in early 2018, for the first time in 18 years of operation in Indonesia, IOM could no longer cover the costs of asylum seekers and refugees in immigration detention in Indonesia. Consequently, the remaining asylum seekers and refugees incarcerated until then were released.

Because of the funding cuts, IOM also had to limit the number of beneficiaries of its migrant care program covering those living in alternatives of detention. IOM capped the number of beneficiaries to 9,000 persons. After March 2018 IOM accepted no new admissions of asylum seekers and refugees into its care program, even though some within that cohort of 9,000 have been resettled and others repatriated since 2018.[4] In 2020 the number of beneficiaries was 1,000 short of the 9,000 cap.

The new IOM care policy excludes not only newly arrived migrants but also those who had been in Indonesia for much longer but have avoided detention so far. The imposition of a limit on the number of people under IOM care has not only cemented two classes of refugees – those supported by IOM and those left to their own devices who are now increasingly destitute – but has also created a new hierarchy of refugee deservingness. While the end of punitive incarceration in immigration detention centres signals a positive development, the new policy can only function well if enough alternatives are provided and if they are open to all those in need. Limiting available spots and privileging one group of refugees over others will give rise to envy and, potentially, unrest.

While this article acknowledges the positive changes in Indonesia's decarceration policies, it takes a critical view by scrutinising some unintended side effects of the policy shifts and by pointing to a number of old and new dilemmas that have been (re)produced by the recent policy shifts. First of all, I emphasise once again that it is often wrongly assumed that alternatives to detention are the opposite of the detention regime. This is not the case, as they serve the very same purpose of containing asylum seekers and refugees, albeit in a larger area than in a tiny detention cell (Missbach 2017). This article shows why alternatives to detention in Indonesia remain part of the wider containment regime sponsored by Australia, despite Indonesia's good intentions of reducing the hardship of incarceration in detention centres. Even when they were released from detention, asylum seekers and refugees were not able to leave Indonesia, unless they were chosen for resettlement in a resettlement country or agreed to repatriation (McNevin and Missbach 2018). In this regard the Indonesian case study illustrates clearly that immigration detention is not the only "necessary adjunct' of the state's power to control immigration' (Costello 2015, 143), as irregular onward migration can be prevented by other means, such as by imposing many requirements that inhabitants of community shelters in Indonesia must meet to avoid the risk of redetention (Missbach 2017). The immobilisation of asylum seekers and refugees in Indonesia is now primarily achieved through containment techniques that favour self-regulation and self-discipline and the threat of potential (re)detainment rather than through immigration detention as the first instance of migration management.

Second, I hope to shed light on the 'continuum of unfreedom' inherent in alternatives to detention in Indonesia and, therefore, to add a new layer to my previous critique. Despite being released from detention, asylum seekers and refugees remain widely segregated from the Indonesian host society. While their social integration is not welcomed, their legal and economic integration is in fact prohibited. The Indonesian government does not offer local integration to refugees, despite the UNHCR's endorsement of local integration as one of three possible durable solutions for refugees, next to resettlement and repatriation.[5] For asylum seekers and refugees this means that they experience a perennial lack of freedom and basic human rights as long as they are in

Indonesia. I make use of the concept of 'continuum of unfreedom' in analysing the various dimensions of exclusion.

Continuum of unfreedom has so far been used mainly to theorise different dimensions of precarity within the realms of forced labour and the exploitation of migrant labour (Lewis et al. 2015) and in regard to everyday control of migrants who are victims of domestic violence by quasi-state agents (Cassidy 2019). In this article I use the concept of continuum of unfreedom to capture the categorical exclusion of refugees from legal integration into the local host society, which is accompanied by the withholding of basic rights, such as the right to work, and thus results not only in prolonging their precarity but also in fostering dependency. The inability to legally generate income makes refugees dependent on help, including single acts of charity, regular aid, and external support from friends and kin. The prohibition on working legally also creates a new hierarchy between refugees deemed 'deserving' of help and those deemed 'undeserving', with the latter being deliberately pushed into further destitution, as currently witnessed in Indonesia.

This article consists of three parts. I begin with an overview of the previous detention system, its funding and political objectives. I then explain the transition from immigration detention to alternatives to detention, the political reasoning behind it and conditions within community shelters. In the first and second parts I rely first and foremost on my fieldwork observations and data collection in Indonesia, where I have spent more than 24 months since 2010. Finally, I address the consequences of the decarceration policy for refugees who are excluded from alternatives to detention and IOM's migrant care program. Here I offer two potential political reasonings behind the state-supported marginalisation of independent refugees and their exclusion from IOM refugee care. On the one hand such marginalisation and exclusion serve to protect the Indonesian government from further international criticism of its cruel treatment of refugees in detention; on the other hand they help maintain a policy of deterring anyone who might consider Indonesia as a potential safe haven.

Immigration detention

Generally speaking, immigration detention is the practice of confining migrants in prisons, closed camps and other restricted areas while they await the outcome of their immigration status determination (Goodwin-Gill 1986, 194; Ramos 2018, 53).[6] Detaining migrants, including refugees and asylum seekers, consolidates their criminalisation and their alienation from the host society (Grewcock 2010, 196). Moreover, immigration detention impinges upon individual decision-making capacities, prevents them from accessing legal and social services and disrupts families and social networks (Moran, Gill, and Conlon 2013; Oliver 2017; Martin 2019). The detrimental physical and psychological effects of long-term immigration detention have been identified and are well documented all around the world (Grewcock 2010; Edwards 2013; Kalhan 2010; Sampson and Mitchell 2013; Nethery and Silverman 2015; Bloomfield 2016).[7] Cathryn Costello (2015) has noted that 'immigration detention is one of the singularly most disturbing contemporary practices from the point of view of the rule of law and human rights'. Nevertheless, many potential host and transit countries, including Indonesia, have relied on immigration detention for administrative and punitive – sometimes even for 'humanitarian' purposes – thus making immigration detention part of their overall strategy to immobilise asylum seekers and deter other potential asylum seekers from crossing their borders.

The immigration detention system in Indonesia primarily served to prevent the irregular onward migration of asylum seekers and refugees to Australia. As loosely connected 'buffer zones' (Mountz and Loyd 2014, 389), immigration detention centres in Indonesia can therefore be understood as one of many features that enabled Australia's wider externalised and extraterritorial deterrence, exclusion and containment strategies (Mountz 2011; Dastyari and Hirsch 2019). Some observers have described the externally funded immigration detention system in Indonesia as 'incentivised policy transfer' (Nethery and Gordon 2014), for which Australia channels money via the IOM to implement its own border policies outside its national territory (Nethery, Rafferty-Brown, and Taylor 2013).

Looking at Indonesia's track record as refugee-hosting country, one sees that the hospitality Indonesia offered to refugees always had some carceral elements. From the late 1970s until the mid 1990s, Indonesia accommodated more than 100,000 Indo-Chinese displaced after the Vietnam War on the small island of Galang close to Singapore, rather than allowing them to roam freely through the archipelago. From the late 1990s asylum seekers from Iraq, Iran, Afghanistan, Pakistan, Sri Lanka and, more recently, Somalia and Myanmar started coming to Indonesia, albeit in much smaller numbers than the Indo-Chinese in the preceding decades (Missbach 2016). In the 2000s, Indonesia by and large refrained from interfering with asylum seekers transiting in Indonesia (Missbach 2015). As more and more people arrived in Australia by boat, the Australian government offered substantial funding for the arrest and detention of asylum seekers in Indonesia, and Indonesia adopted a more hands-on approach. Under a tripartite Regional Cooperation Agreement (RCA) between Australia, Indonesia and the IOM, Australia agreed to financially support Indonesian security and immigration forces in arresting and detaining transiting asylum seekers and refugees, while the IOM was to provide the necessary care (food, health, daily necessities) to those in detention.

Although immigration detention in Indonesia was often viewed as a form of administrative confinement, rather than punitive incarceration, the differences between detention centres and prisons in terms of their architecture, location and security measures, as well as the day-to-day experience of the detainees, tended to be negligible. Between 2008 and 2013, the Indonesian government repurposed its existing immigration detention centres, originally built to host foreign criminals awaiting deportation, for the detention of asylum seekers and refugees.

Indonesia's Law on Immigration (No. 6/2011), implemented in May 2011, made no mention of asylum seekers or refugees because they were not considered legal categories for migration purposes. Foreigners without valid passports and visas were required to be placed in detention indefinitely, although exemptions were made for children, sick or elderly people, women about to give birth, or victims of human trafficking or smuggling. Arrested asylum seekers who wanted to apply for asylum had to do so from within the detention centres. Only those who had been granted refugee status could be released from immigration detention, and, even then, their release was very much at the discretion of immigration officials and often involved bribes.[8] Later their release also depended on the availability of places in community shelters. Direct referral to alternatives to detention and thus to IOM's care program was not possible. In this regard, immigration detention became a precondition for referral to non-custodial alternatives to detention, reinforcing the close concatenation of detention and its alternatives and placing alternatives to detention as an essential ingredient of the detention regime.

Indonesia has 13 immigration detention centres with a combined maximum capacity of 1,700. Despite Australian-funded refurbishment and extensions, the immigration detention centres were notoriously overcrowded, with up to 3,000 detainees.[9] Additional offers from Australia to increase detention capacity were rejected when it was found that resettlements was not proceeding fast enough. Basically, the Indonesian government began to realise that the more asylum seekers and refugees they arrested and detained, the longer they would stay in Indonesia, which was definitely not in Indonesia's political interests. Facing international criticism about the poor conditions in its detention centres and widespread violation of the human rights of detained asylum seekers, Indonesia looked for options other than detention. In 2014, Indonesia became one of 12 countries for which a national action plan for the adoption of the guiding objectives of the UNHCR's Beyond Detention agenda was prepared (UNHCR 2015; Edwards 2016; Setiadi and Siagian 2019). Interestingly, even before joining this project to trial alternatives to detention, Indonesia had already put in place some options for non-custodial accommodation of refugees (Missbach 2017).

As the Indonesian government became more open to alternatives to detention, something rather paradoxical happened following Australia's adoption of a new turn-back policy under Operation Sovereign Borders in September 2013. Almost all the asylum seeker boats that left Indonesia for Australia were promptly sent back by Australian authorities (Chia, McAdam, and Purcell 2014). With irregular boat crossings suppressed successfully, the length of time asylum seekers waited in Indonesia started to increase. From late 2013 onwards, hundreds of asylum seekers, who had so far managed to avoid immigration detention, could no longer support themselves and began to surrender to Indonesian authorities, asking to be detained. With no more boats reaching Australia, asylum seekers and refugees became desperate enough to swap their freedom for a roof over their heads and regular meals. To make matters worse, in November 2014 Australia announced its intention to decrease its annual intake of refugees from Indonesia. Immigration detention centres in several Indonesian cities saw a rush of asylum seekers begging to be detained, nevertheless hoping that their time in detention would be short and that they would be released into alternatives to detention promptly.

Although recognised refugees were now transferred to community shelters more frequently, as the IOM kept arranging for their capacity to be extended, immigration centres could sometimes not cope with the many new asylum seekers wanting to be detained. In early 2018, for example, approximately 300 asylum seekers and refugees began to camp on the footpaths in front of the Kalideres detention centre in Jakarta, where immigration officials, citing a lack of capacity, had refused to take them in (Bemma 2018). Even after the Kalideres detention centre had released all detained asylum seekers and refugees in late 2018, new asylum seekers continued to camp outside, hoping to attract attention to their destitution and the lack of care.

Alternatives to detention

So far there is no authoritative definition of what determines an alternative to detention (Bloomfield 2016). Some international NGOs have determined that alternatives to detention include a range of policies and practices employed by states to manage immigration that fall short of incarceration and protect rights and dignity (Sampson and Mitchell 2013; Sampson 2019). Others consider them to be little more than non-custodial accommodation that allow minimal freedom of movement and still rely on surveillance (Kahlan 2010). Julia Morris remarked that detention rights' reforms that seek to ameliorate restrictive policies through humanitarian-based solutions with more humane facility standards are nothing more than a 'normative cover' (Morris 2016, 51) and a 'moral veneer' of the overall politics of forced immobility (Morris 2016, 66). Providing less carceral and more humane forms of detention is an improvement, but does not necessarily contribute to abolishing restrictive migration dogma or to ending containment policies per se. Rather, because people living in alternatives to detention are far from enjoying the same rights as citizens, they prolong their unfreedom.

In Indonesia, alternatives to detention comprise a number of housing options, including purpose-built new accommodation, repurposed former hotels and student dormitories. As mentioned in the previous section, in order to be transferred to alternatives to detention and thus to benefit from the IOM care scheme, refugees need to be referred to IOM by the Indonesian migration authorities. When released from immigration detention, asylum seekers and refugees usually have no choice about which of the alternatives to detention they are placed in. The task of allocating appropriate shelters falls to the IOM. If potential shelters meet the IOM's basic standards, IOM then needs to get the approval of the local government. Finding suitable accommodation has been challenging for the IOM, not least because many local governments have been unwilling to host refugees, as they fear potential religious tension, social envy and cultural misunderstandings.

Financial costs for accommodation in alternatives to detention (including guards and electricity to some extent, but not water, gas or internet access) have so far been covered entirely by the IOM.[10] Conditions in alternatives to detention vary widely and depend heavily on local government authorities and their local regulations and services.[11] Some alternatives to detention I have visited over the years have been clean and renovated, while others were cramped and decrepit. Families with small children usually get a room to themselves, while single people share a room with another person. Alternatives to detention also offer better access to services, such as health care, religious institutions and psychological support. Some local governments started allowing refugee children to attend local primary schools. An adult living in the shelters receives a monthly stipend from the IOM of Rp1.25 million (US$90) to buy food, clothes and all other necessities; each child receives about half that amount. IOM also covers medical treatment for the chronically ill and medical emergencies. Finding employment and any form of income-generation are still not allowed. The prohibition to work is probably the most significant barrier for those who might otherwise be more open to local integration.

Refugees in alternatives to detention must sign a declaration in which they agree to comply with Indonesian law and to report regularly to the local authorities. The declaration restricts their mobility by prohibiting them to go to airports and seaports (Missbach 2017). Asylum seekers and refugees who leave the shelter for more than two days without prior permission are blocked from re-entering and lose all services and payments they had been entitled to. Some people learned these rules the hard way, as they were not fully aware of the draconian consequences of, for example, their visits to friends or family in another city.

Each shelter has additional rules in place, usually displayed in several languages at the shelter's entry. While some rules are quite straightforward, others are kept deliberately vague, giving the local authorities more discretionary power over the shelters' inhabitants. Individual cases of non-compliance created precedents for punishment that have ensured high levels of self-discipline and submissive behaviour among the inhabitants.[12] Particularly, the risk of readmission to immigration detention centres has enhanced compliance with the regulations.

Rules have changed over time, with many shelters recently imposing more restrictive regimes, causing them to resemble detention centres more and more. From this point of view, new rules have acted as invisible walls and intensified self-discipline among the inhabitants. In some cases, however, the degradation of service provision and the introduction of more restrictions have also goaded refugees into protesting in public. For example, when an 8pm curfew and limitations on leaving the shelter during the day were introduced in all of the shelters in Makassar in early 2018, refugees took to the streets and their protests were widely reported beyond Makassar.

Alternatives to detention do offer refugees, objectively speaking, better conditions of accommodation and coverage of their basic material needs, but many refugees have become increasingly desperate because of the uncertainty and lack of options that they have been experiencing over long periods of time. This is illustrated in the account of Assodulah Amiri, a refugee who has been waiting for resettlement to a third country for eight years:

> The situation here is worse than in an immigration detention centre. When I was there, I saw the door was locked for 24 hours and I admitted that I was in prison, and I had a hope that I would be released to freedom. But, when I was transferred to IOM accommodation, things became more complicated day by day as I realised that I had been sent to an infinite open prison with no certainty of my future. I am treated as an unwanted person, less than a human being. This system is designed for refugees to give up and go back to our countries or die slowly in stress and anxiety (Joniad 2020).

Another refugee, who has been living in Indonesia for six years, expressed similar frustration:

> We are frustrated and exhausted due to this unending waiting game of resettlement, confined in an open prison and effectively denied their fundamental human rights, such as the right to work, right to education, and right to movement (SBS 2019).

There is no sign of any durable solutions for refugees currently waiting in Indonesia. Any chance of resettlement in third countries is slim, as those countries have decreased significantly their annual resettlement quotas since 2014. In 2018, only 400 people or three per cent of the total refugee and asylum seeker population in Indonesia were resettled (Cochrane 2018). Australia, which used to accept the largest numbers from Indonesia, has further minimised its annual intake. Moreover, autonomous onward migration, such as by boat, is also no longer a viable option because of Australia's turn-back policies (Chia, McAdam, and Purcell 2014; Missbach 2019). This leaves refugees in Indonesia with a choice between continuing to endure the ongoing limbo, with all its uncertainties and lack of rights, or opting for repatriation to their countries of origin, which, more often than not, are neither safe nor prepared to reintegrate large numbers of returnees.

With voluntary assisted repatriation the only durable option on offer for these refugees; any chance for them to make proper and meaningful choices in their lives has been removed. The demoralising absence of choice and truly durable solutions has an immensely negative impact on their mental health, as high levels of depression and reports of suicide attest. Consequently, it is not surprising that some refugees refer to Indonesia as an 'open prison'.

Creating undeservingness

While most refugees were pleased to leave detention, one somewhat paradoxical yet tragic case has been reported from Manado (North Sulawesi), which illustrates the anxieties of those asylum seekers who have had their protection claims rejected but are unable to return to their country of origin. They may be released from detention eventually, but they have no access to any kind of proper institutional support or care arrangements and cannot pursue proper integration into Indonesian society, which leaves them in continued unfreedom.

In February 2019, Sajjad, a 24-year old Afghan man, set himself alight in the Manado detention centre and died shortly after. Sajjad and his family had come to Indonesia 20 years earlier and spent the last nine years in detention in Manado. Their application for asylum was rejected twice, but, unwilling to return to Afghanistan, the family stayed on in Indonesia. For unknown reasons, the family rejected repeated offers from the UNHCR to reopen their case, therefore keeping their status as rejected asylum seekers. In the Manado detention centre, they occupied an entire floor and enjoyed some privileges other detainees did not have, for reasons that remain unknown. Sajjad, for example, attended high school and university in Manado, even earning a degree. Following the decision to release all refugees from the detention centre, Sajjad's family barricaded themselves in their quarters. When immigration officers forced their way in, Sajjad set fire to himself (Panigoro 2019).

Although this case is extreme, it is indicative of a challenge that is likely to become more pressing in the next few years – what to do with rejected asylum seekers who have exhausted all available legal avenues for protection in Indonesia,[13] but cannot leave Indonesia. Under the Law on Immigration (No. 6/2011), irregular migrants can be detained for up to ten years. The law also provides for the detention of rejected asylum seekers pending their removal from Indonesia. However, as already mentioned, from 2018 the IOM ceased covering the expenses of immigration detention. After the maximum ten-year stay in immigration detention, asylum seekers whose claims have been rejected must be released into the community.

While voluntary assisted repatriation is, in theory, available to rejected asylum seekers, many are unable to take up this offer.[14] Some rejected asylum seekers, for example, Iranians, might be open to repatriation but find it impossible to acquire valid travel documents from their embassy. Many simply refuse the option for repatriation outright, as they fear that their lives will be in danger once they return. While the IOM funds voluntary assisted repatriation, it does not provide funding for the deportation of rejected asylum seekers. Indonesian authorities claim that they can organise only a small number of deportations, as they lack funding.

The exact number of rejected asylum seekers currently in Indonesia is unknown. Some may have merged into the local community, but still lack full citizen's rights; others may have moved elsewhere, for example to Malaysia, to look for work; others may have been trafficked or vanished without trace.

The second group of intentionally marginalised people are refugees who had managed to avoid detention before the Indonesian relaxed its detention policies in 2018 and asylum seekers who arrived in Indonesia after March 2018, when the IOM stopped accepting new asylum seekers into its care program. They have no access to the services provided under IOM care or any public service available to Indonesians.[15] Without access to free accommodation in alternatives to detention, they have to find and pay for their own housing. Many are now homeless and sleep in mosques or tents in front of the UNHCR office.

More than 5,000 asylum seekers and refugees are excluded from any form of institutionalised care (under IOM) and their presence is widely overlooked by the responsible Indonesian policy makers and their implementing partners. While the UNHCR has offered these independent refugees voluntary assisted repatriation, very few have accepted the offer. Excluding people from a range of community services and leaving their needs unattended will not only intensify their socio-economic hardship but also push some of them into criminal activity and into a hyper-precarious existence. Living in limbo might become a de facto fourth and all-too-durable 'solution' for these refugees.

Dividing the asylum seekers and refugees currently in Indonesia into the 'deserving' and 'undeserving' serves two rather different political ends. Releasing all formerly detained refugees and catering to the basic needs of these 'deserving refugees' helps Indonesia demonstrate its commitment to temporary refugee protection and, therefore, silences any further international criticism. On the other hand, disadvantaging and marginalising the 'undeserving' group helps send out a stern warning to potential asylum seekers who might be considering coming to Indonesia in the near future.

Conclusion

This article has explained why and how Indonesia has shifted away from arbitrary and indefinite immigration detention, opting instead for alternatives to detention. While refugees and asylum seekers released from detention centres now enjoy a wider radius of mobility, their freedom of movement is not absolute, as their rights are still restricted and they are still deprived of their liberty. Asylum seekers and refugees are still essentially being held back in Indonesia. Although non-custodial community shelters are generally perceived as a more humane option for accommodating refugees than detention, they are essentially a component of a containment regime in Indonesia that is intended to immobilise refugees and deter their self-organised onward movement. In this regard, carceral migration management does not end with the release of refugees and asylum seekers from detention centres, but continues in more subtle forms in the alternatives to detention which are subject to intense surveillance.

Although Indonesia's shift to decarceration is laudable, the policies associated with it do not go far enough, as refugees are still excluded from many basic rights, such as the right to work. With very few resettlement options available to them and the inability to either organise their own onward migration and integrate into Indonesian society, refugees and asylum seekers in Indonesia continue to be marginalised and deprived of their rights, but to different extents. While the basic material needs of those living in alternatives to detention are met, others struggle to survive in the streets. The absence of meaningful choices and durable solutions for refugees stuck in Indonesia therefore contributes to a continuum of unfreedom outside the walls of immigration detention centres.

Notes

1. The term 'open prison' has been used by asylum seekers in Indonesia to describe their living conditions outside immigration detention (see, for example, Morse 2019). I have decided to adopt their term as an emic category.
2. Indonesia has been a primary focus for Australian funding of the IOM. Between 2001 and 2016, Australia provided A$238 million to IOM for its Indonesian projects, with the vast majority of those funds dedicated to migration control and migrant care (Hirsch and Doig 2018).
3. See circular letter by Director of Immigration No IMI-UM.01.01–2827 on *Pengembalian Fungsi Rumah Detensi* [Restoring the original function of immigration detention centres], dated 30 July 2018.
4. According to an IOM representative, IOM care is now available only for asylum seekers intercepted at sea (interview, Jakarta, July 2018).
5. Indonesia is not a State party to the *1951 Convention relating to the Status of Refugees* or its *1967 Protocol*, nor has it signed the *1954 Convention relating to the Status of Stateless Person*. While Indonesia has generally respected the principle of *non-refoulement*, the return of a small number of asylum seekers to countries where they could have faced persecution has been reported since 2013.
6. More recent definitions of immigration detention acknowledge a broader spectrum of carceral factors. Martin (2019) defines it as 'an assemblage of practices, discourses, and material infrastructures that are connected to wider institutional, financial, legal, and geopolitical networks' in support of migration control.
7. The socio-psychological damage that results from prolonged immigration detention cannot be stressed often enough. Nils Melzer, UN Special Rapporteur on torture and other cruel, inhumane or degrading treatment or punishment, has stated that 'grossly inadequate detention conditions can even amount to torture if they are intentionally imposed, encouraged or tolerated by States for reasons based on discrimination of any kind, including based on immigration status, or for the purpose of deterring, intimidating, or punishing migrants or their families, coercing them into withdrawing their requests for asylum, subsidiary protection or other stay, agreeing to "voluntary" return, providing information or fingerprints, or with a view to extorting money or sexual acts from them' (Melzer 2018, 7).
8. During informal interviews with IOM officers it became clear that immigration detention centres had become hotbeds of corruption that drained asylum seekers and refugees of their limited resources in return for favours or even escape. The centres also submitted inflated receipts and demands to the IOM (Missbach 2015).
9. Between 2012 and 2017, I visited six of the 13 detention centres, usually for a couple of hours each visit. In some detention centres I could talk quite freely to detainees; in others I was escorted by guards all the time, making open discussion more challenging. In general, I was also able to have proper interviews with the heads of detention or at least informal chats with some of their staff.
10. Similar to the corruption that was common in detention centres, owners of shelters have complained that they had to pay bribes of up to 40% of their income from the IOM to third

parties to maintain their eligibility as contractors (field observation, Makassar, February 2018).

11. During a visit to alternatives to detention on Batam island in 2019, I learned from the refugees living in repurposed hotels that the air conditioning had recently been cut off. Although all rooms were equipped with air conditioners, IOM wanted to save on electricity costs and to get people out of the shelters and socialising on the streets (field observation, Batam, April 2019).
12. Field observation, Makassar, February 2018.
13. Every rejected asylum seeker can submit one appeal. Claims for asylum are not necessarily rejected because they are weak; more often than not they are rejected because of a lack of proper legal advice or the inability to understand the bureaucratic procedures and requirements.
14. Those willing to be repatriated receive free air travel and US$2,000 from the IOM, using funds provided by the Australian government, to resume their lives in their countries of origin.
15. A few faith-based NGOs have stepped in to provide monthly care to highly vulnerable people or emergency care, but they cannot match the services and financial support that the IOM provides.Source: Presentation by UNHCR of its work to support the government of Indonesia in protecting refugees, Workshop on 'Presidential Regulation No. 125 of 2016 on the Treatment of Refugees and Asylum-seekers in Indonesia: Opportunities and Challenges', Depok, 20–21 March 2019.

Disclosure statement

No potential conflict of interest was reported by the author.

References

Amnesty International. 2012. "Indonesia: Asylum-Seeker Tortured to Death in Detention." (Amnesty International Public Statement ASA 21/008/2012), 2 March

Asher Lazarus, H., and D. Cameron. 2018. "Outsourcing Control: The International Organization for Migration in Indonesia." *International Journal of Human Rights* 22: 681–708. doi:10.1080/13642987.2017.1417261.

Bemma, A. 2018. "Refugees in Indonesia Told to Assimilate but Not Settle." *Refugees Deeply* February. 9.https://deeply.thenewhumanitarian.org/refugees/articles/2018/02/09/refugees-in-indonesia-told-to-assimilate-but-not-settle

Bloomfield, A. 2016. "Alternatives to Detention at a Crossroads: Humanisation or Criminalisation?" *Refugee Survey Quarterly* 35 (1): 29–46. doi:10.1093/rsq/hdv018.

Cassidy, K. 2019. "Where Can I Get Free?: Everyday Bordering, Everyday Incarceration." *Transactions of the Institute of British Geographers* 44 (1): 48–62. doi:10.1111/tran.12273.

Chia, J., J. McAdam, and K. Purcell. 2014. "Asylum in Australia: 'Operation Sovereign Borders' and International Law." *Annual Australian Yearbook of International Law* 32: 33–64.

Cochrane, J. 2018. "Refugees In Indonesia Hoped for Brief Stay: Many May Be Stuck for Life." *New York Times*, 26 January.

Costello, C. 2015. "Immigration Detention: The Grounds beneath Our Feet." *Current Legal Problems* 68 (1): 143–177. doi:10.1093/clp/cuv015.

Dastyari, A., and A. Hirsch. 2019. "The Ring of Steel: Extraterritorial Migration Controls in Indonesia and Libya and the Complicity of Australia and Italy." *Human Rights Law Review* 19: 435–465.

Edwards, A. 2013. "Detention under Scrutiny." *Forced Migration Review* 44: 4–6.

Edwards, A. 2016. "From Routine to Exceptional: Introduction to UNHCR's Global Strategy–Beyond Detention 2014–2019: Supporting Governments to End the Detention of Asylum-Seekers." *Refugee Survey Quarterly* 35: 128–133. doi:10.1093/rsq/hdv019.
Goodwin-Gill, G. S. 1986. "International Law and the Detention of Refugees and Asylum Seekers." *International Migration Review* 20: 193–219. doi:10.1177/019791838602000204.
Grewcock, M. 2010. *Border Crimes: Australia's War on Illicit Migrants*. Federation Press: Sydney.
Human Rights Watch. 2013. *Barely Surviving: Detention, Abuse and Neglect of Migrant Children in Indonesia*. New York: Human Rights Watch.
Joniad, J. N. 2020. "Refugees Stuck in Indonesia are Experiencing a Mental Health Crisis." *BuzzFeed.News* February. 21.
Kalhan, A. 2010. "Rethinking Immigration Detention." *Columbia Law Review Sidebar* 110: 42–58.
Lewis, H., P. Dwyer, S. Hodkinson, and L. Waite. 2015. "Hyper-precarious Lives: Migrants, Work and Forced Labour in the Global North." *Progress in Human Geography* 39 (5): 580–600. doi:10.1177/0309132514548303.
Martin, L. 2019. "Carceral Mobility and Flexible Territoriality in Immigration enforcement&#x201D." In *Handbook on Critical Geographies of Migration*, edited by M. Katharyne, R. Jones, and J. L. Fluri, 244–253. London: Edward Elgar Publishing.
McNevin, A., and A. Missbach. 2018. "Luxury Limbo: Temporal Techniques of Border Control and the Humanitarianisation of Waiting." *International Journal of Migration and Border Studies* 4 (1/2): 12–34. doi:10.1504/IJMBS.2018.091222.
Melzer, N. 2018. *Report of the Special Rapporteur on Torture and Other Cruel, Inhuman or Degrading Treatment or Punishment (A/HRC/37/50)*. New York: United Nations.
Missbach, A. 2015. *Troubled Transit: Asylum Seekers Stuck in Indonesia*. ISEAS: Singapore.
Missbach, A. 2016. "Detaining Asylum Seekers and Refugees in Indonesia." In *Detaining the Immigrant Other: Global and Transnational Issues*, edited by R. Furman, D. Epps, and G. Lamphear, 91–104. New York: Oxford University Press.
Missbach, A. 2017. "Accommodating Asylum Seekers and Refugees in Indonesia: From Immigration Detention to Containment in 'Alternatives to Detention'." *Refuge* 33 (2): 32–44. doi:10.7202/1043061ar.
Missbach, A. 2019. "Asylum Seekers' and Refugees' Decision-making in Transit in Indonesia: The Need for In-depth and Longitudinal Research." *Journal of the Humanities and Social Sciences of Southeast Asia* 175 (4): 419–445.
Missbach, A., and F. Sinanu. 2013. "Life and Death in Detention." *Inside Indonesia* 113 (July–September). https://www.insideindonesia.org/life-and-death-in-immigration-detention
Moran, D., N. Gill, and D. Conlon, eds. 2013. *Carceral Spaces: Mobility and Agency in Imprisonment and Migrant Detention*. Ashgate: Farnham, Surrey.
Morris, J. 2016. "In the Market of Morality: International Human Rights Standards and the Immigration Detention 'Improvement' Complex." In *Intimate Economies of Immigration Detention: Critical Perspectives*, edited by D. Conlon and N. Hiemstra, 51–69. London: Routledge.
Morse, I. 2019. "'open Prison': The Growing Despair of Refugees Stuck in Indonesia." *Aljazeera* March. 4.
Mountz, A. 2011. "The Enforcement Archipelago: Detention, Haunting, and Asylum on Islands." *Political Geography* 30 (3): 118–128. doi:10.1016/j.polgeo.2011.01.005.
Mountz, A., and J. Loyd. 2014. "Transnational Productions of Remoteness: Building Onshore and Offshore Carceral Regimes across Borders." *Geographica helvetica* 69 (5): 389–398. doi:10.5194/gh-69-389-2014.
Nethery, A., B. Rafferty-Brown, and T. Savitri. 2013. "Exporting Detention: Australian-funded Immigration Detention in Indonesia." *Journal of Refugee Studies* 26: 88–109. doi:10.1093/jrs/fes027.
Nethery, A., and C. Gordon. 2014. "Australia–indonesia Cooperation on Asylum-seekers: A Case of 'Incentivised Policy Transfer'." *Australian Journal of International Affairs* 68: 177–193. doi:10.1080/10357718.2013.841122.

Nethery, A., and S. Silverman, eds. 2015. *Immigration Detention: The Migration of a Policy and Its Human Impact*. New York: Routledge.
Oliver, K. 2017. *Carceral Humanitarianism: Logics of Refugee Detention*. Minneapolis: University of Minnesota Press.
Panigoro, I. (2019). "Sajjad, Imigran Afghanistan yang Bakar Diri di Rudenim Manado Meninggal Dunia„ [Sajjad, Afghan immigrant who self-immolated at Manado detention centre passed away], Tribun Manado, February 13 . Accessed 4 December 2020. https://manado.tribunnews.com/2019/02/13/breaking-news-sajjad-imigran-afghanistan-yang-bakar-diri-di-rudenim-manado-meninggal-dunia?page=all Accessed 4 December 2020.
Ramos, S. 2018. ""Icebox: The Logistics of Detention"." *Footprint* 23: 53–68.
Rung, D. L. 2020. "Processes of Sub-citizenship: Neoliberal Statecrafting 'Citizens,' 'Non-citizens,' and Detainable 'Others'." *Social Sciences* 9 (1): 1–30. doi:10.3390/socsci9010005.
Sampson, R. 2019. "The Biopolitics of Alternatives to Immigration Detention." In *Handbook on Critical Geographies of Migration*, edited by K. Mitchell, R. Jones, and J. L. Fluri, 255–264. London: Edward Elgar Publishing Limited.
Sampson, R., and G. Mitchell. 2013. ""Global Trends in Immigration Detention and Alternatives to Detention: Practical, Political and Symbolic Rationales"." *Journal on Migration and Human Security* 1: 97–121. doi:10.1177/233150241300100302.
SBS. 2019. "Australia Urged to Help Refugees Stranded for Years in Indonesia." *SBS News*, 5 August.
Setiadi, W., and S. Mario Johanes Caesar. 2019. "The Implementation of Alternatives to Detention to Handle the Problems of Refugees in Indonesia." *Padjadjaran Jurnal Ilmu Hukum* 6 (1): 128–150.
United Nations High Commissioner for Refugees (UNHCR). 2015. *Beyond Detention: A Global Strategy to Support Governments to End the Detention of Asylum-seeker and Refugees.* 2014–2019. *National Action Plan – Indonesia*. Geneva.
United Nations High Commissioner for Refugees (UNHCR). 2016. *Progress Report Mid-2016. Beyond Detention: A Global Strategy to Support Governments to End the Detention of Asylum-Seekers and Refugees*, 2014–2019. Geneva.
United Nations High Commissioner for Refugees (UNHCR). 2019. *Progress Report 2018: A Global Strategy to Support Governments to End the Detention of Asylum-Seekers and Refugees*, 2014–2019. Geneva: United Nations High Commissioner for Refugees.

ICE comes to Tennessee: violence work and abolition in the Appalachian South

Michelle Brown

ABSTRACT
By way of a case study of a key Trump-era Immigration and Customs Enforcement (ICE) workplace raid amidst the arrival of 287(g) programs in Eastern Tennessee, this article places the violence of the carceral state in relation to the ongoing work of emancipation in the American South. It 1) reconceptualizes immigration enforcement as a key locus for intensifying the carceral state's power via a specific form of violence work and 2) maps the manner in which horizons of abolition take shape in the shadow of this violence. The radical reimagining of immigration as the abolition of policing, detention, and borders is linked to everyday grassroots efforts that seek to counter the pervasive state violence of 287(g) policies. Distinct forms of relational care have slowed and, in some cases, halted the political dominance of carcerality, drawing upon historic emancipatory projects of Southern abolition democracy.

Introduction: ICE comes to Tennessee

In 2018, Tennessee passed one of the nation's most extreme anti-immigration laws (HB2315), reinforcing its national reputation as one of the Southern US states at the forefront of enacting and valorizing Trump policy. The 'mass deportation bill,' as it was popularly known, prohibited state and local government officials from adopting sanctuary policies. The bill passed in the legislature less than a month after what was, at the time, the largest workplace ICE raid of the Trump era, occurring at an East Tennessee meatpacking plant, in a small rural town a little over half an hour from Knoxville, where 97 immigrants from Mexico and Guatamala were detained. Knox County was the only jurisdiction in the state at the time to have in place a controversial 287(g) contract, a partnership with ICE at the federal level, received the previous year, that allowed them to expand local immigration enforcement authority. All of these events had been augmented by insistent demands of local government for the expansion of policing powers, including the use of the jail for immigrant processing and detention; a demand for infrastructural police resources, including a 40 USD million new department headquarters; and a call for new jail construction at another 40 USD million while contracting for profit with Securus Technologies to end in-person visitation. While these kinds of patterns exemplify changes in the carceral state at the local level across the US, they also bring to the fore the manner in which immigration enforcement is increasingly used in new immigrant destinations in the South to justify and buttress the expansion of the carceral state at key levels of municipal governance. In this convergence, Eastern Tennessee emerged as an interior hub for border control and its abolition in the Appalachian South.

The majority of immigrants that ICE arrested the day of the workplace raid were detained solely for being in the country illegally. ICE had conducted a joint operation with Homeland Security, the Internal Revenue Service and the Tennessee Highway Patrol on the grounds that a family-run cattle slaughter facility had allegedly evaded taxes, filed false returns, and hired 'illegal' immigrants. The work day had just begun, a day that, ordinarily, would be made up of the bloody work of decapitating, skinning and butchering cattle, all in close proximity to dangerous chemicals, when suddenly dozens of armed ICE agents flooded the scene while a helicopter circled above. Panicked workers tried to flee or hide, wedging themselves under tables, between beef carcasses, with one man resisting capture by hiding in a freezer. Many were cornered, called racial slurs at gunpoint, and restrained with plastic zip ties. Eventually, they were driven to a National Guard armory where they were questioned and detained. Later that evening, family members would assemble nearby in the hopes of finding out the fate of loved ones. Many were children – 160 had a parent arrested that day – and the effects of the raid radiated across generations of immediate and extended families well beyond the original 97. The Latinx community that had been in the region since the early 1990s, when the South had taken shape as a new immigrant destination, that day, were terrified. Over the next weeks, the classrooms of Grainger County emptied as families refused to send their children to school for fear of deportation. Teachers were devastated. Church pastors were shaken. And a significant subset (but certainly, not all) of the white community, 77% of whom had voted for Trump in the 2016 election, found itself up close to and troubled by the violence of immigrant detention, deportation and the racializing logics of police and the carceral state.

The show of police force at a factory facing labor violations in a working class community, a town whose very air is defined by the industrialized factory farming stench of slaughter houses, reveals much about the function and definition of police in the rural context of a carceral state whose focus has shifted to immigration. In communities across the US, federal initiatives like the 287(g) program have incentivized partnerships with ICE, empowering local law enforcement to act as federal immigration authorities in exchange for funding and training. While research has investigated the development, evolution and variable effects of 287(g) programs at the county level (Wong 2012; Coleman 2007, 2012; Arriaga 2017; Armenta 2017), these relationships remain under-theorized in relation to the sheer violence of criminal justice and community efforts to resist these harms. 287(g) agreements are currently geographically clustered[1] in the United States in a handful of major cities, at the Texas/Mexico border, and in the South (Winders 2007; Armenta 2017; Arriaga 2017). The Tennessee case is exemplary of the variable geopolitical configurations of carceral power and control (Armenta 2012, 2017) where 287(g) allows for a flexible, adaptable expansion of police power that can focus on a range of issues such as 'gang suppression,' 'workplace violations,' 'human trafficking,' 'tax violations,' and so on.

In Knox County, the longstanding Sheriff Jimmy 'JJ' Jones had played a key role in advocating tirelessly for 287(g) partnerships, applying as early as 2009 to the program. His efforts, in turn, mobilized local immigrant rights advocates to focus their efforts via a multipronged campaign against 287(g). Sheriff Jones' application was denied in 2013. He responded with a visceral kind of punitive outrage, making national news when he publicly stated that 'I will continue to enforce these federal immigration violations with or without the help of U.S Immigration and Customs Enforcement (ICE). If need be, I will stack these violators like cordwood in the Knox County Jail until the appropriate federal agency responds' (Terkel and Foley 2013). After the presidential election of 2016 and the Trump win, Jones and the Sheriff's office received approval from ICE for the program in 2017. Tennessee augmented the police power of 287(g) with a number of initiatives, including House Bill (HB) 2315 whose provisions included prohibiting municipal governments authorities from *refusing* to comply with federal immigration officials, such as immigration detainers from ICE; and rendering local governments that establish 'sanctuary city' policies as ineligible for state funding.

Local organizers rallied in response to these concerns. Allies of Knoxville's Immigrant Neighbors (AKIN) noted how 287(g) made the city 'a geographical hub for immigrant detainees, who are arrested on charges in nearby jurisdictions and brought to Knox County' (Conley and Ansley 2019). They also mapped how deputized and designated officers assumed new roles related to detention and deportation proceedings, with a 300% spike in immigrant detainees at the local jail in the month after the program's implementation (Ibid). Their platform of opposition borrowed heavily from empirical research and the work of immigration scholars in the community (who were routinely doxed and threatened) and strategically used social media and relationships with local news organizations to demonstrate 287(g) to be 'a flawed and controversial program' … one that was expensive,[2] led to indiscriminate deportation of people who posed no threat to community safety,[3] encouraged racial profiling,[4] eroded trust between immigrant communities and local law enforcement,[5] and falsely portrayed the entire undocumented community as a danger to society[6]" (AKIN's website). It is within this framework of the local that a deeper abolitionist analysis of the everyday would take shape.

Violence work, immigration, and the South

Two kinds of national visibility emerged out of the conjuncture of the raid, 287(g)'s local implementation,[7] and grassroots coalitional organizing: 1) the sheer materiality and intensification of the violence of police and the carceral state became, temporarily, apparent as a story of the carceral South; and 2) a ground-up counter-movement of community care and resources at the local level was organized – and celebrated – as neighbors, institutions and organizations sought to support the families whose lives had been devastated. The first, an appearing – as opposed to disappearing – of state violence exemplifies what Walia refers to when she argues bordering is a practice that is both exterior and interior to the nation-state. As with the workplace ICE raid, 'The internalization of borders is happening in so-called public institutions – schools, hospitals, transit – that are operating as checkpoints and either denying migrants access and often acting as border guards to detain and report people to immigration authorities' (2019, 13). Another way of thinking about this internalization is as a kind of performance enacted by state agents, migrants, and the communities who both host and are hostile to them, what Wonders (2006) refers to as 'border performativity.' For Weber, such practices are evidence of how border controls infiltrate everyday worlds via a 'structurally embedded border' that also 'reflexively creates the conditions for its dispersed and performative nature' (2019, 229), a transversality that expresses the potential to shift reference points away from state-centric perspectives. The latter emphasizes sites of struggle and resistance that interrupt the territorial control of the state and privileges 'fugitive events and moments' (Soguk and Whitehall 1999) that, through unauthorized border crossings, including community resistance and sanctuary, create key points of meaning in larger exclusionary contexts.

The shifting role of immigration enforcement at various scalar levels, including the local, reveals the importance of critical policing and prison studies to understandings of the carceral state, including an under-theorization of police in relationship to state violence. The carceral state, as a construct, seeks to be a more expansive term than mass imprisonment, and one that scholars use to describe the historically unprecedented expansion of criminal justice, specifically, the penal sector of the state, alongside the dramatic downsizing of social welfare in the United States in the post-civil-rights era. As Beckett writes, 'the term "carceral state"' works 'to call attention to the expanding role of penal institutions, broadly defined, in the lives of the poor and in communities of color (e.g. Hernandez, Muhammad, and Thompson 2015). Scholarship showing that penal intervention matters even absent incarceration provides support for this conceptual framework' (2018, 37). Massification has come to define the entire criminal justice system – mass criminalization, mass imprisonment, mass surveillance, etc. – and the amassing of satellite social service agencies and nonprofits, with total spending on corrections by the federal and state government quadrupling in the carceral era to roughly 80 USD billion, surpassing in many state budgets spending on higher education and health care (Schoenfeld 2018; Aviram 2015). Jail expansion, increased budgetary resources for police and sheriff's offices, as well as federal grants, contracts and reimbursements are, at the municipal level, increasingly and flexibly linked to anti-immigrant positions. A logical phase of carceral capitalism, immigrant detention is presented as the next 'key market' for the prison-industrial-complex by way of municipal and county budgets. Policing, and its present relation to immigration and border control, is a practice and technology fused to the entrance, expansion and maintenance of a carceral state.

However, as with prison construction and the promise of economic boom for rural counties, these gains have not shown up, as anticipated, at the local level, with 287(g) programs often leaving the county to pay for program costs when federal reimbursements fail (Arriaga 2019). Electoral politics around sheriffs, prosecutors, and city council have become key sites for pushback by coalitions that have waged successful anti-287(g) campaigns, ending ICE contracts in key counties in the South (Arriaga 2019). These kinds of carceral investments are now national targets with numerous reports including the Movement for Black Lives Invest/Divest platform (Akbar 2017) reshaping popular consciousness and emergent radical municipal politics, evident in city council movements and peoples' assemblies, as organizers demand divestment from police and jails and pursue power at the municipal and state level. These radical municipalist movements (Gellatly and Rivero 2017) are committed to providing an infrastructure that allows for power building at the community level, including meaningful provisions of safety and security, a governance from below. As McDowell and Fernandez write, divestment, grounded in the US in the work of groups like BYP100, Youth for Justice in Los Angeles, and Law for Black Lives, is an important tactic in efforts to disband and disarm the police, one that seeks 'to reallocate spending on law enforcement to *life giving* services and institutions' (2018: online first, pagination unavailable at time of writing). Such efforts aim to build and expand a diversified set of practices, processes, and institutions, that can, in the present, extract concessions from the state and crowd out its dominance and control – All in a move to stop the placement of people in cages (Loyd, Mitchelson, and Burridge 2013).

Abolitionist aims take shape in direct relationship to the violence of the carceral state, and specifically the police. In this manner, discussions of abolition beg the question of what exactly police are (Wall 2016; Seigel 2018), including ICE, and how immigration and the carceral state are inseparable from the nature, function, and extensionality of police power. 287(g) programs make explicit the vast complex of relations embedded in the concept of police, which is more of an assemblage and intentional multi-level scaling of authority and force than a set of relations between institutions or agencies. Police power exhibits an amorphous, creeping quality, one that Seigel describes as 'vast blank, organized by historical-cultural norms, structured by institutional forms, and made more plastic by a great degree of individual officer discretion ....nothing l(ying) outside of its essential limitless scope' (Seigel 2018, 7–8). As Armenta writes of the period in which 287 (g) was active in Nashville, Tennessee, 'the sheriff's office did not run the program "how it was set up to do." They ran it as they wanted ... to punish Latino immigrants for being undocumented' and without any intention of including public and community input (2017, 128). Coleman and Steusse insist ' ... the particular challenge posed by the devolution of immigration enforcement – or the translation of immigration control into a general law enforcement problem that concerns police and sheriffs – is that, for those who are not subject directly to its violences, it is tough to scrutinize in a proximate sense, and moreover very difficult to substantiate in terms of practice ... where extra-ordinary violences are folded into fugitive, transitory, and fluid routines, landscapes, labor, social reproduction, etc.' (2016, 529–530). This is especially true in Southern rural contexts, those sites, where McClanahan and Linnemann write, we find that the 'darkness on the edge of town,' is 'a materially dark and isolated landscape that allowed the violence of police to be unleashed without the concern of visibility' (2018, 518). Here, 'the willful ignorance or disavowal of the ongoing harms and horrors of increasingly quotidian rural technologies of power facilitate the uninterrupted construction of social order through the normalization of rurality as a geography of harm' in which prisons, CAFOs (concentrated animal feeding operations), slaughterhouses, coal mines, and police violence go unseen (516). This kind of state violence spans both spectacular and ordinary routinized forms of dispossession, destruction, and premature death in intergenerational forms specific to the carceral. Central to this account is the manner in which state actors and institutions commit or abet racial violence in the reproduction of durable systems of inequities framed as protection, safety, and service.

The irony here, as border criminologists and others have made clear (Aas and Bosworth 2013), is that crimmigration, securitization, and states of emergency in relation to border crossings are made up of policies, practices and technologies that impose increasingly harsh suffering on migrants. Securitization itself makes border crossings exponentially more deadly (Weber and Pickering 2011). And a new form of 'legal violence' has taken shape where the threat and reality of detention and deportation make family separation a normalized component of daily life across institutions for many who cross borders (Menjívar and Abrego 2012). Coleman and Stuesse (2016) refer to 287 (g) programs specifically as instrumental in the creation of 'a climate of terror' (58). In the US South, this convergence takes shape against a geographic backdrop of shifting racial compositions of urban and rural counties that have become new destinations for largely Latinx immigrants. Criminologists continue to make clear immigration influx in rustbelt cities and rural areas across the US has, counter to popular portrayals, been an important force in stabilizing economies and crime rates even as anti-immigration stances have intensified (Bauer 2019). Within this framework, the transformation of policing and the carceral state in its most contemporary forms relates expansion, justification, and institutional persistence to immigration enforcement and increasingly volatile political questions of inclusion and expulsion from the polity (Bosworth, Franko, and Pickering 2018).

The prefigurative work of abolition

A discussion of reconceptualizing borders and immigration through violence work is, however, incomplete without attention to movement building around ending violence, specifically the prefigurative work of abolition and the various related forms it takes at local levels (Aiken et al. 2019). As Strunk and Leitner write, 'Most of the academic literature on local immigration enforcement has elaborated on the diffuse, ubiquitous and often paralyzing nature of the biopolitical power of the state vis-à-vis undocumented immigrants. In contrast, in this article, we focus on the contestations that challenge and go beyond repressive state power. We conceive of these not simply as a reaction to state techniques of power, but as productive and affirmative power that promotes alternative imaginaries and institutional change' (Strunk and Leitner 2013, 62). What constitutes an abolitionist approach is a critical question in this work. Foundationally, for abolitionists, contestation and struggle matters, even when those efforts fall short of dramatic social or institutional change or the transformation of power. Abolition is both a lived practice and an analytical space that, minimally, allows for various forms of inclusive understanding of citizenship and community to take shape through alternative ways of ensuring public safety, an always unfinished, reflexive project of principled struggle. These forms span, in practice, messily from policies and proposals that ultimately are reformist and co-opted (as with the use of 'sanctuary cities' to justify abortion restrictions [Stanley-Becker 2019]), to radical configurations that surface community power as protection.

In our case, the raid at Bean Station galvanized the community of Morristown and the surrounding areas. By all accounts, in the hours and days after the raid, a remarkable form of community solidarity took shape in Eastern Tennessee. As Appalachian historian Elizabeth Catte writes "Residents responded with such swiftness and purpose that the New York Times labeled it 'a town that fought back" (2019, 64). A local attorney shared across social media in the hours after the raid:

> Several people have inquired so with the benefit of having just arrived back from Morristown, an update. First, what is needed: Believe it or not, more lawyers. *If you are

> a lawyer of any kind* please consider spending part of your day at St. Patrick's Catholic Church hall in Morristown. You don't have to be an immigration lawyer, you just need to know your usual bs about filling out forms properly. There are real immigration lawyers there to guide you. Translators are available but *translators are also needed and welcome*. Notaries: You are needed for Power of Attorney documents; lots of the detainees had stuff in their names to which their families need access. To give you some idea of the scale of need, something like 100 people were rounded up and shipped out to detention centers in Alabama and Louisiana. Multiply that by the number of spouses and kids left behind. What you should know about them: They are poor, they are heartbroken, and they are terrified. I'm not sharing my personal anecdotes from today, just take my word for it. As for stuff: Wow, Morristown is a town full of decent people. Food was being delivered and passed around, and I wonder if there is anything left in the local Walmart. HOWEVER, you know how it is when something blows up: a lot of attention at first. So please stay tuned in case the material need comes back. And thanks to everybody who inquired and who helped. And, as always, #fuckICE. (Salty language, pearl clutchers, but we live in an evil empire so it fits.)

In the midst of improvised triage, the community focused on the immediate needs and suffering of immigrant families and their work mirrored a kind of pragmatic prefigurative abolition first response – in particular, one that potentially disappears the police – and, in this case, is a response TO police violence. As Seigel writes, 'The things police do that do not have to do with "crime" could – and should – be done by other bodies: social workers, emts, fire fighters, traffic directors, garbage collectors, counselors, neighborhood associations, friends, and so on. That, not so incidentally, is the core of a practical, stepwise process of police abolition: begin to give to nonviolent agencies, piece by piece, the tasks currently allocated to men and women in blue' (2018, 7). As Walia writes, 'The main principle I work around in these individual instances is the principle of self-determination. If I am supporting someone facing deportation or partner violence, what do they need? Are there effective alternatives to the state that exist that I can suggest or do they feel the need to engage with the state in order to reduce harm or to access safety?' (2019, 15). The abolitionist imaginary is then an important kind of collective labor and solidarity built in the process of struggle and response – through developing perceptions and beliefs in the very possibility of power, via a political technology and infrastructure of organizing, that achieves forms of solidarity and safety often in what nationally are constructed as intractable political spaces of white supremacy.

These states of emergency point to a kind of care upon which an everyday abolition is contingent, framed within the 'potential to challenge the legitimacy of the state directly. That is, by taking over basic state functions, like emergency response, these practices could lead to a dual power situation wherein neighborhoods could self-organize outside of the system, much like the Black Panther Party's community self-determination programs' (McDowell and Fernandez 2018). These kinds of acts and practices fundamentally shift the day-to-day ways of life for individuals, families and communities in a manner in which the community is not simply being acted upon but is working against state violence to sustain life. And they are already central ways of existence for those designated as within the frame of irregular and unauthorized immigrant life in the US. Of course, a white supremacist counterinsurgent effort, inseparable from particular forms of racialized misogyny, seeks to violently put down these efforts. Across the US, efforts to surface care are increasingly criminalized, whether leaving water for migrants in desert borders, the criminalization of protest, bans from campus and public common spaces, and the sudden materialization of the sheer force of the state in detention and deportation. These historic conjunctures of uprising and counterinsurgency mark the contours of a larger abolition project of self-determination and remembrance where community power building seeks to disrupt the carceral and settler colonial state.

As Segrave argues, careful attention to forms of differential inclusion, 'offers a useful conceptual map for examining the everyday subversion of the nation-state's bordering practices "from below"' (2019, 206). In that sense, the push for 287(g) and the raid that occurred in its midst mobilized a kind of historic resistance led by a coalition of immigrant and refugee organizations, including the Tennessee Immigrant and Refugee Rights Coalition (TIRCC, founded in 2003), Bridge Refugee Services, Centro Hispano, Allies of Knoxville's Immigrant Neighbors (AKIN), Mijente and ConMijente, Face to Face Knox, and a number of groups working in conjunction with other regional labor and abolition organizations including the Highlander Research and Education Center, No Exceptions Prison Collective, Jobs With Justice – East Tennessee, The Poor People's Campaign of Tennessee, Resist ICE Nashville. These groups interfaced with a variety of health, education, defense attorney, domestic/sexual violence advocates, and faith-based organizations, forming temporary networks of support and direct action. This regional work took shape against a recurrent national narrative of the region as impoverished, retrograde and fundamentally politically conservative. And yet, in the hours after the raid, organizers raised 60,000 USD for the targeted immigrant families.

This kind of movement work is situated in the arc of a much longer history of the region, one whose understanding of abolition is foundational to its relationship to the transatlantic slave trade, labor, and racial capitalism. Cross-border activism and challenges to the transnational prison-industrial-complex are foundational to abolition efforts and its key constructs of the South. In the project of Southern survival and radical power, organizers from across coalitions draw from shared histories and longterm power building efforts to work across differences toward principled struggle (Catte 2018, 2019; Harkins and McCarroll 2019; Woodard-Henderson 2017, 2019). The notion of the South that they rely upon is one embedded in a construct that is at once local and global – they draw on coalitions and alliances with migrant workers and freedom movements from across Central, South, and Latin America as well as Africa. For instance, the arrival of People's Assemblies is rooted geographically and ideologically in these contexts and, like the first Southern Movement Assembly in 2012, have, in the US, taken shape predominantly in the South. Emergent spaces for meetings, strategy sessions and freedom circles, assemblies pursue a radical imagining of city politics (Gellatly and Rivero 2017), safety, housing, education, youth power, immigrant justice, healthcare, economic alternatives, environmental change, and international solidarity. In just over a decade, they have incorporated thousands of people into their work. The South materializes in other ways too: organizers rely upon the work of community building being done on the south side of Chicago (Ransby 2019) or Detroit, spaces that intersect with neoliberal dispossession and low income, racialized social life. The South, always, is defined by its border work: the outmigration of its young people and the arrival of a growing new immigrant and African American population, thereby making abolition in relation to immigrant and racial justice key features of the new South (Conley 2013).

Here, material and epistemological interventions take shape in a variety of forms: campaigns, direct actions, and various politics of refusal (non-participation, boycotts, occupations, sanctuary); strategies and tactics to build key coalitions and solidarities via local and regional politics; grassroots electoral organizing; facilitated trainings, workshops and convergences; a new media presence built upon podcasts, webinars, toolkits and curricula, all of which are producing an intensively heightened public presence. Just a few examples include grassroots efforts and campaigns to abolish/end cash bail (Southerners on New Ground [SONG] 2017); prisoner strikes, such as the Free Alabama Movement which launched a national strike across 12 states, 29 prisons, and 24,000 people (Berger 2016; Chase 2015); and moratorium projects on prison construction and jail expansion, such as the fight against a new federal prison sited on a coal mine in Letcher County, Kentucky. Prisoners and organizers from local and regional groups such as the Letcher Governance Project, Fight Toxic Prisons, the Prison Ecology Project, and the Abolitionist Law Center have built an impressive and ongoing resistance against the prison that halted construction on the most expensive federal prison in US history. Sited in Eastern Kentucky, where 8 prisons form the heart of Central Appalachia's extensive prison geography, organizers actively imagine alternative economic futures that fuse Appalachian justice and anti-prison activism, advocating 'for a just and diversified regional economy that is not built on fossil fuel industries and prisons' (Ryerson and Schept 2018).

In Knoxville, organizers had committed themselves to providing a community buffer to 287(g)'s terror. These efforts focused on support and shelter for those directly affected, building, across ten years of 287(g) threat, an infrastructure of emergency first response (whether in response to detention, deportation, or release). They also worked to maintain a regular presence at city council and public meetings. They showed up at a nondescript cul-de-sac strip malls where ICE check in facilities materialized (what they named Wednesday Witnessing). And they pursued a popular form of education, establishing a media and public relations network, a clear social media presence, and providing frequent community, campaign, and educational events. Eventually, efforts took shape to build their own database to scrape daily data posts by the county on immigrants who were being processed at the local jail.

Importantly, organizers also strategically relied upon the law. In response to efforts to expand the jail, organizers worked with prisoners to launch a class action lawsuit from the jail and AKIN brought forward a lawsuit against the Sheriff's Office which had refused to provide access to public jail records that might better reveal the impact of 287(g). Furthermore, current bills on the table in 2019 reflect efforts to counter the state's harsh turn on immigration, seeking to relieve state and local governments from some of the more disastrous provisions: SB0931/HB110 seeks to exempt key agencies such as police, health services, and education institutions from asking questions and/or enforcing laws related to identity status. SB0507/HB0558 would require the state to reimburse localities and municipalities for expenses incurred in the enforcement, including costs of litigation. Finally, in a class action lawsuit launched by seven people targeted by the Bean Station ICE Raid (who had worked at the plant for a combined 38 years) and the Southern Poverty Law Center, plaintiffs argue the raid violated the Fourth Amendment on unreasonable search and seizure and excessive force and the Fifth Amendment right to equal protection – all on the basis of racial profiling: law enforcement detained only those workers who appeared to be Latino and didn't question their immigration status until after detaining them.

These efforts all follow generationally from histories of care and survival strategy that are specific to the region and the intersection of immigrant, racial and labor justice, forms of insurgent safety (McDowell 2019) and efforts directed at movement-building, research, radical education, and cultural work. In this way, abolition work is both directly stated (Abolish ICE) and other times, in its reliance upon the law and the necessity of the state, strategic and reformist. It models how abolition itself manifests as a response to state violence (not yet its own way of being) and does so through a variety of not unproblematic liberal scripts and forms. In the end, it materializes ephemerally as a moment in which to take note of elements of world-inhabiting that might be used to end the violence of racialized life and the state. Communities, organizers, and the state are caught in a continuous effort to materially and discursively shift the terms on which safety is configured. Organizing efforts, whether openly abolitionist or reformist, are increasingly more carefully framed in a manner so as not to leave power intact, nor expand the carceral footprint of harm, or reinforce punitive ideologies and capacities. New forms of accountability in the analysis of violence and borders take shape. And the abolitionist efforts in Eastern Tennessee take shape amidst local and regional efforts to end money bail, build community defense in court, stop school pushout, and build grassroots and community power through socialist and independent political power. This represents a significant convergence of work by rural socialists, queer and trans organizers, immigrant communities, labor organizers, and new Black power movements whose tactics originate out of struggles that have always already been taking place in the everyday imagining practices of Black, Southern, and Appalachian communities past, present and future. And this is happening in the state of Tennessee, the state with the longest life sentences with parole, some of the worst and most obstructionist voting restoration processes for those convicted of a felony, a resurgent death penalty, and a region whose state actors welcomed ICE.

Conclusion

At the heart of immigration and abolition is a politics of refusal grounded in belonging and the freedom of mobility. It takes shape against the efforts of a toxic, dangerous state, that requires immense amounts of labor and energy to withstand and survive. These spaces model how racialized communities survive the end of the world. Abolition materializes only in the destruction of a society that could produce the kind of superfluousness performed by state violence in relation to borders. It arrives, in fact, only at the end of the world. As Fred Moten asks 'What is, so to speak, the object of abolition? Not so much the abolition of prisons but the abolition of a society that could have prisons, that could have slavery, that could have the wage, and therefore not abolition as the elimination of anything but abolition as the founding of a new society' (2004, 114).

What this looks like is pre-modeled on a day in which the world-as-it-is-known ends for a community of immigrant workers, with families torn apart and terror taking shape. In all of this, a community that had largely supported electoral issues dedicated to anti-immigration paradoxically found itself in a politics of land, relationship, and reciprocity. This required a recognition, as Indigenous scholar Glen Coulthard insists, that 'Our claims to land and conceptions of nationhood are not based on an understanding of land that is something to be exploited or horded to the exclusion of others. Land is a relationship based on the obligations we have to other people and the other than-human relations that constitute the land itself' (Walia 2015). Grounded in a kind of temporal shared belonging, the violence of the state and capital left them struggling for a different and oppositional kind of self-determination in a moment of trauma. Fraught, flawed, and not without its liberal mythologies of charity and problematic forms of care, an impulse for an otherwise briefly formed at a specific conjuncture of internalized border violence. Understanding the long project of land, labor and Southern emancipation and its counterinsurgencies is of vital importance strategically in the struggle for abolition as transformation hinges upon the possibility of weaving together practices that are variable and localized – tuned in to the conditions of historical sites of violence, like the South and Appalachia. Furthermore, enclosure and occupation take variable forms across the planet even as new forms of social life are imagined and take shape, contextually, contingently. As multiple forms of abolition, coalition, and violence materialize across geographic regions and the globe, critical and nuanced accounts of the local possibilities of transformative justice within neoliberal racial capitalism are urgent. Abolition's long history, from transatlantic slavery to multiple forms of detention, criminalization, incarceration and policing is inseparable from the importance of place and the improvised local, temporal practice of freedom.

Notes

1. See US National Mapp of 287(g) agreements @ https://www.ilrc.org/national-map-287 g-agreements
2. 'For instance, a report by researchers at the University of North Carolina on the costs and consequences of 287(g) in that state found that the program's first year of operation in Mecklenburg County cost $5.3 million, and in Alamance County $4.8 million. More recently, the American Immigration Council reports that Sheriff Ed Gonzalez of Harris County, Texas has announced he is terminating that county's 287(g) agreement and will reallocate the program cost of $675,000 and put it toward other priorities, such as raising the department's clearance rates of major crimes. Aside from operating costs such as paying personnel to carry out federal law enforcement duties, 287(g) significantly increases the risk of liability for participating jurisdictions. In one case that drew national attention, Nashville/Davidson Metro Government ended up paying hundreds of thousands of dollars to settle a civil rights case brought by Juana Villegas, a pregnant woman who was forced to labor in shackles after being arrested for driving without a license.[vi] Most observers agree that the sizeable settlement in her case played a large role in Sheriff Daron Hall's decision to terminate Nashville's 287(g) agreement in 2012.' (AKIN website)
3. 'Despite commonplace assurances by those in charge of 287(g) programs that they focus on getting rid of dangerous criminals who threaten community safety, over the lifetime of the 287(g) program nationwide, numbers show that a startling number of those deported were originally brought in on minor charges. In 2011, the Migration Policy Institute reported that a shocking half of 287(g) activity focused on people accused of misdemeanors and traffic offenses.[vii] Closer to home, a 2012 report on Davidson County's 5-year experiment with 287(g) found that the vast majority of 287(g) deportation proceedings there (some 10,000 over the five years) were triggered by non-violent, misdemeanor crimes, many of which never even resulted in a conviction, most of them minor traffic charges.[viii] AKIN's analysis of police-ICE collaboration in the Knox County jail indicate that, over a one-year period, 90% of people brought into the jail with ICE holds were charged with a misdemeanor, including 22% who were charged with nothing more severe than a traffic offense.[ix]In 287(g) jurisdictions, immigrant families are torn apart, business activities are disrupted, and community networks are shredded, all with little benefit but major cost to the larger community.' (AKIN website)
4. '287(g) exacerbates and encourages biased policing practices. Public officials in some 287(g) jurisdictions have made overtly racist statements and have supported blatantly discriminatory

practices. But infamous rogue jurisdictions like Maricopa County in Arizona or Alamance County in North Carolina are hardly the only problem. A study of Davidson County's 287(g) program found that during its 5-year lifetime, from 2007 to 2012, racial profiling and bias based on appearance, ethnicity or language skills had affected many Metro Nashville residents at key points including police stops, at the point of arrest, and at the moment of booking. Sheriff Jones claimed that his officers "never have and never will" engage in racial profiling of Knox County residents.[xi] However, Knox County officers, like those elsewhere, are not immune to conscious and unconscious racial bias. Residents in Knox County have complained for years and continue to complain that profiling by local law enforcement officers is a problem.[xii] Of course, Sheriff Jones should express opposition to racial profiling, but his denial that there was even a challenge raises far more questions than it answers. Although Jones argued that he "won't let things happen and get out of hand like they have in other places,"[xiii] he offered no plan to avoid civil rights abuses. Sheriff Jones' refusal to acknowledge the potential for a problem in Knox County was, in the words of the Rev. Dr. John Butler, president of the Knoxville Chapter of the NAACP, "inconsistent with taking leadership to identify, address and train officers for the actual eradication of racial profiling."[xiv] Sheriff Spangler should publicly articulate any efforts KCSO has undertaken to address concerns of racial profiling.' (AKIN website)

5. '287(g) drives a wedge between immigrant communities and local law enforcement officers. This exacerbates vulnerabilities of already marginalized communities as immigrant victims and witnesses of crime avoid police for fear of immigration consequences. Sheriff Jones said that he understands how difficult it is to cultivate community trust, stating, "We work very hard in [minority] communities to gain that trust . . . and they trust us to do just what I said: be good stewards and make sure there are no shortcuts taken and make sure there are no prejudices, no biases and no racial profiling."[xv] However, based on the Sheriff's refusal to engage transparently with the community around 287(g), his dehumanizing "cordwood" statement following rejection of the previous 287(g) application, and his denial of the existence of a single instance of racial profiling in Knox County, we doubt that minority communities in Knox County agree that the Sheriff earned their trust. Changes both rumored and real in immigration enforcement have already heightened fear and have increased mistrust between local law enforcement and the immigrant community. Implementation of the 287(g) program and the detention bed contract have only exacerbated that divide. Sheriff Spangler should work to address the gap in community trust left by his predecessor.' (AKIN website)
6. "ICE claims that 287(g) removes dangerous criminal immigrants by screening for immigration violations among those taken into participating jails. Similarly, Sheriff Jones stated to the press, 'If you're here illegally, and you're a law abiding citizen, you'll never know 287(g) exists.'[xvi] This point has been echoed by Sheriff Spangler, who argued, 'If you're not out doing something you're not supposed to be doing, you have nothing to worry about. . . we're not going to be out looking for people who are undocumented or illegal.'[xvii] However, research clearly indicates that the program acts as an indiscriminate funnel, sucking in immigrants picked up on minor charges, and putting them into deportation proceedings. In fact, Sheriff Jones appeared to concede this issue in the 'Needs Assessment' he submitted to ICE in February 2017 to indicate his continued desire to join the 287(g) program. This document – made public only through records requests filed by advocates – indicates that the top five reasons foreign-born people are arrested and brought into the Knox County jail under current practice do not fit the picture of a program that will only be ridding the community of dangerous criminals. Of the five leading charges, three are traffic offenses (Driving without a License, Driving without a License in Possession, Driving while Privilege Suspended) and two are offenses related to alcohol (Driving Under the Influence and Public Intoxication).[xviii]Perhaps even more telling, KCSO reports that approximately 20 immigrant prisoners per month (or 240 per year) are presently the subject of ICE detainers in Knox County. However, they estimate that under a 287(g) agreement, Knox County would turn over 1800 detainees per year (or 150 per month). This is a huge increase. Simple math says that unless KCSO has been failing to apprehend over a thousand dangerous criminal

immigrants every year, they will not be able to meet this steep new quota without pulling in over a thousand non-dangerous immigrants under the new regime." (AKIN website)

7. For additional accounts of the raid, see: Jordan (2018). ICE Came for a Tennessee Town's Immigrants. The Town Fought Back. *The New York Times*. Accessed at https://www.nytimes.com/interactive/2018/06/11/us/tennessee-immigration-trump.html on 1 May 2019; Wickendon (2018). ICE Comes to a Small Town in Tennessee. *The New Yorker*. Accessed at https://www.newyorker.com/podcast/political-scene/ice-comes-to-a-small-town-in-tennessee on 1 May 2019.

Disclosure statement

No potential conflict of interest was reported by the author.

References

Aas, K. F., and M. Bosworth, Eds.. 2013. *The Borders of Punishment: Migration, Citizenship, and Social Exclusion*. London: Oxford University Press.

Aiken, S., S. J. Silverman, H. Walia, K. Pate, and S. Benslimane. 2019. "Can We End Migrant Detention?" *Policy Options*. Accessed June 10. https://policyoptions.irpp.org/magazines/may-2019/can-we-end-migrant-detention/on

Akbar, A. 2017. "Toward a Radical Imagination of Law." *New York University Law Review* 93: 405–479.

Armenta, A. 2012. "From Sheriff's Deputies to Immigration Officers: Screening Immigrant Status in a Tennessee Jail." *Law & Policy* 34 (2): 191–210. doi:10.1111/j.1467-9930.2011.00359.x.

Armenta, A. 2017. *Protect, Serve, and Deport: The Rise of Policing as Immigration Enforcement*. Berkeley, CA: Univ of California Press.

Arriaga, F. 2017. "Relationships between the Public and Crimmigration Entities in North Carolina: A 287 (G) Program Focus." *Sociology of Race and Ethnicity* 3 (3): 417–431. doi:10.1177/2332649217700923.

Arriaga, F. 2019. "Banking on Immigrants." Scalawag. Accessed 27 May 2019. https://www.scalawagmagazine.org/2019/05/north-carolina-ice/?fbclid=IwAR1Ip4ECzArCQpsXDfUDKf5dHaQ_b7lXZHv2KVJqYw5MzAuw_BoglAXjhSo

Aviram, H. 2015. *Cheap on Crime: Recession-era Politics and the Transformation of American Punishment*. Berkeley, CA: University of California Press.

Bauer, M. 2019. "Trump Is Lying about Immigrant Crime – And the Research Proves It." *Southern Poverty Law Center*. Accessed 1 June 2019. https://www.splcenter.org/news/2019/05/17/trump-lying-about-immigrant-crime-and-research-proves-it

Beckett, K. 2018. "The Politics, Promise, and Peril of Criminal Justice Reform in the Context of Mass Incarceration." *Annual Review of Criminology* 1: 235–259. doi:10.1146/annurev-criminol-032317-092458.

Berger, D. (2016). "Rattling the Cages." *The Jacobin*. Accessed 11 May 2019. https://www.jacobinmag.com/2016/11/prison-strike-slavery-attica-racism-incarceration/on

Bosworth, M., K. Franko, and S. Pickering. 2018. "Punishment, Globalization and Migration Control: 'Get Them the Hell Out of Here." *Punishment & Society* 20 (1): 34–53. doi:10.1177/1462474517738984.

Catte, E. 2018. *What You are Getting Wrong about Appalachia*. Cleveland, OH: Belt Publishing.
Catte, E., Ed. 2019. ""Introduction." Forum: Left Elsewhere: Finding the Future in Radical Rural America." *Boston Review* 9. Accessed 08 April 2020. http://bostonreview.net/forum/elizabeth-catte-finding-future-radical-rural-america
Chase, R. T. 2015. "We are Not Slaves: Rethinking the Rise of Carceral States through the Lens of the Prisoners' Rights Movement." *The Journal of American History* 102 (1): 73–86. doi:10.1093/jahist/jav317.
Coleman, M. 2007. "Immigration Geopolitics beyond the Mexico–US Border." *Antipode* 39 (1): 54–76. doi:10.1111/j.1467-8330.2007.00506.x.
Coleman, M. 2012. "The "Local" Migration State: The Site-specific Devolution of Immigration Enforcement in the US South." *Law & Policy* 34 (2): 159–190. doi:10.1111/j.1467-9930.2011.00358.x.
Coleman, M., and A. Stuesse. 2016. "The Disappearing State and the Quasi-Event of Immigration Control." *Antipode* 48 (3): 524–543. doi:10.1111/anti.12209.
Conley, M., and F. Ansley. 2019. "What Is 287(g) and Why Do We Oppose It (Updated)." *Allies of Knoxville's Immigrant Neighbors*. June 1. https://weareakin.wordpress.com/2019/03/05/what-is-287g-and-why-do-we-oppose-it-updated/on
Conley, M. E. 2013. "Immigrant Rights in the Nuevo South: Enforcement and Resistance at the Borderlands of Illegality." Doctoral Dissertation. Knoxville, TN.
Davis, A. Y. 2011. *Abolition Democracy: Beyond Empire, Prisons, and Torture*. New York, NY: Seven Stories Press.
Du Bois WEB. 1935. *Black Reconstruction in the United States, 1860–1880*. New York: Atheneum.
Gellatly, J., and M. Rivero. 2017. "Radical Municipalism: Fearless Cities." *Stir to Action*. Accessed 23 May 2019. https://www.stirtoaction.com/article/fearless-cities
Harkins, A., and M. McCarroll. 2019. *Appalachian Reckoning: A Region Responds to Hillbilly Elegy*. Morgantown, WV: West Virginia University Press.
Hernandez, K. L., K. G. Muhammad, andH. A. Thompson. 2015. "Introduction: Constructing the carceral state." *J. Am. Hist.*102(10): 18–24.
Lakin, M. 2019. "UT Professor and AKIN Activist Sues Knox Sheriff for Records on 287(g) Deal with ICE." *Knoxville News Sentinel*. Accessed June 10. https://www.knoxnews.com/story/news/local/2019/04/25/knox-sheriff-lawsuit-ice-cooperation-287-g/3555250002/
Loyd, J. M., M. Mitchelson, and A. Burridge, Eds. 2013. *Beyond Walls and Cages: Prisons, Borders, and Global Crisis*. Athens GA: University of Georgia Press.
McClanahan, B., and T. Linnemann. 2018. "Darkness on the Edge of Town: Visual Criminology and the "Black Sites" of the Rural." *Deviant Behavior* 39 (4): 512–524. doi:10.1080/01639625.2017.1407111.
McDowell, M. G. 2019. "Insurgent Safety: Theorizing Alternatives to State Protection." *Theoretical Criminology* 23 (1): 43–59. doi:10.1177/1362480617713984.
McDowell, M. G., and L. A. Fernandez. 2018. "'Disband, Disempower, and Disarm': Amplifying the Theory and Practice of Police Abolition." *Critical Criminology* 26 (3): 373–391. doi:10.1007/s10612-018-9400-4.
Menjívar, C., and L. Abrego. 2012. "Legal Violence: Immigration Law and the Lives of Central American Immigrants." *American Journal of Sociology* 117 (5). doi:10.1086/663575.
Moten, F., and S. Harney. 2004. "The University and the Undercommons: Seven Theses." *Social Text* 22 (2): 101–115. doi:10.1215/01642472-22-2_79-101.
Ransby, B. 2019."The Rising Black Left Movement Behind Chicago's Historic Elections." *The Nation*. Accessed 30 May 2019. www.thenation.com/article/chicago-election-mayor black-lives-matter/
Ryerson, S., and J. Schept. 2018 "Building Prisons in Appalachia." *Boston Review*. Accessed 25 May 2019. http://bostonreview.net/law-justice/sylvia-ryerson-judah-schept-building-prisons-appalachia
Schoenfeld, H. 2018. *Building the Prison State: Race and the Politics of Mass Incarceration*. Chicago, IL: University of Chicago Press.
Segrave, M. 2019. "Theorizing Sites and Strategies of Differential Inclusion: Unlawful Migrant Workers in Australia." *Theoretical Criminology* 23 (2): 194–210. doi:10.1177/1362480619827527.

Seigel, M. 2018. *Violence Work: State Power and the Limits of Police*. Durham, NC: Duke University Press.

Soguk, N., and G. Whitehall. 1999. "Wandering Grounds: Transversality, Identity, Territoriality, and Movement." *Millennium* 28 (3): 675–698. doi:10.1177/03058298990280030301.

Southerners on New Ground. 2017 May 16. "A Labor of Love: Black Mama's Bail Out Action Reflection." Accessed September 1. http://southernersonnewground.org/2017/05/a-labor-of-love/

Stanley-Becker, I. 2019. "Five Men Outlaw Abortion in a Texas Town, Declaring a 'Sanctuary City for the Unborn'." *Washington Post*. Accessed June 14. https://www.washingtonpost.com/nation/2019/06/13/waksom-texas-outlaws-abortion-five-men/on

Strunk, C., and H. Leitner. 2013. "Resisting Federal–Local Immigration Enforcement Partnerships: Redefining 'Secure Communities' and Public Safety." *Territory, Politics, Governance* 1 (1): 62–85. doi:10.1080/21622671.2013.769894.

Terkel, A., and E. Foley. 2013. "Tennessee Sheriff Ready To Stack Undocumented Immigrants In Jail 'Like Cordwood'." *Huffington Post*. Accessed 1 May 2019. https://www.huffpost.com/entry/immigrants-cordwood-jj-jones_n_3795634?guccounter=1&guce_referrer=aHR0cHM6Ly93d3cuZ29vZ2xlLmNvbS8&guce_referrer_sig=AQAAAAxMNiHxN2XkT-Qyr3r2KK6QCCWo2LTKDHFtpWdPsWEHowBLEv0GkulsuSH5qmM8Hbysh7tUTuUQGeJtnUaqSR59-eSkULZ_WrdxpP3JP6UEO7iC107pZ-hk9C1oX5VXrv4pSk3uAsUoTcS1ylAfHMxxgdYYtKITKI3-8yRe_zAR)

Walia, H. 2013. *Undoing Border Imperialism*. Vol. 6. New York: Ak Press.

Walia, H. 2015. "'Land Is a Relationship': In Conversation with Glen Coulthard on Indigenous Nationhood." *Rabble*. Accessed 1 June 2019. http://rabble.ca/columnists/2015/01/land-relationship-conversation-glen-coulthard-on-indigenous-nationhood

Wall, T. 2016. "Ordinary Emergency: Drones, Police, and Geographies of Legal Terror." *Antipode* 48 (4): 1122–1139. doi:10.1111/anti.12228.

Weber, L. 2019. "From State-centric to Transversal Borders: Resisting the 'Structurally Embedded Border' in Australia." *Theoretical Criminology* 23 (2): 228–246. doi:10.1177/1362480618819795.

Weber, L., and S. Pickering. 2011. *Globalization and Borders: Death at the Global Frontier*. Dordrecht: Springer.

Wickendon, D. 2018. "ICE Comes to a Small Town in Tennessee." *The New Yorker*. Accessed 1 May 2019. https://www.newyorker.com/podcast/political-scene/ice-comes-to-a-small-town-in-tennessee

Winders, J. 2007. "Bringing Back the (B)order: Post-9/11 Politics of Immigration, Borders, and Belonging in the Contemporary US South." *Antipode* 39 (5): 920–942. doi:10.1111/j.1467-8330.2007.00563.x.

Wonders, N. A. 2006. "Global Flows, Semi-permeable Borders and New Channels of Inequality." In S. Pickering, and L. Weber, Eds., *Borders, Mobility and Technologies of Control*. 63–86. Dordrecht: Springer.

Wong, T. K. 2012. "287 (G) and the Politics of Interior Immigration Control in the United States: Explaining Local Cooperation with Federal Immigration Authorities." *Journal of Ethnic and Migration Studies* 38 (5): 737–756. doi:10.1080/1369183X.2012.667983.

Woodard-Henderson, A.-L. 2017 September 1. "How We Can Organize The South To Save The Country." *Huffington Post*. Accessed 21 May 2019. https://www.huffpost.com/entry/organize-the-south-save-the-country_b_59a9699ce4b0dfaafcefc442

Woodard-Henderson, A.-L. 2019. ""Legacies of Resistance." Forum: Left Elsewhere: Finding the Future in Radical Rural America." *Boston Review* 9 (44.1). Accessed 08 April 2020. http://bostonreview.net/forum/finding-future-radical-rural-america/ash-lee-woodard-henderson-legacies-resistance

Migrant justice as reproductive justice: birthright citizenship and the politics of immigration detention for pregnant women in Canada

Salina Abji[1] and Lindsay Larios

ABSTRACT

This research develops an analytical framework for theorizing the lived experiences of pregnant women in immigration detention, and then applies this framework in considering possibilities for transforming citizenship and the allocation of rights. We focus on the Canadian case, examining the 2.5-year detention of a refugee claimant who was detained while 3 months pregnant. In line with feminist intersectional and critical migration scholars, we argue that immigration detention is a form of structural violence against non-citizens that is gendered, raced, and classed. However, our analytical framework extends existing scholarship by centring reproductive justice as a key axis along which the structural violence of non-citizenship is enacted. Our findings are thus critical of reforms to detention that frame pregnant women as biologically vulnerable: we instead argue for a structural understanding of vulnerability that centres reproductive justice as a fundamental component of migrant justice in envisioning a decarceral future.

In February 2013, the Canadian Border Services Agency (CBSA) detained Glory Anawa, a refugee claimant from Cameroon. Glory was pregnant at the time: she had fled to Canada out of fear that she would be subject to female genital mutilation as a result of having a child out of wedlock (Browne 2015; CBC 2015). Glory was held at the immigration detention centre in Toronto and gave birth to a baby boy on 25 August 2013, whom she named Alpha. A Canadian citizen by birth, Alpha spent his first 2 years in an immigration detention centre because the Canadian government refused to release Glory, despite media reports of their detention in national news along with activists' calls to either release them or provide alternatives to detention. According to media reports, Glory was subsequently removed in November 2015 with her Canadian-born child in tow (Cain 2016).

In this research, we centre the lived experiences of detainees like Glory, asking what such cases illuminate about the structural violence of immigration detention (Esposito et al. 2019). While such cases are increasingly the subject of activist campaigns and media coverage, there is comparatively little scholarship analyzing the intersections between migrant justice and reproductive rights in the immigration detention system (although see Arshad et al. 2018; Hartry 2012a; Messing et al. 2020). Likewise, a growing body of scholarship examines issues of gender and immigration detention – for example, in the context of Greece (Esposito et al. 2019; Bosworth et al. 2016; Bosworth et al. 2018), Italy (Esposito et al. 2016), and Portugal (Matos and Esposito 2019), yet few have focused specifically on pregnancy or examined immigration detention as a site of reproductive injustice. Due to a significant and growing grey literature examining the experiences of pregnant women and children in immigration detention (e.g. Kraft-Stolar 2015; Ashdown and James 2010) and health-studies literature examining experiences of pregnancy and birth for migrant women in Canada and beyond (e.g. Almeida et al. 2013; Munro *et al.* 2013), we believe this is an issue that calls for more focused scholarly attention.[2] We argue that scholarly attention to pregnant women in detention – as well as other sub-populations who may be fewer in numbers in detention but are nevertheless present – can help deepen a structural analysis of immigration controls in ways that mobilize rather than close-off possibilities for transformational change. Our project is therefore two-fold: (1) to develop an analytical framework for theorizing the lived experiences of pregnant women in detention and the resultant implications for a structural analysis of immigration controls; and (2) to apply this analytical framework in considering possibilities for transformational change in the Canadian context and beyond.

To meet these objectives, we offer a theoretically informed reading of Glory Anawa's experiences in detention to show how current migration scholarship on detention falls short in explaining the intersecting forms of structural violence that pregnant women detainees like Glory experience in an increasingly securitized immigration system. In doing so, we draw from two distinct literatures: feminist intersectional scholarship on reproductive justice (Ross 2017; Larios 2019a) as well as political theories of citizenship that challenge the allocation of rights by virtue of a birthright 'lottery' (Bosniak 2006; Shachar 2009; Abji 2017). By combining insights from feminist intersectional and citizenship literatures to develop our analytical framework, we argue that immigration detention is a growing site where reproductive rights as fundamental human rights are being systematically violated, with particular implications for women of colour from the global south. Scholarly critiques of detention, we argue, must therefore account for the multiple forms of structural violence that shape migrant (in)justice in detention – not only across race, gender, class and other axes of difference (Bosworth et al. 2018; Esposito et al. 2019), but also in terms of the embodied and material realities of social reproduction experienced by individuals, families, and communities as they interface with immigration controls.

With our analytical framework developed, we then turn to a discussion of possibilities for transformational change that centre reproductive justice and the inequalities of birthright citizenship as fundamental components of a migrant justice framework. Here we reflect on recent reforms to the Canadian immigration detention system introduced by the federal government and the Canadian Border Services Agency in 2017. We argue that the CBSA's naming of pregnant women as one of several 'vulnerable' groups where detention is to be 'avoided' should be a cause for suspicion rather than celebration by those seeking to advance migrant justice. Indeed, we show how state discourses of vulnerability as biological rather than structural – as in the case of the

CBSA's framing of pregnant women – work to undermine access to reproductive justice while reinforcing racialized and gendered framings of black and brown men as criminalized threats to the security of the Canadian public (Razack 2007). Moreover, we question opaque state promises of 'detention avoidance' as a proposed reform, arguing that such practices constitute carceral technologies that reinforce rather than protect against migrant vulnerability. The research thus advances an important distinction between detention avoidance and detention abolition, arguing that the former should not be presented as a 'softer' version of the latter but rather as operating in opposition to logics of migrant justice.

Our paper concludes with a discussion of what migrant justice as reproductive justice might look like in a world where Glory and Alpha's structural vulnerabilities are centred rather than systematically violated. Taking the Canadian case as an illustration, we point to both the possibilities and limitations of abolitionist claims to end immigration detention. In doing so, our discussion highlights the risks of critiquing birthright citizenship in a context where alternative models for rights allocation are not in place – leading to, for example, a potential dove-tailing with right-wing, anti-immigrant efforts to curtail the already-limited benefits of birthright citizenship in Canada (Abji 2017; Larios 2019b). Ultimately, we align ourselves with an abolitionist vision of migrant justice and extend this vision by calling for new models of rights and membership that address deeply embedded inequalities of birthright citizenship and gendered social reproduction in contemporary societies.

From reproductive to birthright justice: advancing feminist intersectional approaches to immigration detention

Reproductive justice is an intersectional feminist framework developed by Black feminist activists and scholars in the US in the 1990s.[3] Reproductive justice centres the claim that 'all fertile persons and persons who reproduce and become parents require a safe and dignified context for these most fundamental human experiences' (Ross and Solinger 2017, 9). To this end, three rights, in particular, are emphasized: (1) the right to *not* have a child; (2) the right to have a child; and (3) the right to parent children in healthy environments. Importantly, the framework grounds these reproductive rights in a structural analysis of gendered, racialized, and class-based oppressions, among other intersecting axes. Activists who coined the approach aimed to move beyond the pro-choice/pro-life dichotomy popularized through reproductive rights discourse and politics to this day, which fails to capture the reproductive challenges and realities facing racialized women, in particular, and other marginalized people, more generally (Price 2010; Ross 2017; Smith 2005). Instead, Black and other women of colour feminists offered a systemic analysis of the ways in which racialized and poor women's reproductive choices have been used as battlegrounds in the shaping of (white) national identity and nation-building projects (Anthias et al. 1992; Hartry 2012b; Roberts 1997; Ross 2017).

In applying a reproductive justice framework in our study, we join these activists and scholars in emphasizing the structural effects of white supremacy, settler colonialism, global capitalism, and hetero-patriarchy in differentially affecting the reproductive rights of marginalized groups across multiple axes of difference (Glenn 2015; Stasiulis and Bakan 2005; Ross 2017; Walia 2013). In our project, we emphasize the salience of reproductive justice as a citizenship issue. To build our analytical model, we draw from three strands of citizenship studies: research on the effects of precarious non-citizenship for diverse migrant groups (Goldring and Landolt 2013); a growing sub-field on the securitization of citizenship and borders in a crimmigration era (Stumpf 2006); and scholarly debates on the politics of birthright (Bosniak 2006; Shachar 2009). In what follows, we bring these strands of citizenship studies into conversation with scholarship on reproductive justice, in order to tease out the structural vulnerabilities experienced by pregnant women in immigration detention.

Reproductive justice in citizenship studies: developing our analytical framework

At their foundation, reproductive rights are a core component of substantive citizenship: to have autonomy over one's reproductive choices as well as access to the basic necessities required for parenting are fundamental pre-conditions for full participation in public life.[4] The extent to which citizens have access to substantive membership is thus an important question examined by scholars studying the intersections between citizenship and race, gender, class and other axes of difference (Kymlicka 1995; Marshall 1950; Yuval-Davis 1997). Our analytical model is thus grounded in feminist critiques of social reproduction, and the ways in which the rearing and care for children is profoundly gendered, raced, and classed (Glenn 1992; Laslett and Brenner 1989).

To this foundational critique, we call attention to the salience of immigration status as a key axis of oppression that intersects with gender, race, class and other axes in structuring access to reproductive rights. Thus, the second layer of our analytical model (beyond social reproduction) focuses on precarious non-citizenship[5] as a fundamental *source* of inequality (Landolt and Goldring 2015; De Genova 2002; Stasiulis and Bakan 2005; Goldring et al. 2009). For example, migration scholars have shown the differential access to health care and employment that migrants with precarious immigration status may experience, depending on an assemblage of contingent and variable factors, which has significant implications for reproductive rights (Oxman-Martinez et al. 2005; Larios 2019a).

To this literature on differential access to reproductive rights for non-citizens, we add attention to a growing body of literature examining the securitization of borders and criminalization of migrant populations – or what some have coined a 'crimmigration' system (Stumpf 2006; Armenta 2017; Menjívar et al. 2018). In her study of pregnant women detainees in the US, for example, Hartry documents the prevalence of right-wing populist discourse that criminalizes pregnant women (often racialized) as 'birth tourists' or as having 'anchor babies' to 'fraudulently' obtain access to US citizenship (2012a; see also Buhler 2002; Nyers 2006; Arshad et al. 2018). She links this political discourse to regulatory attempts to scale back access to citizenship by birthright – specifically, to the allocation of citizenship on the basis of *jus soli* or birth on US territory (2012a, 60). Attacks on birthright citizenship work to scapegoat migrant mothers in a context of the neoliberalization of the state under global capitalism (2012a, 72). Within this crimmigration system, immigration detention features as a key site where reproductive rights are systematically undermined – not only in the discretionary power of border officials to target pregnant women for deportation and detention – but also in the failure of the state to provide access to abortion or basic healthcare services for pregnant detainees leading in many instances to miscarriages, infant deaths, and/or denial of access to abortion (2012a; see also Messing et al. 2020; Rabin 2009). Hartry (2012a) thus adds an important dimension to the analytical framework we develop in this paper, namely, the notion of 'birthright justice', which captures both the attacks on birthright citizenship by right-wing groups, and the particular ways in which the rights of pregnant detainees are systematically denied in the crimmigration system.

While Hartry's pivotal work offers a compelling critique of birthright (in)justice, in our framework, we expand this critique to ask what justice might look like for non-citizen parents and their citizen-born children? In other words, to what extent is birthright citizenship a 'just' system worth fighting for? We thus add a third layer to our analytical framework, which calls the very system of birthright allocation into question as a long-term goal for reproductive justice in a decarceral future. In doing so, we foreground ongoing debates on the politics of birthright and attempts by scholars and activists to re-theorize and/or to decolonize citizenship as a first step in radically transforming systemic inequalities (Shachar 2009; Isin 2012). In terms of birthright citizenship, political theorists in the 1990s and early 2000s began to question the allocation of citizenship by birthright in a context of global migration and an expanding human rights regime (Shachar 2009; Benhabib 2006; Bosniak 2006; Sassen 2006). Growing disparities between citizens and non-citizens in global cities led some to point to fundamental contradictions in how Western liberal democracies are constructed. As Shachar explains, the allocation of citizenship by birthright – whether by *jus soli* (territory) or by *jus sanguinis* (descent) – has been naturalized as an apolitical distribution of citizenship across symmetrical state units, each "represented as different colour-coded areas on the world map" (2009, 378). What this masks, however, is the "slippage between an abstract right to membership and its concrete materialization … [in] the inequality of *actual* life chances attached to membership in specific political communities" (Shachar 2009, 377, original emphasis). Individuals born to less wealthy states, for example, have a significantly higher chance of "witnessing or themselves suffering infringements of basic human rights" (Shachar 2009, 378). In effect, the allocation of citizenship by birthright in an unequal world exposes a fundamental contradiction at the heart of liberal democracies: namely, that despite purporting to act in the name of universal principles, the distribution of rights vis-a-vis state-centred citizenship is fundamentally illiberal, "the modern equivalent of feudal privilege – an inherited status that greatly enhances one's life chances … akin to a'birthright lottery'" (Carens 1987, 252; see also Anderson 2000; Basok 2009; Benhabib 2006; Butler and Spivak 2007; Bosniak 2006; Sassen 2006). Thus, when we use the term birthright justice, we refer both to the rights of non-citizens to access birthright citizenship for their children in the short term (Hartry 2012a), as well as the need for longer-term transformation of rights allocation altogether. In short, we seek an abolitionist alternative to birthright citizenship – an alternative that guarantees rights on the basis of one's status as a *person* rather than one's birthright in an unequal world (Shachar 2009; Abji 2018).

In our project, we thus bring a reproductive justice lens to such debates in citizenship studies, and we ask what the implications of birthright justice might be for pregnant women detainees in a crimmigration system. We apply this framework to the Canadian case, where there is growing attention to crimmigration but virtually no attention to pregnant women detainees (although see Buhler 2002). The Canadian case is also key in so far as recent attempts to reform the detention system have included pregnant women as a vulnerable group. Our attention to reforms thus extends work by Hartry and others to consider possibilities for transformational change beyond even so-called progressive systems like birthright citizenship. In what follows, we outline the methodological approach that informs our theoretical reading of Glory Anawa's experience in detention and the limitations of recent reforms to detention in Canada.

Methodology

To develop an analytical framework for examining the lived experiences of pregnant women in detention, we apply a reproductive justice lens to our reading of Glory Anawa's experiences in detention and subsequent detention reforms. Importantly, our analysis of Glory's experience is illustrative rather than representative: we offer a theoretically informed reading of her story garnered from a sample of 48 artefacts including media interviews, newspaper articles, policy papers, advocacy campaigns, and legal case documents. To analyze these artefacts, both authors conducted independent thematic analysis and then developed a shared reading through dialogue and exchange. Our interpretation of data is also grounded in our respective larger research projects in Toronto and Montreal, respectively (Abji 2017; Larios 2019a, 2019b). Abji's project examined the intersections between migrant justice and gender-based violence and included ethnographic fieldwork among migrant rights activists in Toronto (2011–2015). Larios' research examines precarious immigration status as a reproductive justice issue in Canada using narrative interviews with migrant women living in Montreal (2018–2019).

In line with other feminist epistemologies of violence, our approach is less concerned with establishing 'objective truths' of Glory's experiences, and rather focuses on unpacking the social processes that shape how accounts of violence are constructed and interpreted by differently positioned actors within a larger social context (Razack 2017; Menjívar 2011). As such, we acknowledge that details of her case as told in public reports are framed as part of larger narratives, and as such are not the same as first-person accounts. At the same time, we take insight from scholars like Bosworth and Kellezi (2017) and others, who point to the potential harms and challenges of eliciting first-hand accounts from detained migrants, including concerns over privacy, confusion over the role of researchers, and potential harms from the research process itself. We thus focus on publicly available details of her case as a sufficient-yet-limited approach for theoretical analysis while mitigating against potential harms that more intrusive methods might produce.

Analyzing Glory's story: reproductive justice and the structural violence of immigration detention

Glory Anawa was detained by the CBSA upon arrival in Canada in February 2013. According to media reports, she had filed a refugee claim at the border and was held by a CBSA officer as a 'flight risk' because her identity documents were not from her country of origin, Cameroon (Browne 2015; Gros 2017). While the details of her refugee claim are private, in a media interview with the CBC, Glory described how she had fled Cameroon after being threatened with female genital mutilation – a form of gender-based violence (2015). As she explained to the interviewer: 'I was just hoping that the Canada immigration or the Canada authorities would help me because I cannot let anyone mutilate me, because my life is at risk. And I have seen this happen and the women will die, but nobody will care because my government does not really get involved about things like these.'

It is unclear whether or not the CBSA officer who processed her claim was made aware of the fact that Glory was three-months pregnant at the time. Nevertheless, soon after Glory was detained, she decided to withdraw her claim and was subsequently served with a removal order (or deportation order). Like many asylum-seekers whose claims are voluntarily withdrawn or rejected, Glory remained caught in a limbo with Canadian authorities seeking to remove her and her home country refusing to issue travel documents (EIDN 2014). As a result, Glory was held indefinitely at the Toronto Immigration Holding Centre, a medium-security facility near the Toronto airport and a dedicated facility for 'foreign nationals' awaiting deportation.

On 25 August 2013 Glory gave birth to a baby boy at a local hospital, whom she named Alpha. Glory and Alpha spent 2.5 years in detention and were the subject of advocacy efforts against the detention of children (Gros 2017) as well as abolitionist campaigns against all detention of immigrants (EIDN 2014). In 2015, Glory was also part of a legal challenge *Chaudhary vs. Canada* filed by four appellants detained in Ontario where the Ontario Superior Court of Appeals affirmed the right of long-term detainees to apply for direct *habeas corpus* relief at court (Molnar and Silverman 2016)[6] While *Chaudhary* was arguably a positive outcome for detainees in Ontario, for Glory and Alpha this did not translate into their release or their right to stay on humanitarian and compassionate grounds. Glory and baby Alpha were subsequently removed to Cameroon in November 2015 (Cain 2016), their current whereabouts unknown to us. In what follows, we start by pointing to forms of injustice that all non-citizens are subject to in the Canadian detention system, and then apply our framework to trace the multiple layers of structural violence that pregnant women like Glory experience in a crimmigration system.

Crimmigration and migrant (in)justice in Canada: situating Glory's story

Migration scholars have pointed to the structural violence of immigration detention that asylum-seekers like Glory experience in a crimmigration system (Esposito et al. 2019; Menjívar et al. 2018; Abji 2020; Bergen and Abji 2020). According to Canadian policy, detention is to be used as a 'last resort'; however, critics have pointed to the wide degree of discretion that individual officers have to detain non-citizens (Silverman 2014; Moffette 2018). The grounds for detention are both broad and vague: individuals can be detained if a CBSA officer considers them (i) a 'flight risk', i.e. as someone who is 'unlikely to appear' for their removal, or (ii) a 'danger to the public,' or (iii) if the individual is of unknown identity (Global Detention Project 2018). Significantly, there is also no independent oversight of the CBSA, which means that any complaints against individual officers go to the CBSA and not to an independent body for investigation (UNHCR 2012; United Nations 2015).[7] Indeed, by the CBSA's own admission, roughly one-third of detainees held in 2009–2010 were failed asylum-seekers like Glory, considered 'low-risk' by officials at the time of their detention (Global Detention Project 2018; EIDN, 2014). What this in effect means is that people are being detained in part because their stated fear of returning (where they may face death, harm, or human rights abuses) could easily lead to an officer considering them a flight risk and then detaining them.

The Canadian detention system also includes the controversial practice of holding detainees in prisons when they cannot be accommodated in administrative holding centres (Silverman 2014). Roughly 40–60% of detainees are held in prisons, despite having committed no crime under Canadian criminal law, where they are subject to punitive conditions including strip searches, handcuffing for transportation, limited time outside, and solitary confinement (Gros and Van Groll 2015). These punitive conditions are even further exacerbated in the Canadian case, where migrants can be held indefinitely as there are no current time limits on detention as in other immigrant-receiving countries (Track and Paterson 2017; GDP 2018). While detainees have their cases reviewed by the Immigration and Refugee Board (IRB) every 30 days, adjudicators require 'clear and compelling reasons' to depart from previous decisions leading to what some have called a 'kafkaesque' system (Gros and Paloma 2015; Fine 2017; see also Bosworth and Kellezi 2017). The impacts of this on Glory come through in her CBC interview: 'It's very, very hard,' Glory describes, 'I just feel like I'm trapped in here. I'm in a difficult situation. Every time I go to court, for one, they don't have any new reason [to depart from previous decisions], so they just keep me here.' Indeed, the indefinite nature of detention has been compared to psychological torture and is widely regarded by the UN and international human rights organizations as an arbitrary and unjust deprivation of human liberty (Gros and Paloma 2015; Track and Paterson 2017).

Advancing a reproductive justice approach to Glory's story: social reproduction, birthright justice, and the allocation of rights

While migration scholars have drawn important attention to the human rights violations rampant in the detention system in Canada and elsewhere, few have considered reproductive rights as a key dimension along which detainees like Glory are exposed to structural violence. Indeed, there is a burgeoning academic and grey literature documenting the forms of discrimination that migrant women experience in detention (e.g. Bosworth et al. 2018; Brané and Wang 2013; Esposito et al. 2019; Molnar and Silverman 2018; NIJC 2014; Rabin 2009). Detained women are more likely to be asylum-seekers compared to men; they are more likely to be single-parents compared to men, with less overall social support in mitigating the effects of incarceration for themselves and their families; and women are more likely than men to report experiencing domestic violence or sexual assault prior to detention (Bosworth et al. 2018; Brané and Wang 2013; Esposito et al. 2016; National Immigrant Justice Center (NIJC) 2014; Rabin 2009). While prone to being represented as passive victims of migratory processes, women in detention have described their migration in terms of resistance and personal agency – for example, as a choice they made in order to find safety and provide for themselves and their children, sometimes in response to gendered structural violence in their countries of origin (Bosworth et al. 2018; Esposito et al. 2019). Regardless of their personal narratives, representations of migrant women consistently fall back on gendered national stereotypes of particular migrant women as highly sexualized, naive, and/or untrustworthy, broadly criminalizing migrant women as a subject position (Bosworth et al. 2016; Bosworth et al. 2018; Esposito et al. 2016). In the Canadian case, there is a significant lack of publicly available data on the number of men, women, and trans people in detention, let alone on the numbers of pregnant detainees, miscarriages, abortions, childbirths, or the prevalence of sexual violence[8] in detention more broadly.[9]

By centring reproductive justice for non-citizens in our analytical framework, we can see how immigration detention as an institution is embedded in broader systems of gendered and racialized social reproduction. While no formal CBSA guidelines exist on the housing of parents with young children, we know anecdotally that children are housed with mothers in a gender-segregated system. Mothers with young children are also faced with an untenable situation: to either keep children detained with them or to give children up to the care of others, including foster care for those with no family ties in Canada (Gros 2017). Until the practice was recently exposed, CBSA did not formally count the children of detained parents in their statistics of detainees, classifying these children as 'visitors' who were 'free to leave' – again, showing the kafkaesque carceral logic of detention only visible when parenting is foregrounded (Gros 2017).

Reproductive injustice for detainees is even more pronounced when we consider the conditions of detention that pregnant and new mothers experience. Grey literature on detention conditions shows a wide degree of discretion and lack of oversight in terms of the right to not have a child (e.g. access to abortion), the right to have a child (e.g. health complications leading to miscarriage, etc.) and the right to raise a child in healthy environments (Kraft-Stolar 2015; Rabin 2009).[10] Glory provides a vivid account of mothering within a detention centre, describing how mothers are responsible for their children 24/7 with no respite and few resources. Since the bathroom in Glory's detention cell has no door, she describes how baby Alpha will wander into the facilities and play in the toilet seeking entertainment unless under constant supervision. While Glory can have access to formula for Alpha, she has to request it and is not allowed to prepare it herself or see it prepared. Glory was given no medical or social support for breastfeeding. She laments that Alpha's first words were 'radio check' – the call that guards frequently made while changing shifts, saying: 'Those are the things he's used to because that's the only life he knows.' Mothering clearly structures the conditions of her incarceration and how she navigates it. 'When he smiles, it keeps me going', Glory explains, 'But in the inside, I feel, I cry every time. But I just can't cry in front of him to let him feel down. I try to do the best that I can' (CBC 2015).

While these are unique details to Glory's story, scholarship on mothering while incarcerated affirm that these conditions are systemic and widespread (Roth 2017). Lack of perinatal care and support reveals not only the ways in which '[w]omen in prison are often considered unworthy of motherhood' (Roth 2017, 290), but also how the detention system, like the prison system, is an androcentric system designed around the needs of male citizens with systemic inequalities for women, trans, and non-citizens embedded in how the system functions. While we do not have statistics for the number of pregnant women in detention, Glory points to the fact that there are others: 'I see other inmates with babies. Other ladies here with children. We have telephones, two couches and a tv and a few toys for the children to play around with' (CBC 2015).

Beyond the conditions of detention, attention to reproductive rights also exposes how detainability itself is gendered, raced, and classed. Here, we draw from the second layer of our analytical framework to show how access to birthright citizenship is itself criminalized for non-citizen women. For instance, the reproductive choices of racialized women from the global south can themselves become grounds for their detainability. Hartry (2012a) argues that the discretionary power afforded to individual officers can lead to racial and gendered profiling of women of colour from the global south – whether conscious or not, such micro-level decisions draw from deeply embedded notions of women of colour's reproduction as a threat to nation-building projects (80). Critical migration scholarship examining the European context have highlighted how gendered and racialized stereotypes mean detained women are commonly viewed through a lens of presumed sexual promiscuity and as present in the country only to find a husband or work in the sex trade (Andrijasevic 2009; Bosworth et al. 2016). In the crimmigration context, tropes of women of colour as 'bad mothers' and 'welfare queens' are heightened through right-wing attacks on immigrant women's supposed 'birth tourism' and their children as 'anchor babies' (Hartry 2012a). While such discourses are less pronounced in the Canadian case, there is mounting evidence of similar criminalizing narratives among right-wing populists (Brean 2012; Buhler 2002; Winter 2014).[11] For example, the right-wing Conservative government in power between 2006 and 2015 began openly characterizing pregnant women as 'birth tourists' and their children as 'passport babies' while implementing a series of regulatory changes limiting access to citizenship across most categories of migration (Brean 2012; Bhuyan et al. 2014; Larios 2019b). Such narratives make women like Glory more vulnerable to detention because they are more likely to be seen as flight risks or threats to border sovereignty, requiring their detention and deportation (Hartry 2012a).

But it is not only about the conditions of detention and detainability that result from the crimmigration of birthright for non-citizen women. Our framework adds a third layer, which can help us to see how the allocation of rights itself is structurally problematic. While we can think about reproductive rights as human rights, they are allocated through a state-centred system. So the likelihood of reproductive rights is dependent on where one is born, like a lottery system if you will. Western states that benefit from colonialism and global capitalism arguably have the capacity to provide access to healthcare etc. although such rights may be more accessible for some residents compared to others. For women from the global south, histories of colonial exploitation combined with the ravages of global capitalism are one vector along which reproductive justice is structured transnationally. These intersect with localized hetero-patriarchal systems, '(re) produc[ing] interlocking systems of oppression' (Esposito et al. 2019, 412). As supported by other critical migration studies, gendered inequality in the form of violence or economic barriers, for example, are frequently cited as factors in women's migration (Bosworth et al. 2018). In Glory's case, she was making reproductive choices in a context of FGM and other forms of gender-based violence. We can think of her decision to migrate as a reproductive strategy to exercise bodily autonomy in the context of gender-based violence.

The inequalities in rights allocation also shape interactions between parents and children at the micro-level. As a non-citizen giving birth on Canadian territory, Glory and baby Alpha were a mixed-status family. This means that in theory at least, they had differential access to rights, despite being deeply connected as parent and child. Mixed-status families bring to the fore the deeply embedded privileges of birthright citizenship in a state-centred human rights system. As much as the limited rights that baby Alpha had were under attack by anti-immigrant groups, it nevertheless raises questions about the limitations of liberal citizenship as a conduit for human rights, and whether this is ultimately a source of justice over the long term. In explaining her own frustrations parenting her citizen-child, Glory shows how mixed-status families get caught in the bureaucratic assemblage that ultimately penalizes families like hers'. As she explained: 'The security guards took me to the clinic to get [Alpha's] two months needles, his four months needles, his six-month needles. And then when he was 1 year old, the manager of the facility told me that they have changed the rules. That he is a Canadian citizen, and nobody is supposed to escort him to the hospital. And I told them that I was arrested from the airport, I do not know anybody in Canada. Because of that they refused to let my son have his one-year needle. Until last week, he got his one-year needle and the doctor was not very happy about [the delay in Alpha's care]. And those kinds of things make me really frustrated.' Glory's frustrated account of trying to access health care for her child shows how the difference in status between non-citizen mother and citizen child becomes a structural barrier, undermining her capacity to parent her child in a healthy environment.

Taken together, our analysis of Glory and baby Alpha's accounts of detention traces multiple layers of structural violence that they experienced, from the conditions of their detention, to the contexts in which pregnant women are rendered detainable through criminalizing notions of migrant women as reproductive threats and flight risks. By foregrounding reproductive justice through attention to social reproduction and crimmigration-related attacks on birthright citizenship, our analysis contributes to migration scholarship on the structural violence of immigration controls. However, we also add a third layer to our analysis, by tracing the ways in which birthright privilege itself structures Glory's life chances: leading her to choose migration as a reproductive justice strategy for her family, while at the same time undermining her ability to provide care for her child as part of a mixed-status family. In what follows, we consider the implications of this analysis for social change. We start by considering recent reforms to the immigration detention system that identify pregnant women as a vulnerable group, and then offer an exploratory discussion of what justice might look like if birthright citizenship itself were scrutinized by scholars and activists advancing migrant justice.

Reforming detention: a feminist-abolitionist critique of 'detention avoidance' for pregnant women

In 2016, the Canadian government announced a series of reforms to the immigration detention system following a series of stakeholder consultations (CBC 2016). Reforms included $138M CDN in infrastructure investments and the publication of a new National Immigration Detention Framework, a 20-page document that sets out the intentions of the CBSA in 'strengthening the detention system and developing more alternatives to detention' (CBSA 2017). This reform came on the heels of a number of controversies and activist campaigns including reports of children being held in detention, as well as reports of at least 16 deaths in detention between 2000 and 2017 (Global Detention Project (GDP) 2018; Molnar and Silverman 2018). The framework mentions pregnant women once, in an opening paragraph that sets out the CBSA's approach to 'vulnerable groups':

"**Generally**, immigration detention is **avoided** for children or other **vulnerable groups** such as **pregnant women**, elderly persons, persons who are ill or disabled or persons with behavioural or mental health issues ..." (CBSA 2017, our emphasis).

It is unclear to what extent the inclusion of pregnant women as a vulnerable group had to do with activist campaigns against the detention of Glory. There is no mention of pregnant women in the CBSA's own summary of stakeholder consultations (CBSA 2017). Likewise, in the CBSA's broader guidelines, pregnant women are only mentioned once in terms of instructions to CBSA officers to not use handcuffs when transporting pregnant women. Outside of this, there are no public policy documents on the detention of pregnant women in Canada.

Migration scholars have long been critical of the uses of vulnerability to reinforce good/bad migrant dichotomies (Golash-Boza and Hondagneu-Sotelo 2013; Yukich 2013). The framing of certain migrants as vulnerable reinforces the notion of other migrants as risky and these are often gendered and racialized framings. In the case of immigration detention, we can be critical of attempts to frame women and children as particularly vulnerable given that the majority of detainees are racialized men from the global south (Golash-Boza 2016). Likewise, the major absence of any significant policies or guidelines on how detention is to be avoided for pregnant women, or the concrete practices that might protect their vulnerabilities, further bolsters arguments that this is simply a superficial response that ultimately reinforces larger discourses of criminalization of racialized men in the Canadian crimmigration system.

While such critiques of the good/bad migrant dichotomy are indeed useful, our analysis of Glory's and Alpha's lived experiences of detention suggest that we need to push further in our analytical frameworks. The risk here for scholars is to *not* talk about pregnant women in detention at all and, by virtue of that, we stop acknowledging the multiple structural forces at work that differentially affect detainees across gender and gender identity, race, nation, class, sexuality and so on. The question for us is how to do this work without dove-tailing with dominant discourses that frame racialized men from the global south as criminals and security threats.

The reproductive justice framework offers an important vantage point from which to situate our critiques using a structural analysis. For example, we suggest that the CBSA's framing of pregnant women quoted above implies a biological understanding of vulnerability compared to the structural understanding of vulnerability that underlies a reproductive justice approach. We can see this in the discursive placement of pregnant women in the CBSA's list of vulnerable populations (2017). The grouping begins with children as the first vulnerable group identified, suggesting that this is the most salient group associated with vulnerability. Pregnant women are then placed next in how vulnerability is constructed for the 'other vulnerable groups' that must be considered in addition to children. Their placement beside children in this way suggests an underlying logic of biological vulnerability: 'pregnant women' is the signifier used, not 'mothers with young children' or other possible signifiers, which implicitly reinforces the idea that the vulnerability stems from the woman's bodily housing of the fetus rather than structural vulnerabilities associated with social reproduction or the care work often imposed on mothers. It also individualizes the experiences of detainees, rather than acknowledging that it is relational, that we know children are there because their mothers are there. Likewise, the CBSA's stated policy against handcuffing pregnant women as the only other mention of this group suggests biological vulnerability, where pregnancy is a temporary physical state that makes the practice of handcuffing medically risky.

The framing of the solution to addressing vulnerability is also instructive here. Nowhere in the framework is it made clear how the state will 'avoid' detention of vulnerable groups. Instead, the general public are to trust that CBSA officers will use their discretion to uphold the rule of law. What that means in practice, however, is often expedited deportation rather than regularization of asylum-seekers like Glory, and by extension, their Canadian-born children. In her study on the US case, Hartry found, for example, efforts among border officers to deport pregnant women more quickly, often leading to increased likelihood of being held in detention to avoid flight risk (2012a). While there is a lack of available data on the Canadian case, this logic of removal is already implied in how the CBSA frames its own attempts to avoid detention. For example, in the same opening paragraph where pregnant women are identified, the CBSA (2017) concludes by stating 'However, where safety or security is an issue, immigration detention is considered for the shortest time possible and *primarily focused on supporting the removal* of those individuals.' In the Canadian lexicon, 'removal' is used as a softer word to convey deportation (Lefebvre and Bourbeau 2019). The notion of *faster* removal as a solution to pregnant women's vulnerability only makes sense in a context where the sovereign authority of states to include or exclude is normalized and left unquestioned. When we as scholars and activists resist where and how the lines are drawn, we also risk reinforcing the power of the state as the arbiter of rights and membership (Abji 2017; 2018). We can thus question reforms that use the language of 'detention avoidance' by the CBSA as constituting a carceral technology, which draws from sovereign authority of the state to prioritize its own interests in cases where that authority stands in conflict with the human rights of non-citizens.

Discussion: the politics of detention abolition in Canada and beyond

In a sense, scholars and activists are caught in a catch-22 when it comes to pushing for detention reforms. By focusing on strategic reforms for groups that the public might find more salient, for example, by centring women and children, such efforts work to reproduce criminalization of the majority of detainees who also experience structural vulnerabilities. In the case of pregnant women in Canada, the proposed reforms do little to address the structural vulnerabilities, making the case for reforms even less desirable compared to transformation – or abolition – of the system altogether. Thus, when we consider what birthright justice might look like, we refer both to the rights of non-citizens to access birthright citizenship for their children in the short term (Hartry 2012a), as well as the need for longer-term transformation of rights allocation altogether. In short, we seek an abolitionist alternative to birthright citizenship – an alternative that guarantees rights on the basis of one's status as a person rather than one's birthright in an unequal world (Shachar 2009; Abji 2018).

While we align ourselves with abolitionist politics, we pause here to offer two cautions. First, we need a way to think about and talk about birthright in a context where anti-immigrant and right-wing governments are criminalizing this issue. Here's the dilemma – on the one hand, the allocation of citizenship by birthright is a fundamental source of structural inequality (Shachar 2009). So when we fight to retain birthright citizenship for migrant families who have children in Canada or elsewhere, we reinforce this foundational source of inequality in the current interstate system. But if we are vocal in our rejection of birthright citizenship – if we reject citizenship or try to decolonize it – is there a risk of dove-tailing with this political moment where birthright is being targeted by the right but for very different reasons? Ultimately what we call for is more work that imagines and blueprints what an alternative way of organizing rights and membership might look like in a de-carceral future. Here we draw inspiration from abolitionist and anti-border activists and scholars working to pre-figure what a world without prisons and detention centres might look like in the everyday practices of movement-building (Incite! 2006; Walia 2013; García Hernández 2017; Ritchie & Martensen 2020).

Second, in imagining abolitionist alternatives, we insist that our visions for migrant justice must also include reproductive justice. There are decades of feminist work on social reproduction that we can draw from and find ways to bring analytically into our models (Laslett and Brenner 1989; Kofman and Raghuram 2018). So if we are imagining a de-carceral future, what does that mean in a context when the reproduction of some families is privileged over the reproduction of others? What does that mean for the unequal division of labour where the work of social reproduction largely performed either as unpaid work by women or as underpaid and precarious work by racialized and migrant women (Glenn 1992)? Ultimately, this is about the multiple and intersecting structural vulnerabilities that are at play and we need to keep pushing our analytical frameworks to be able to account for this complexity.

Conclusion: Migrant Justice as Reproductive Justice

Our analysis of Glory Anawa's experiences in immigration detention in Canada highlighted forms of structural violence that pregnant women may experience in detention at the intersections of migrant justice and reproductive rights. Honouring her story along with the story of her citizen-born child, Alpha, who spent the first 2.5 years of his life in detention prior to deportation, we developed an analytical framework for examining such cases as evidence of structural vulnerability (rather than biological vulnerability). Our analytical framework both applied and extended Hartry's notion of birthright justice as a contemporary form of injustice experienced by (often racialized) non-citizen women whose reproductive choices are criminalized, leading to a scaling back of the rights afforded to non-citizens who have children on US soil.

While we show how Hartry's notion of birthright justice applies to the experiences of detainees like Glory in Canada, we argue that the 'justice' in birthright justice should also account for more long-standing inequalities inherent to the birthright system in the first place. We argue that scholarly critiques of detention must therefore account for the multiple forms of structural violence that shape migrant (in)justice in detention – not only across race, gender, class and other axes of difference, but also in terms of the embodied and material realities of social reproduction experienced by individuals, families, and communities as they interface with immigration controls.

Notes

1. Equal co-author. Authors are listed alphabetically.
2. At the same time, we agree with critical migration scholars who have been rightly cautious not to sensationalize the detention of women and children in ways that reproduce criminalizing narratives of the predominantly racialized-male population of detainees (Golash-Boza and Hondagneu-Sotelo 2013). Our focus on structural analysis is thus an attempt to bring scholarly attention to pregnant detainees without reinforcing criminalizing narratives.
3. Now operating under the name *SisterSong Women of Color Reproductive Justice Collective*, the movement for reproductive justice builds on a rich legacy of Black women's activism in the United States, tracing back to the civil rights movements and key organizations, such as the

Combahee River Collective (1974) and the *Black Women's Health Imperative* (1984) (Bond Leonard 2017; Ross 2017).

4. Here, we build on a Marshallian notion of social citizenship (1950), while recognizing that reproductive rights were not included in his original formulation. Feminist scholars have offered important critiques of the implicit androcentrism in how early theories of citizenship were formulated (Ong 2006; Stasiulis 1999; Yuval-Davis 1997)
5. Coined by Landolt and Goldring (2015), precarious non-citizenship refers to the 'dynamic, multi-scalar assemblage' that shapes access to citizenship for immigrants with precarious immigration status along contingent and indeterminate pathways. The approach challenges dichotomous conceptions of citizen/non-citizen, which they argue are socially constructed.
6. As Molnar and Silverman (2016) explain, '*Chaudhary* provides an alternative to Canada's provisions for parole or bail for detainees ... The decision provides important theoretical and practical steps towards justice: the ancient criminal-justice protection of *habeas corpus* is being wedged into modern legal thinking' (2).
7. The Liberal government ear-marked funds for an arms-length monitoring unit for CBSA in its 2019 budget, following decades of activist organizing and at least 16 reported deaths in immigration detention since 2000 (Molnar and Silverman 2018; Tunney 2019). However, at the time of writing, no such body exists in Canada.
8. A recent journalist investigation found five reported allegations of sexual assault within the CBSA between 2016–2018 but no details were available on the outcome or actions taken (Swain et al. 2019).
9. In terms of demographics, earlier accounts from scholars suggest that roughly 70–75% of detainees are male, and that racialized men from the global South are the dominant group in detention in Canada (Pratt 2005).
10. This is true for all incarcerated mothers, but there are particularities for immigrant mothers in a detention system (Ross and Solinger 2017).
11. While right-leaning governments have historically taken the lead politicizing the issue of birth tourism, it is not a wholly partisan issue. The Trudeau Liberal government committed to investigating the issue further in response to a 2018 report suggesting an increase in birth tourism across Canada (Griffith 2018; see also Wright 2018). Problematically, this report includes births by international students, workers, and other temporary residents under the birth tourism label, problematizing all births by foreign mothers as potentially fraudulent (Larios 2019b).

Acknowledgments

With respectful gratitude to Glory and Alpha Anawa: may your story help others. We also gratefully acknowledge comments from the editors and three anonymous reviewers, as well as participants of the De-Carceral Futures workshop at Queen's University, who provided generative feedback on this paper. This research was supported by funding from the Social Sciences and Humanities Research Council (SSHRC).

Disclosure statement

No potential conflict of interest was reported by the authors.

References

Abji, S. 2017. *"Emerging Logics of Citizenship: Activism in Response to Precarious Migration and Gendered Violence in an Era of Securitization."* Toronto: University of Toronto. Doctoral dissertation http://hdl.handle.net/1807/97099

Abji, S. 2018. "Postnational Acts of Citizenship: How an Anti-border Politics Is Shaping Feminist Spaces of Service Provision in Toronto, Canada." *International Feminist Journal of Politics* 20 (4): 501–523. doi: 10.1080/14616742.2018.1480901.

Abji, S. 2020. "Punishing Survivorship and Criminalizing Survivors: A Feminist Intersectional Approach to Migrant Justice in the Crimmigration System." *Studies in Social Justice* 14 (1): 67–89. doi: https://doi.org/10.26522/ssj.v2020i14.2158.

Almeida, L. M., J. Caldas, D. Ayres-de-Campos, D. Salcedo-Barrientos, S. Dias, *et al.* 2013. "Maternal Healthcare in Migrants: A Systematic Review." *Maternal and Child Health Journal* 17 :1346–1354. doi:10.1007/s10995-012-1149-x.

Anderson, K. 2000. "Thinking 'Postnationally': Dialogue across Multicultural, Indigenous, and Settler Spaces." *Annals of the Association of American Geographers* 90 (2): 381–391. doi:10.1111/0004-5608.00201.

Andrijasevic, R. 2009. "Sex on the Move: Gender, Subjectivity and Differential Inclusion." *Subjectivity* 29 (1): 389–406. doi:10.1057/sub.2009.27.

Anthias, F., N. Yuval-Davis. 1992. *Racialized Boundaries: Race, Nation, Gender, Colour, and Class and the Anti-racist Struggle.* New York: Routledge.

Armenta, A. 2017. "Racializing Crimmigration: Structural Racism, Colorblindness, and the Institutional Production of Immigrant Criminality." *Sociology of Race and Ethnicity* 3 (1): 82–95. doi:10.1177/2332649216648714.

Arshad, F., M. Haith-Cooper, P. Palloti. 2018. "The Experiences of Pregnant Migrant Women in Detention: A Qualitative Study." *British Journal of Midwifery* 26 (9): 591–596. doi:10.12968/bjom.2018.26.9.591.

Ashdown, J., and M. James. 2010. "Women in Detention." *International Review of the Red Cross* 92 (877): 123–141. doi:10.1017/S1816383110000226.

Basok, T. 2009. "Counter-hegemonic Human Rights Discourses and Migrant Rights Activism in the US and Canada." *International Journal of Comparative Sociology* 50 (2): 183–205. doi:10.1177/00207152 08100970.

Benhabib, S. 2006. *Another Cosmopolitanism: The Berkeley Tanner Lectures.* Oxford: Oxford University Press.

Bergen, H., and S. Abji. 2020. "Facilitating the Carceral Pipeline: Social Work's Role in Funnelling Newcomer Children from the Child Welfare System to Jail and Deportation." *Affilia: Journal of Women and Social Work* 35 (1): 34–48.

Bhuyan, R., B. Osborne, S. Zahraei, S. Tarshis. 2014. "Unprotected and Unrecognized: Canadian Immigration Policy and Violence against Women 2008-2013" *Migrant Mothers Project* Accessed 16 March 2020. http://www.migrantmothersproject.com/report/

Bond Leonard, T. M. 2017. "Laying the Foundations for a Reproductive Justice Movement." In *Radical Reproductive Justice: Foundations, Theory, Practice, Critique,* edited by L. Ross, E. Derkas, W. Peoples, L. Roberts, P. Bridgewater, 39–49. New York: Feminist Press.

Bosniak, L. 2006. *The Citizen and the Alien: Dilemmas of Contemporary Membership.* Princeton: Princeton University Press.

Bosworth, M., A. Fili, S. Pickering. 2016. "Women's Immigration Detention in Greece: Gender, Control and Capacity." In *Immigration Detention, Risk and Human Rights*, edited by M. J. Guia, R. Koulish, V. Mitsilegas, New York: Springer. 157–170.

Bosworth, M., A. Fili, S. Pickering. 2018. "Women and Border Policing at the Edges of Europe." *Journal of Ethnic and Migration Studies* 44 (13): 2182–2196. doi:10.1080/1369183X.2017.1408459.

Bosworth, M., and B. Kellezi. 2017. "Doing Research in Immigration Removal Centres: Ethics, Emotions and Impact." *Criminology & Criminal Justice* 17 (2): 121–137. doi:10.1177/1748895816646151.

Brané, M., and L. Wang. 2013. "Women: The Invisible Detainees." *Forced Migration Review* 44 (September): 37–39.

Brean, J. 2012. "Tories Look to Eliminate 'Passport Babies'; Undermines Value of Citizenship, Kenney Says." *National Post*, Canada: March 6. https://nationalpost.com/news/canada/passport-babies-canada

Browne, R. 2015. "What are Babies Doing behind Bars in Canada?" *Macleans Magazine*. https://www.macleans.ca/news/canada/what-are-babies-doing-behind-bars-in-canada/

Buhler, S. 2002. "Babies as Bargaining Chips - in Defence of Birthright Citizenship in Canada." *Journal of Law and Social Policy* 17: 87–114.

Butler, J., and G. C. Spivak. 2007. *Who Sings the Nation-state?* New York: Seagull Books.

Cain, P. 2016. *Immigration Detention 'Woefully Unsuited for Children,' Report Charges.*. Global News. September 22. https://globalnews.ca/news/2953723/immigration-detention-woefully-unsuited-for-children-report-charges/

Carens, J. H. 1987. "Aliens and Citizens: The Case for Open Borders." *Revolutionary Politics* 49 (2): 25–73.

CBC. 2015. "Glory Anawa Shares Her Story from an Immigrant Detention Centre." DNTO. CBC Radio, January 24. https://www.cbc.ca/radio/dnto/glory-anawa-s-shares-her-story-from-a-immigrant-detention-centre-1.2926970

CBC. 2016. *"Canada's Immigration Detention Program to Get $138M Makeover."* CBC News. Montreal: August 15. https://www.cbc.ca/news/canada/montreal/goodale-immigration-laval-1.3721125

CBSA. 2017. "Cbsa's New National Immigration Detention Framework: A Summary Report of the Framework and Stakeholder Roundtable Discussions (Aug - Dec 2016)." Canada Border Services Agency,January. http://www.cbsa-asfc.gc.ca/agency-agence/consult/consultations/nidf-cnmdi/menu-eng.html

Chaudhary V. Canada. 2015. ONSC 1503 (CanLII). http://canlii.ca/t/ggkl4

De Genova, N. 2002. "Migrant 'Illegality' and Deportability in Everyday Life." *Annual Review of Anthropology* 31: 419–447. doi:10.1146/annurev.anthro.31.040402.085432.

End Immigration Detention Network (EIDN). 2014. *Indefinite, Arbitrary and Unfair: The Truth about Immigration Detention in Canada*. Toronto: End Immigration Detention Network. June https://endimmigrationdetention.files.wordpress.com/2014/06/truth-about-detention-report_eidn.pdf

Esposito, F., C. R. Quinto, F. De Masi, O. Gargano, P. A. Costa. 2016. "Voices of Nigerian Women Survivors of Trafficking Held in Italian Centres for Identification and Expulsion." *International Migration* 54 :133–149. doi:10.1111/imig.12253.

Esposito, F., J. Ornelas, S. Scirocchi, C. Arcidiacono. 2019. "Voices from the Inside: Lived Experiences of Women Confined in a Detention Center." *Signs: Journal of Women in Culture and Society* 44 (2): 403–431. doi:10.1086/699344.

Fine, S. 2017. "Ontario Judge Frees Refugee Claimant, Calls Detention Kafkaesque." *Globe & Mail*. August 14. https://www.theglobeandmail.com/news/national/ontario-judge-frees-refugee-claimant-calls-detention-kafkaesque/article35988726/

Glenn, E. N. 1992. "From Servitude to Service Work: Historical Continuities in the Racial Division of Paid Reproductive Labor." *Signs: Journal of Women in Culture and Society* 18 (1): 1–43. doi:10.1086/494777.

Glenn, E. N. 2015. “Settler Colonialism as Structure: A Framework for Comparative Studies of US Race and Gender Formation.” *Sociology of Race and Ethnicity* 1 (1): 52–72. doi:10.1177/2332649214560440.

Global Detention Project (GDP). 2018. *“Immigration Detention in Canada: Important Reforms, Ongoing Concerns.”*. Geneva: Global Detention Project. June https://www.globaldetentionproject.org/immigration-detention-in-canada-important-reforms-ongoing-concerns

Golash-Boza, T. 2016. “The Parallels between Mass Incarceration and Mass Deportation: An Intersectional Analysis of State Repression.” *Journal of World-Systems Research* 22 (2): 484–509. doi:10.5195/JWSR.2016.616.

Golash-Boza, T., and P. Hondagneu-Sotelo. 2013. “Latino Immigrant Men and the Deportation Crisis: A Gendered Racial Removal Program.” *Latino Studies* 11 (3): 271–292. doi:10.1057/lst.2013.14.

Goldring, L., C. Berinstein, J. K. Bernhard. 2009. “Institutionalizing Precarious Migratory Status in Canada.” *Citizenship Studies* 13 (3): 239–265. doi:10.1080/13621020902850643.

Goldring, L., and P. Landolt, eds. 2013. *Producing and Negotiating Non-Citizenship: Precarious Legal Status in Canada*. Toronto: University of Toronto Press.

Griffith, A. 2018. “Hospital Stats Show Birth Tourism Rising in Major Cities.” *Policy Options*, November 22. Montreal, QC: Institute for Research of Public Policy. Accessed online: https://policyoptions.irpp.org/magazines/november-2018/hospital-stats-show-birth-tourism-rising-in-major-cities/

Gros, H. 2017. *“Invisible Citizens: Canadian Children in Immigration Detention.”*. Faculty of Law. University of Toronto: International Human Rights Program. https://ihrp.law.utoronto.ca/sites/ihrp.law.utoronto.ca/files/PUBLICATIONS/Report-InvisibleCitizens.pdf

Gros, H., and V. G. Paloma. 2015. *“‘we Have No Rights’: Arbitrary Imprisonment and Cruel Treatment of Migrants with Mental Health Issues in Canada”*. Faculty of Law. University of Toronto: International Human Rights Program. http://ihrp.law.utoronto.ca/utfl_file/count/PUBLICATIONS/IHRP%20We%20Have%20No%20Rights%20Report%20web%20170615.pdf

Hartry, A. S. 2012a. “Birthright Justice: The Attack on Birthright Citizenship and Immigrant Women of Color.” *NYU Review of Law & Social Change* 36 (57): 57–101.

Hartry, A. S. 2012b. “Gendering Crimmigration: The Intersection of Gender, Immigration, and the Criminal Justice System.” *Berkeley Journal of Gender, Law & Justice* 27 (1): 1–27.

Hernández, G., and C. César. 2017. “Abolishing Immigration Prisons.” *Boston University Law Review* 97 (1): 245–300.

Incite! Women of Color against Violence. 2006. *Color of Violence: The INCITE! Anthology*. Boston: South End Press.

Isin, E. F. 2012. “Citizenship after Orientalism: An Unfinished Project.” *Citizenship Studies* 16 (5–6): 563–572. doi:10.1080/13621025.2012.698480.

Jacqueline, O.-M., J. Hanley, L. Lach, N. Khanlou, S. Weerasinghe, V. Agnew. 2005. “Intersection of Canadian Policy Parameters Affecting Women with Precarious Immigration Status: A Baseline for Understanding Barriers to Health.” *Journal of Immigrant and Minority Health* 7 (4): 247–258. doi:10.1007/s10903-005-5122-2.

Kimberly, M., C. Jarvis, M. Munoz, V. D’Souza, L. Graves. 2013. “Undocumented Pregnant Women: What Does the Literature Tell Us?” *Journal of Immigrant and Minority Health* 15 (2): 281–291. doi:10.1007/s10903-012-9587-5.

Kofman, E., and P. Raghuram. 2018. “Gender, Migration and Social Reproduction.” In *Handbook on the International Political Economy of Gender*, edited by J. Elias and A. Roberts, 427–440. Northampton: Edward Elgar Publishing.

Kraft-Stolar, T. 2015. *Reproductive Injustice: The State of Reproductive Health Care for Women in New York State Prisons*. New York: Correctional Association of New York.

Kymlicka, W. 1995. *Multicultural Citizenship: A Liberal Theory of Minority Rights*. New York: Oxford University Press.

Landolt, P., and L. Goldring. 2015. “Assembling Noncitizenship through the Work of Conditionality.” *Citizenship Studies* 19 (8): 853–869. doi:10.1080/13621025.2015.1110280.

Larios, L. 2019a. "A Critical Feminist Look at Reproductive Justice for Migrant Women in Canada." Paper presented at the International Conference on Public Policy (ICPP4). Concordia University, Montreal, QC. June 26-28. https://www.ippapublicpolicy.org//file/paper/5d001796d3a65.pdf

Larios, L. 2019b."Re-imagining Immigration through the Ethics of Care: Reproductive Justice and Precarious Status Migration in Canada." Paper presented at the International Conference on Public Policy (ICPP4). Concordia University, Montreal, QC. June 26-28. https://www.ippapublicpolicy.org//file/paper/5d00056f7647d.pdf

Laslett, B., and J. Brenner. 1989. "Gender and Social Reproduction: Historical Perspectives." *Annual Review of Sociology* 15 (1): 381–404. doi:10.1146/annurev.so.15.080189.002121.

Lefebvre, C., and P. Bourbeau. 2019. *"Emergence and Disappearance: Has Deportation Been Removed from Canadian Laws?"*. Paper presented at the Laval University Workshop on Migration and Security. Quebec City: March 26.

Marshall, T. H. 1950 [1965]. "Citizenship and Social Class." In *Class, Citizenship, and Social Development: Essays by T. H. Marshall*, 71–134. Garden City, NY: Doubleday Publishing.

Matos, R., and F. Esposito. 2019. "Women's Experiences of Border Crossing: Gender, Mobility, and Border Control." *International Journal of Migration and Border Studies. Special Issue: Workshop Bordering a View from Portugal Migration and Border-Making in Portugal.* 5 (4): 371–391. doi:10.1504/IJMBS.2019.105809.

Menjívar, C. 2011. *Enduring Violence: Ladina Women's Lives in Guatemala*. Berkeley: University of California Press.

Menjívar, C., A. Gómez Cervantes, D. Alvord. 2018. "The Expansion of 'Crimmigration', Mass Detention, and Deportation." *Sociology Compass* 12 :1–15. doi:10.1111/soc4.12573.

Messing, A., R. E. Fabi, J. D. Rosen. 2020. "Reproductive Injustice at the US Border." *American Journal of Public Health* 110 (3): 339–344. doi:10.2105/AJPH.2019.305466.

Moffette, D. 2018. "'The Jurisdictional Games of Immigration Policing: Barcelona's Fight against Unauthorized Street Vending'." *Theoretical Criminology*. doi:10.1177/1362480618811693.

Molnar, P., and S. J. Silverman. 2016. "Cracks Where the Light Gets In: Recent Legal Breakthroughs in Detention and Crimmigration in Canada." Metropolitics, December 7. http://www.metropolitiques.eu/Cracks-Where-the-Light-Gets-in.html

Molnar, P., and S. J. Silverman. 2018. "How Canada's Immigration Detention System Spurs Violence Against Women." *The Conversation*, April 15. https://theconversation.com/how-canadas-immigration-detention-system-spurs-violence-against-women-95009

National Immigrant Justice Center (NIJC). 2014. *"Eliminating the Detention Bed Quota Helps Women."*. Chicago: National Immigrant Justice Center. https://www.immigrantjustice.org/sites/immigrantjustice.org/files/Bed%20Quota%20Impact%20%202014%2004%2023_FINAL%20MM_1.pdf

Nyers, P. 2006. "The Accidental Citizen: Acts of Sovereignty and (Un)making Citizenship." *Economy and Society* 35 (1): 22–41. doi:10.1080/03085140500465824.

Ong, A. 2006. "Mutations in Citizenship." *Theory, Culture and Society* 23 (2–3): 499–531. doi:10.1177/0263276406064831.

Pratt, A. 2005. *Securing Borders: Detention and Deportation in Canada*. Vancouver: UBC Press.

Price, K. 2010. "What Is Reproductive Justice? How Women of Color Activists are Redefining the Pro-Choice Paradigm." *Meridians: Feminism, Race, Transnationalism* 10 (2): 42–65. doi:10.2979/meridians.2010.10.2.42.

Rabin, N. 2009. "Unseen Prisoners: A Report on Women in Immigration Detention Facilities in Arizona." *Georgetown Immigration Law Review*. Discussion Paper No. 09-01. https://ssrn.com/abstract=1327841

Razack, S. 2007. *Casting Out: The Eviction of Muslims from Western Law and Politics*. Toronto: University of Toronto Press.

Razack, S. H. 2017. "Human Waste and the Border: A Vignette." *Law, Culture and the Humanities: 1-13* 17438721774952. doi:10.1177/1743872117749524.

Richie, B. E., and K. M. Martensen. 2020. "Resisting Carcerality, Embracing Abolition: Implications for Feminist Social Work Practice." *Affilia* 35 (1): 12–16. doi:10.1177/0886109919897576.

Roberts, D. E. 1997. *Killing the Black Body: Race, Reproduction, and the Meaning of Liberty*. New York: Pantheon Books.

Ross, L. J. 2017. "Trust Black Women: Reproductive Justice and Eugenics." In *Radical Reproductive Justice: Foundations, Theory, Practice, Critique*, edited by L. J. Ross, E. Derkas, W. Peoples, L. Roberts, P. Bridgewater, 58–85. New York: Feminist Press.

Ross, L. J., and R. Solinger. 2017. *Reproductive Justice: An Introduction*. Oakland: University of California Press.

Roth, R. 2017. "'She Doesn't Deserve to Be Treated like This': Prisons as Sites of Reproductive Justice." In *Radical Reproductive Justice: Foundations, Theory, Practice, Critique*, edited by L. J. Ross, E. Derkas, W. Peoples, L. Roberts, P. Bridgewater, 285–301. New York, NY: Feminist Press.

Sassen, S. 2006. "The Repositioning of Citizenship and Alienage: Emergent Subjects and Spaces for Politics." In *Migration, Citizenship, Ethnos*, edited by M. Bodemann and G. Yurdakul, 13–33. New York: Palgrave Macmillan.

Shachar, A. 2009. *The Birthright Lottery: Citizenship and Global Inequality*. Cambridge: Harvard University Press.

Silverman, S. 2014. "In the Wake of Irregular Arrivals: Changes to the Canadian Immigration Detention System." *Refuge* 30 (2): 27–34. doi:10.25071/1920-7336.39616.

Smith, A. 2005. "Beyond Pro-choice versus Pro-life: Women of Color and Reproductive Justice." *NWSA Journal* 17 (1): 119–140.

Stasiulis, D. 1999. "Feminist Intersectional Theorizing." In *Race and Ethnic Relations in Canada*, 16th ed., edited by P. S. Li (ed.), 347–397. Toronto: Oxford University Press.

Stasiulis, D., and A. B. Bakan. 2005. *Negotiating Citizenship: Migrant Women in Canada and the Global System*. Toronto: University of Toronto Press.

Stumpf, J. 2006. "The Crimmigration Crisis: Immigrants, Crime, and Sovereign Power." *American University Law Review* 56 (2): 367–419.

Swain, D., A. Wesley, and S. Davis. 2019. "Harassment, Sexual Assault among Alleged Misconduct by Border Agents Investigated by CBSA." *CBC News*. February 4. https://www.cbc.ca/news/canada/cbsa-files-abuse-atip-1.4999473

Track, L., and J. Paterson. 2017. "Oversight at the Border: A Model for Independent Accountability at the Canada Border Services Agency." *British Columbia Civil Liberties Association (BCCLA)*. https://bccla.org/wp-content/uploads/2017/06/FINAL-for-web-BCCLA-CBSA-Oversight.pdf

Tunney, C. 2019. "Budget Includes Watchdog Agency for Border Officers." *CBC News*. March 20. https://www.cbc.ca/news/politics/cbsa-independent-watchdog-1.5063543

United Nations. 2015. "International Covenant on Civil and Political Rights." Committee on Human Rights. CCPR/C/CAN/CO/6. https://tbinternet.ohchr.org/_layouts/15/treatybodyexternal/SessionDetails1.aspx?SessionID=899&Lang=en#sthash.XzzyC1Bz.dpuf

United Nations High Commissioner for Refugees (UNHCR). 2012. "Detention Guidelines: Guidelines on the Applicable Criteria and Standards Relating to the Detention of Asylum-seekers and Alternatives to Detention." http://www.unhcr.org/refworld/docid/503489533b8.html

Walia, H. 2013. *Undoing Border Imperialism*. Oakland: AK Press.

Winter, E. 2014. "(Im)possible Citizens: Canada's 'Citizenship Bonanza' and Its Boundaries." *Citizenship Studies* 18 (1): 46–62. doi:10.1080/13621025.2012.707010.

Wright, T. 2018. "Ottawa Studying 'Birth Tourism' in Light of New Data Showing Higher Non-resident Birth Rates." *The Globe and Mail*, November 22. https://www.theglobeandmail.com/canada/article-ottawa-studying-birth-tourism-in-light-of-new-data-showing-higher/

Yukich, G. 2013. "Constructing the Model Immigrant: Movement Strategy and Immigrant Deservingness in the New Sanctuary Movement." *Social Problems* 60 (3): 302–320. doi:10.1525/sp.2013.60.3.302.

Yuval-Davis, N. 1997. "Women, citizenship and difference." *Feminist Review* 57(1): 4–27.

Immigration status and policing in Canada: current problems, activist strategies and abolitionist visions

David Moffette

ABSTRACT

Bridging prison and immigration justice is of utmost importance, and an obvious and strategic point of encounter for dialogue among activists and scholars working on these issues is immigration detention. But as penal and carceral abolitionists have taught us, we cannot tackle prison injustice without addressing broader issues in policing, criminal law and other means of coercive social control. Taking my cues from this work, I suggest that we move upstream and look at the role of immigration policing in detention and deportation. The article draws from records obtained mostly through Access to Information (ATI) and Freedom of Information (FOI) requests to map out collaboration between the Canada Border Services Agency (CBSA) and municipal police forces in Toronto, Montreal and Vancouver. In looking for ways to limit police involvement in internal border control, the article discusses strategies to promote a culture of non-collaboration with immigration enforcement and build alternative means of ensuring community safety and well-being in the spirit of police and border abolitionism.

Introduction

This special issue aims to contribute reflections and strategies for the project of abolishing immigration detention (Aiken and Silverman, this issue). To do so, I argue that we need to engage with other pieces of the carceral and border enforcement archipelago (Foucault 1995 [1977]; Mountz 2011) and study dispersed bordering practices that contribute to controlling and limiting the presence of non-citizens within nationalized spaces (Sharma 2006; Moffette 2018). In this article, I contribute to this project by mapping out the role of municipal police officers in the policing of people with precarious immigration status in Canada and by showing how the theoretical and normative underpinning of penal abolitionism should logically extend to the issue of everyday policing, on the one hand, and to the issue of immigration control, on the other. These two sets of questions intersect in the context of immigration policing.

Legally, the control of the presence of non-citizens in Canada falls under the jurisdiction of the Canada Border Services Agency (CBSA). Indeed, the CBSA is the primary force tasked with controlling the entry and presence of non-citizens. Municipal police forces have no jurisdiction over non-citizens *qua* non-citizens. But while the CBSA partakes in targeted raids at people's homes (supported by police officers to enforce entry warrants), as well as open raids at workplaces or roadsides, it is common for people without status or with precarious immigration status to be detained by the CBSA after an interaction with a police officer whose job has officially nothing to do with immigration enforcement. Arguably, the existence of distinct law enforcement units specialized in immigration and border control is mostly a North American phenomenon (e.g. CBSA in Canada, ICE in the United States). But even in countries where regular police officers perform this work, this task is often attributed to a specific unit or branch of the national police force (e.g. the Immigration Division of the Home Office in the UK, the Immigration and Borders Commission of the National Police in Spain) and it is generally understood that police corps of smaller administrative units in charge of everyday policing (territories, provinces, regions, cities) are not primarily responsible for the control of immigration status. Even in countries without a distinct immigration enforcement unit, this task is jurisdictionally understood as a federal or national power. And yet, what research on the devolution of immigration control in the United States (Varsanyi 2008, 2010; Provine et al. 2016; Armenta 2017) or my mapping of police-CBSA collaboration show is that immigration policing is deployed on various scales, by a number of actors that are not readily identifiable as border security professionals. This form of immigration policing – in the Canadian context – is the object of this article.

The article draws from records obtained through Access to Information (ATI) and Freedom of Information (FOI) requests, transcripts of a Coroner's inquest, as well as stories collected for a previous project, to study collaboration between the CBSA and municipal police forces in Toronto, Montreal and Vancouver. It also discusses activists' efforts – including some that I have been a part of – to promote a culture of non-collaboration with the CBSA and to try to limit municipal police involvement in immigration control. The article begins and ends with reflections on abolitionist thought and praxis and contributes to this special issue by arguing that we need to engage seriously with the question of police abolition in order to find ways to abolish detention.

Conceptual moves: from prison abolition to immigration policing abolition

Bridging prison and migrant justice appears at once logical and urgent. In many ways, people involved in these struggles already have much in common. Indeed, penal abolitionist movements and radical migrant justice movements share similar analyses of state violence, surveillance, and the policing and control of racialized communities (Davis and Dent 2001; Escobar 2008; Loyd, Burridge, and Mitchelson 2009/2010; Lytle Hernández 2011; García Hernández 2017; Loyd 2019). Both movements have also found in incarceration a symbol and a crude material manifestation of this violence, one that could potentially shock the public and be central to organizing efforts. Immigration detention is thus an obvious and strategic point of encounter for dialogue among activists and scholars working on these issues. In Canada, there is a recent but growing scholarship on immigration detention focusing on the analysis of its legal regime and modes of operation (e.g.: Pratt 2005; Nakache 2013; Hussan 2014; Silverman and Molnar 2016; Global Detention Project 2018), the detention of children (e.g.: Gros 2017; Kronick, Rousseau, and Cleveland 2018), and the implications of detention for mental health (e.g.: Cleveland and Rousseau 2013; Gros and van Groll 2015). Much of this scholarship is politically located somewhere on the spectrum between detention miminalism and full-fledged carceral abolitionism.

This scholarship is essential, as immigration detention is a central node of the border enforcement archipelago (Mountz 2011) which, in the context of migration, helps secure and reproduce global apartheid (Richmond 1994; Sharma 2007). I suggest, however, that we need to go further and expend the abolitionist analytical and normative lens to also study and challenge immigration policing. Conceptually, this move requires a development of the abolitionist argument along two axes: the first one concerns the question of pain and punishment, and the second one concerns surveillance, states' racial projects rooted in slavery and colonialism, and the control of movement. In what follows, I map out these trajectories to ground my critique of immigration policing within the abolitionist intellectual and activist project.

One of the central tenets of prison and penal abolitionism is the critique of punishment. Theories of punishment all acknowledge that it must include the infliction of pain, and this, regardless of whether their philosophical justifications insist on retaliation, deterrence, rehabilitation, neutralization, or community norm-setting (Pires 2001, 2007). While penal regimes have partly moved away from death penalty and the most violent forms or corporal punishment, the deprivation of liberty through incarceration and financial sanctions are, in criminal law, understood as the infliction of pain or loss (Durkheim 1973; Foucault 1995 [1977]; Christie 1982). The abolitionist critique of state-inflicted pain and suffering takes various forms depending on the justification that is being challenged and the philosophical grounding of the critique (for an overview of such critiques, see Ruggiero 2010). Yet, most of these critiques centre on the criminal law category of *poena*, or formal criminal punishment.

It is well known that immigration law sanctions are administrative in nature and are not legally speaking punishment (*poena*). Indeed, immigration detention and deportation do not officially aim to punish offenders but to regulate access to a country and ensure the removal of people deemed undesirable. But this legal bracketing of immigration law and criminal law as separate entities is the result of an historical jurisdictional division (Blomely 2014; Valverde 2016, Moffette and Pratt 2020). This bracketing should not prevent us from paying attention to other forms of punitive social reaction (Velloso 2013). Indeed, as Feeley (1979) had shown with regard to preventive pre-trial custody in the criminal justice system, measures not legally understood as punishment can nonetheless be experienced as the infliction of pain, and/or be deployed by state actors with the intention to punish. If officially non-punitive preventive custody in the criminal justice system can be conceptualized as punishment, so can administrative detention. This is the argument developed by Stumpf to posit that 'the process is the punishment in crimmigration law' (2013, 58). If punishment goes beyond the criminal law category of *poena* and is present in other forms in immigration legal regulation (Pratt 2005; Bowling 2013; Stumpf 2013; Velloso 2013), the abolitionist critique of state-inflicted pain should logically extend to coercive immigration law.

This is in synch with the broadening trend that started more than 30 years ago among abolitionists. Indeed, while abolitionist movements of the 1970s focused mostly on prisons, they eventually broadened their scope to consider all forms of punishment in the 1980s. If one takes the ICOPA conferences as an example of at least one part of this multi-pronged movement, we see this change reflected in the name of the conference, from the first *International Conference on Prison Abolition* in 1983, to the *International Conference on Penal Abolitionism* as of 1987 (Piché and Larsen 2010). This first broadening move allowed abolitionists to consider other forms of in-community punishment, parole, or police violence as penal threats to be challenged. This would eventually lead to consider non-criminal justice forms of punishment – such as immigration detention – as objects of inquiry and critique for penal abolitionists.

The second axis of the penal abolitionist argument that needs development to justify my critique of immigration policing concerns the issue of white supremacy, surveillance, enclosure and the control of movement. At least two trends within abolitionist thought and praxis charted this path. The first is the long-standing conceptualizing and organizing efforts to explicitly ground the critique of prisons and law enforcement in a struggle against slavery and the control and punishment of Black people. As Childs argued 'today's modern version of mass human warehousing – that is, the penitentiary – represents an extension of, rather than an antithesis to Middle Passage genocide' (2009, 278; cited in Saleh-Hanna 2015, para. 7). Indeed, abolitionists in the United States have shown the historical and philosophical lineage linking chattel slavery, to Jim Crow laws used to police and imprison free Black individuals, to the surveillance and attacks on Black liberation activists, to the current profoundly racialized incarceration crisis and deaths of mostly young Black men at the hands of police (e.g. Davis 2003, 2016; Gilmore 2007; Childs 2009, 2015; Alexander 2012; Saleh-Hanna 2015; Herzing 2016; Ritchie 2017). This abolitionist perspective is particularly strong in the United States, but it is also present in Canada (Sudbury 2008, 2009; Maynard 2017), where connections are also drawn between colonial nation-state building, anti-Indigenous violence, policing and incarceration (e.g. Dhillon 2015; Monchalin 2016; Nichols 2017; Howe and Monaghan 2018). The grounding of the abolitionist critique within a broader reading of colonial state-building, slavery and racism helped in the recent development of solidarities – in analysis and action – between some penal abolitionists and migrant justice and No Borders activists (Davis and Dent 2001; Loyd, Burridge, and Mitchelson 2009/2010; Chase 2019; Loyd 2019).

Another more recent broadening trend that has developed in academic abolitionist writing helps make the case for an abolitionist take on immigration policing. Geographers concerned with mapping out the uneven continuum between spaces of formal confinement and the enclosure of public spaces in neoliberal cities have developed research in carceral geography in order to study how 'techniques and technologies of confinement leach into everyday domestic, street, and institutional spaces' (Moran, Turner, and Schliehe 2018, 670; see also Gill et al. 2018; Martin 2019). This echoed debates already happening outside of academia that had led to the development of *carceral* abolitionism to address forms of coercive control over movement and people that are not formally located in the realm of criminal law: city bylaws prohibiting the use of public space by poor folks, or various forms of immigration controls (Carrier and Piché 2015).

As a result of these efforts, it is today generally accepted that abolitionist theory and praxis need to engage with racialized carcerality more broadly. Taking my cues from this work, I suggest that we move upstream and look at the role of immigration policing in reproducing global apartheid and carceral violence. As Carrier, Piché, and Walby (2019, 329) argue 'abolition of police would in fact be a more logical place for prison and penal abolitionists to begin, given the central role of public police in criminalization.' To abolish prisons, we need to abolish the police, and perhaps the criminal justice system altogether. Similarly, to tackle the violence of immigration detention and deportation, we also need to look at immigration policing (Weber 2013), nationalism and racism (Sharma 2007; Walia 2013), border regimes and global apartheid (Sharma 2007; Walia 2013; Mongia 2018).

Methodology and data

Studying the practices of security actors poses particular challenges with regard to methodology and access (Gusterson 1997; Spivakovsky 2011; Maillet, Mountz, and Williams 2017). For this reason, I mobilized what Gusterson once called a 'polymorphous engagement,' a strategy that overcomes access problems by 'interacting with informants across a number of dispersed sites' and 'collecting data eclectically from a disparate array of sources in many different ways' (Gusterson 1997, 116).

My approach is informed by an activist research methodological ethos (Hale 2001; Speed 2006; Kazansky et al. 2019) as many of my insights build on knowledge acquired and stories collected during a 15-year involvement in migrant justice movements. This project emerged as an attempt to go beyond stories of policing that are too often considered 'anecdotal evidence' and try to document this phenomenon more systematically. The article focuses on Toronto, Montreal, and Vancouver, three big metropolises considered to host most of the undocumented people living in the country (Goldring and Landolt 2013). To map out the collaboration between municipal police and the CBSA, I filed ATI requests to the CBSA, and FOI requests to the Montreal Police Service and the City of Toronto, and collected previously released ATI records from the CBSA.[1] I also obtained the transcript of the Coroner's inquest into the death in immigration detention of Lucía Vega Jiménez in Vancouver in 2013, and featuring the testimonies of a CBSA officer and a Metro Vancouver Transit Police[2] officer who details her arrest by police and everyday police-CBSA collaboration.

Most often used by journalists, access to information remains a 'neglected means of data production in the social sciences' (Walby and Larsen 2011, 31). And yet, this methodological strategy is particularly effective in accessing two important types of records produced by institutional state actors. On the one hand, it allows researchers to access what Gary Marx (1984) calls 'dirty data', that is, data that is produced for internal use and would otherwise be kept secret from the public. On the other hand, it provides access to polished official public discourse, but also to the backstage 'media lines' provided by communication experts to ministers and other officials (Walby and Larsen 2011). While it cannot replace the rich empirical accounts of policing that interviews and ethnography can provide (e.g.: Weber 2013; Villegas 2015; Armenta 2017; Abji 2018; Moffette 2018) – and while it is a 'double-edge sword' with many limits (Rigakos and Worth 2011) – ATI/FOI has been successfully used in the Canadian context by researchers studying the surveillance and policing of queers (Kinsman and Gentile 2009; Walby 2009), social movements (Hewitt 2002; Monaghan and Walby 2017; Boyle and Dafnos 2019), public and private spaces (Lippert and Walby 2019), Indigenous struggles (Dafnos 2012; Howe and Monaghan 2018) and racialized immigrants (Larsen and Justin 2009; Moffette and Gardner 2015). Requests systematically take months to years to be processed, stalking is a common strategy, and records are often heavily redacted or denied (Larsen and Walby 2012), but by piecing together various ATI/FOI records with other data, it is possible to map out policing practices.

Mapping out the municipal policing of immigrants in three Canadian cities

Since its creation in 2003, the CBSA is the main law enforcement institution tasked with controlling entry, enforcing immigration warrants, overlooking immigration detention, and imposing conditions for immigration bail. There is no legal obligation for municipal police officers to inquire about the immigration status of people they interact with or to report this status to the CBSA if they happen to learn information about it – except when enforcing an immigration warrant (Immigration Legal Committee 2008). In what follows, I discuss police-CBSA collaboration 1) as legislated in the *Immigration and Refugee Protection Act* (IRPA), 2) as evidenced through formal memoranda of understanding (MOUs) and joint operations, and 3) as it appears through calls placed by police to the CBSA's Warrant Response Centre (WRC).

Section 142 of the IRPA

While other laws specifically require that police officers enforce them, the *IRPA* does not explicitly give jurisdiction to police officers to enforce its provisions. There is one exception listed in Section 142, which states that 'Every peace officer [...] shall, when so directed by an officer, execute any warrant or written order issued under this Act for the arrest, detention or removal from Canada of any permanent resident or foreign national.' This means that if a police officer enters someone's name into the Canadian Police Information Centre (CPIC) database and an immigration warrant pops up, this person will likely be detained, transferred to the CBSA, and placed in immigration detention. Therefore, contact with police always represents a risk for people without status.

Memoranda of understanding and joint operations

This risk is further exacerbated by police-CBSA collaboration that goes much beyond this legal obligation and is more or less formalized. In Vancouver in 2014, after Lucía Vega Jiménez – an undocumented Mexican immigrant who feared for her life if deported to Mexico – died in immigration detention after being detained for fare evasion by a Transit Police officer (see Gros and van Groll 2015), advocates obtained ATI and FOI records revealing the existence of a formal MOU signed in 2007 between the Metro Vancouver Transit Police and CBSA's Pacific Region Enforcement Centre. The MOU provided 'that assistance and liaison will be provided by CBSA Enforcement Officers to [Transit Police] members for the enforcement of the *IRPA*' and allowed joint operations. A letter from the Chief of the Transit Police to the Transit Police Board also revealed that in 2013, the year Vega Jiménez died, officers had referred 328 cases to the CBSA.[3] Following pressure from activists in the *Transportation Not Deportation* campaign, the official MOU was rescinded in 2015, but it is unclear what level of informal collaboration continued.

In Toronto, where ATI and FOI requests about the existence of MOUs have not yielded results, there is ample evidence of coordinated actions between the CBSA and various policing bodies. One infamous example concerns a number of multi-agency roadside stops to intercept undocumented workers in commercial vehicles in the Greater Toronto Area (GTA). On 14 August 2014, 21 construction workers were arrested in the north end of Toronto in a stint organized by the CBSA Road Investigation units, inspectors of the Ministry of Transportation of Ontario (MTO), inspectors of the Ministry of Environment of Ontario (MOE) and Ontario Provincial Police (OPP). A CBSA internal document released through ATI revealed that in 2014–2015, the CBSA partook in nine such raids in the GTA with 'partners, including Barrie Police Service, Waterloo Regional Police, Ontario Provincial Police, Peel Regional Police, Toronto Police Service, York Regional Police, as well as the [MTO] and [MOE].' The internal document goes on to explain the logic: 'These other agencies have the authority to inspect vehicles, and the CBSA has the jurisdiction should the agency identify any [*IRPA*] violations.' It adds: 'Without the MTO's participation in these initiatives and stopping these vehicles, the CBSA would not have any legal authority to conduct any of the consequent *IRPA* enforcement actions.'[4]

Other records obtained through ATI show how Toronto Licensing Enforcement Unit bylaw officers organized at least one 'training/info session between RCMP, TPS, CBSA and NGOs' with the objective of 'do[ing] joint operations in the future,' 'as part of the adult industry enforcement team focusing on body rubs, strip joints, massage parlors as well as night clubs.'[5] This is consistent with the various instances of collusion documented by *Butterfly – The Asian and Migrant Sex Workers Support Network*, cases in which Toronto bylaw officers used their power of inspection to enter workplaces, TPS officers detained workers for various reasons, and transferred them to the CBSA for violation of their work permits or lack of status (Lam 2018). Indeed, immigrants working in this industry are often in violation of the *IRPA* even if they have a work permit as immigration regulations forbid all temporary residents from 'enter[ing] into an employment agreement [...] with an employer who, on a regular basis, offers striptease, erotic dance, escort services or erotic massages' (SOR/2002-227; s.183(1)b.1), thus making racialized women in this sector an easy target for joint CBSA and Toronto Bylaw raids.

In the case of Montreal, it has been much harder to document formal collaboration agreements or planned joint operations relating to the policing of immigrants. The Montreal Police Service (SPVM) Archives Office – in charge of managing FOI requests – has systematically used a security clause in the provincial FOI legislation to deny all of my requests. In one case, I filed a complaint to the Quebec Access to Information Commissioner and an SPVM lawyer eventually sent me two agreements first denied on this ground – and this, three years after my initial request – to avoid going to the Commission's tribunal. The first is a basic information agreement from 2008 stating information sharing protocols between the SPVM and the CBSA, and the second is an agreement signed in 2015 for the affectation of a CBSA officer to an SPVM investigation unit to assist with regard to 'trans-border crime.'[6] This does not reveal much about the policing of people with precarious status. And yet, migrant justice organizers claim that municipal police officers regularly detain and transfer people to the CBSA (Solidarity Across Borders 2017) and a report produced for the City of Montreal shows that people living with precarious immigration status fear encounters with the police (Lagrange and Ridde 2018).

Calls made to the CBSA warrant response centre

To compensate for this lack of data on formal agreements, I also use calls made to the CBSA Warrant Response Centre (WRC) as a proxy to give us an idea of the extent of police CBSA interactions. In a 2010 document, the CBSA presented this centre, operating 24/7, as 'an important component in effecting removal orders' in the context where the organization considers that 'the process to add an immigration-related warrant to the CPIC system is cumbersome and leads to delays in warrants being transferred to CPIC' (Canada Border Services Agency 2010).

Each time a law enforcement officer calls, the call centre staff logs the call based on the agency calling, and the reason for the call. According to the records obtained through ATI, reasons for calls include 'status check,' 'warrant inquiry,' 'database verification,' 'follow-up calls,' 'previously deported person inquiry,' 'fingerprints requests,' and 'others.' Among these, 'status check' is systematically and by far the most common reason logged for calls placed by police. According to the CBSA's own internal definition of 'status check', 'law enforcement officers may call to verify the immigration status of a subject because they have a *suspicion* a subject may not have legal status in Canada and therefore may be of interest to CBSA.'[7] When the WRC staff considers that this is the basis for the call, it logs it under 'status check.'

The data I have obtained for 2015 to 2019 show that the vast majority of the more than ten thousand calls made annually to the WRC are for status check/status determination. A great number of those calls are by the RCMP, but the majority of them are made by municipal police bodies. The fact that municipal police officers inquire into someone's immigration status through a status check/status determination (and not a 'database verification' or 'warrant inquiry') means that they go beyond what is required from them under *IRPA* s.142. Figures 1 and 2 below show the data for the Toronto Police and the Montreal Police, the two cities where this particular data reveal the highest numbers of calls.

In Montreal, we see a sharp increase in recent years and a total of 3,565 calls in 2019, 88% of them for satus check/status determination. While one might think that this increase is tied to the higher number of asylum seekers crossing the border from the United States in recent years, a SPVM spokesperson told media that it is unlikely and that she does not know why the number of calls has been increasing (Robichaud 2018). In Toronto, while calls have decreased since we first used this data in a report (Moffette and Gardner 2015) and in a public campaign pressuring the TPS in 2015, 3,350 calls were nonetheless placed in 2019, 82% of them for status check/status determination. The numbers are lower for other cities, including Vancouver.

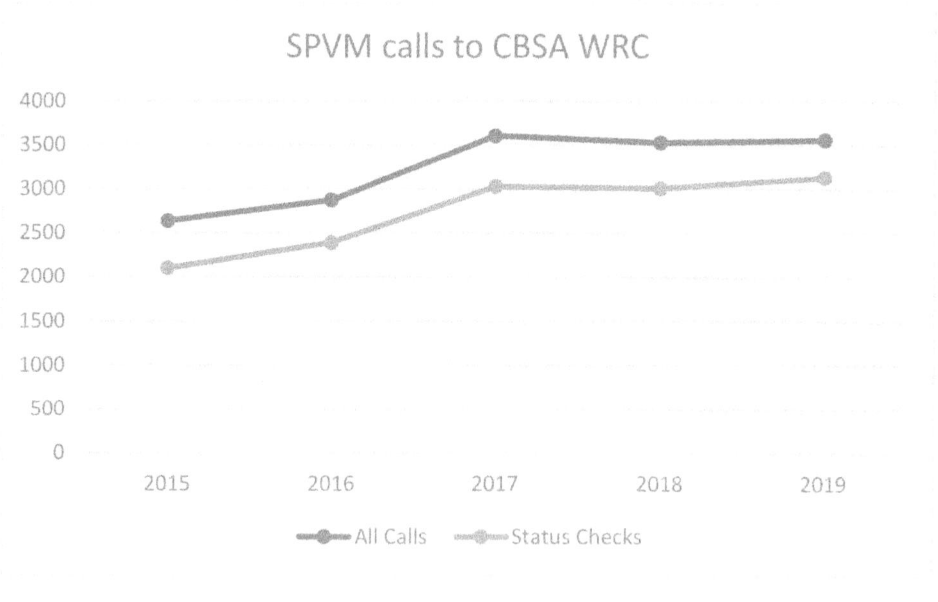

Figure 1. Montreal police service 'status check' calls to the WRC.

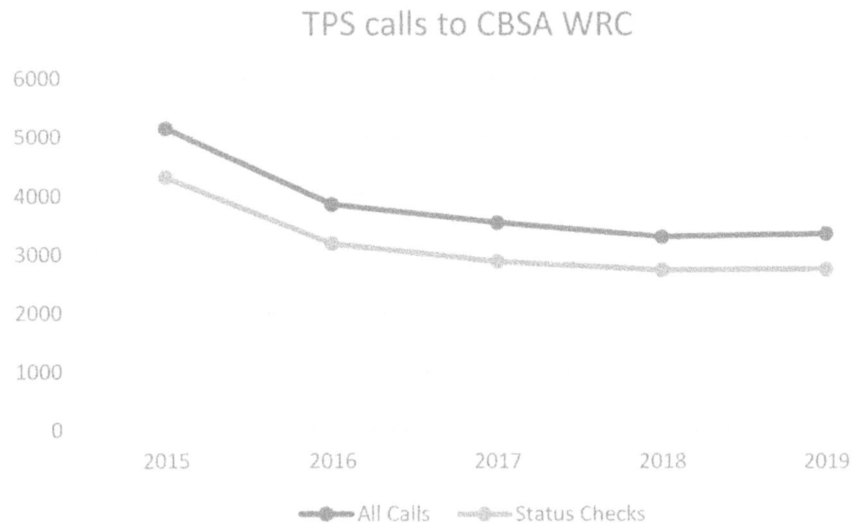

Figure 2. Toronto police service 'status check' calls to the WRC.

This does not certainly mean that interactions are less frequent however, as calls are only one avenue for police to communicate or work with the CBSA on immigration control.

Racial profiling and immigration policing

This data raises a number of serious questions about racial profiling and the grounds on which a police officer develops 'a suspicion a subject may not have legal status in Canada' and decides to contact the CBSA. The CBSA statistical data does not render explicit the grounds for inquiring about immigration status – just that the call is based on a suspicion – but it suggests forms or social and racial profiling (Chan 2011; Wortley and Owusu-Bempah 2011; Bruckert and Hannem 2013).

While legally demonstrating the existence of profiling as a discriminatory biased practice is always difficult due to the lack of data – or to 'data suppression' (Millar and Owusu-Bempah 2011, 653) – we should not get distracted by the question of bias or intent. Indeed, if one conceptualizes race as an assemblage constructed out of various material, discursive and symbolic bits and pieces (M'charek, Schramm, and Skinner 2014), or a 'social profile' as being constituted by a 'constellation of statuses' (Bruckert and Hannem 2013, 298) rendered visible through supposed markers of a particular type of person, it becomes clear that police 'suspicion' cannot but be informed by a number of social and 'racialized risk knowledges' (Pratt and Thompson 2008, 620). This is evident in Weber's (2013, 73) interviews with 776 police officers in New South Wales, Australia. Asked about reasons for deciding to conduct immigration checks, these officers listed 'doubt over identity,' 'foreign documents,' 'unable to speak English,' 'non-Australian accent,' 'foreign name' and 'ethnic appearance' as grounds justifying further inquiry. While 'ethnic appearance' in this case was the least common clue mentioned, and 'doubt over identity' the most common one, it is clear that accent, appearance and foreign documents are assembled together to constitute race.

While such data do not exist in the Canadian context, we find the very same logic at play in the testimony of a Metro Vancouver Transit Police officer at the Coroner's inquest into the death in custody of Lucía Vega Jiménez. The officer was checking everyone's fare when they reached the platform to board public transportation, which Jiménez did not have. He explains:

> I asked her if I could see some identification from her. At that point she stated to me that she didn't have any identification, but she would be willing to give me her name [. . .] I asked for her full name and date of birth, which she gave me. I then ran it on CPIC and PRIME,[8] our police databases, to see if I could confirm the name that she had given me at the time. [This did not yield any result, and so] not being able to confirm it and having the name switched twice, I then decided to – another resource we have to try to identify someone is by contacting CBSA. At that point I contacted CBSA to say that I have – to try to confirm her identification.

When asked by a lawyer why he decided that CBSA might be a good resource to call, he added '[a]t that point I understood that – I could hear that she had an accent when I spoke with her [. . .] And with that there I could tell that she wasn't originally from Canada, and that's why I attempted to identify her by using CBSA.'[9] When the CBSA agent found out who she was and that she did not have status, he instructed the officer to detain her under the *IRPA*, until CBSA officers could pick her up and put her in detention. She ended up taking her life in detention while awaiting deportation. This example shows how the lack of documentation and the foreign accent created the profile of someone who the CBSA may have information about.

Communication and collaboration between police forces and the CBSA mean that urban policing strategies such as carding and racialized policing, while raising issues of racism against racialized residents more broadly, may also impact people with precarious immigration status. As in other contexts (e.g. Varsanyi 2008; Weber 2013; Provine et al. 2016; Armenta 2017; Moffette and Pratt 2020), there is not always a clear distinction here between racialized urban policing and immigration control, and this despite the official jurisdictional division of labour. More broadly, it also means that the mere presence of officers conducting everyday policing activities in our cities, and the interactions and communications between local social services agencies (e.g. shelters or the anti-Violence Against Women sector) or initiatives (e.g. festivals, Pride events, youth programming) increase not only the risk of criminalization in general but also the risk of immigration policing, detention and deportation.

Towards abolition: building a culture of non-cooperation

What my mapping of police-CBSA collaboration shows is that immigration policing is deployed on various scales by a number of actors, and in particular by officers involved in everyday urban policing. This means that migrant justice and anti-deportation work needs to include not only a critique of – and strategies against – formal immigration enforcement but also consider and target other policing bodies operating in our cities.

There are many examples of this type of organizing (Ridgley 2008; Varsanyi 2010). In the three cities discussed in this article, there have been various campaigns opposing immigration policing in recent years. In Toronto in 2004, when a 16-year-old woman from Grenada who had reported an assault to the TPS was detained and transferred to the CBSA because she did not have status, community members organized to fight police collaboration with the CBSA (Deshman 2009). Activists and community members were demanding a '*Don't Ask, Don't Tell*' policy with regard to immigration status; that is, a commitment on the part of the TPS to never inquire about someone's status and, if they were to find out, to never denounce the person to the CBSA. In the end, organizers were only successful in having the TPS agree to the '*Don't Ask*' component and only for 'victims and witnesses of crime' (Toronto Police Service 2008; Deshman 2009). The TPS used *IRPA* s.142 to justify not including a '*Don't Tell*' component. This provision of the *IRPA* seriously limits what local activists can do to impede collaboration. To change it would require challenging the provision at the federal level. But beyond this ground, there is nothing in Ontario law preventing police from choosing not to inquire about people's status, or for the Chief to forbid it (Immigration Legal Committee 2008), and this is what organizers were trying to push for.

This organizing effort against TPS-CBSA collaboration started a series of sectorial campaigns in generally progressive sectors to build a culture of non-collaboration with the CBSA, and to have difficult discussions about reliance on municipal police in some sectors (Berinstein et al. 2006; Nyers 2010; Nail, Kamal, and Hussan 2010). One of the most successful – the *Shelter, Sanctuary, Status* campaign – temporarily forced CBSA to stop lurking near anti-VAW shelters (Nail, Kamal, and Hussan 2010; Abji 2018). When the political timing was ripe – that is, when it was possible to use it as a mobilizing tool – the Toronto Solidarity City Network launched a campaign that led to City Council passing what would be understood as a Sanctuary City policy. Many similar campaigns were then launched across the country. While the policy did not deliver on its promise to provide access without fear for undocumented Torontonians (Hudson et al. 2017), for many organizers, getting a policy passed was not an end in itself. Instead, it was one more tool in trying to promote a culture of non-cooperation and build alternatives for safer cities for all in the spirit of police and border abolitionism (Nail, Kamal, and Hussan 2010; Fortier 2013; Walia 2014; Gardner 2017; Moffette and Ridgley 2018).

As these campaigns develop in various cities, I argue that we should take police abolition and open borders as general compass to assess the strategies we propose. Conceptual arguments and practical strategies for the project of police abolition have been developed by well-known penal abolitionist groups such as *Critical Resistance* since the late 1990s, and a number of collectives – especially in the United States – have developed practical resource kits. More recently, academics and activists have published a number of books highlighting racialized police violence and promoting abolitionist or radical reductionist takes on policing (Camp and Heatherton 2016; Schenwar, Macaré, and Price 2016; Correia and Wall 2017; Ritchie 2017; Vitale 2017). Although still in the minority, some police and prison abolitionist groups such as *INCITE! Women of Color Against Violence* (2008) now include specific discussion about immigration control in their toolkits for resisting law enforcement violence and developing alternatives to policing.

Overall, broader strategies developed by police abolitionist groups apply here as well. There are many resource kits with similar ideas, whose authorship is rather collective, and from which I am borrowing to offer approaches that can be used in this case.[10] A first step is about documenting, exposing and opposing police-induced harm, and CBSA-induced harm, and talking about it within our communities. This has to centrally include exposing and opposing racial profiling, carding, and other forms of racialized policing, regardless of whether it directly impacts people with precarious immigration status (e.g. Wortley and Owusu-Bempah 2011; Madan 2019; Diverlus, Hudson, and Ware 2020). For those of us working with progressive immigration agencies and refugee rights organizations, it means encouraging a broad analysis that extends beyond the impact of detention on immigrants and refugees to also include a critique of the role of policing in colonial state building and white supremacy.

A second set of strategies may focus on securing institutional restrictions of police power. These tactics can aim to restrict police power in general, and its role in immigration control in particular, through legal reform campaigns or litigation. This was the objective, for instance, of the Toronto campaign to prevent police from asking or sharing information about immigration status. They can also aim to financially limit police and immigration enforcement power through divestment and diversion campaigns when police budgets are discussed. This is also important to funnel funding towards alternative harm-reduction initiatives needed for the following set of tactics.

Indeed, a third set of strategies focuses on talking to neighbours and community members about the dangers of calling the police, and developing lists of more appropriate resources that we can access in case of emergency. This is not always easy in the context of austerity and cuts to social services, but alternative rapid response harm-reduction resources are needed to respond to mental health or substance use issues, interpersonal violence, and most problematic or disruptive behaviours that may lead some people to calling the police. It also means raising awareness among local service providers about the criminalizing and immigration risks of communicating with the police, especially in sectors where we generally find allies but where relationships with police services are often institutionalized (such as in the anti-VAW sector; shelters for street-involved people, etc.). Related to this, is the broader need to develop alternative spaces of accountability and restorative justice, an agenda to which the broader penal abolitionist movement has extensively contributed.[11]

Finally – and this is especially important for those of us working specifically in migrant justice movements – we need to build solidarity with criminalized people, and avoid falling for the easy communication strategies of framing immigrants and people with precarious immigration status as 'hard working' and as 'non-criminal.' This recourse to what Loyd (2019) calls 'wages of innocence,' while it may seem like a useful short-term communication strategy to gain popular support, makes it too easy to throw under the bus all people who are criminalized, not employed in a legal waged job, or not useful to police as 'victims or witnesses of crime' (see also Escobar 2008; Moffette and Ridgley 2018). Illegalization and criminalization are similar processes deployed by state actors to border some people out of our communities and we need to address them together.

These strategies are all part of building a culture of non-cooperation with immigration enforcement, of hindering the ability of those who want to help them to do so (especially the police), and of developing alternatives to policing in the spirit of police and border abolition. As immigration policing is often the first link in the chain leading to detention and deportation, we should make it a key site of research and action if we want to fight immigration detention and state-sanctioned coercive control over the movement of people.

Notes

1. In Canada, the right to obtain records from federal agencies is covered by the *Access to Information and Privacy Act* and referred to as Access to Information (ATI), while information from provincial and municipal bodies is covered by provincial laws bearing different names but generally referred to as Freedom of Information (FOI).
2. This service's name has changed many times and appears differently in various documents used here. I am using the current name to avoid inconsistencies.
3. CBSA ATI # A-2014-08770; Transit Police FOI records now available at: https://transitpolice.ca/news/published-foi-requests/#1461268658268-655b45d7-22fc.
4. CBSA ATI # A-2015-01698.
5. CBSA ATI # A-2015-10,948.
6. In French, 'criminalité transfrontalière.' Records with the author.
7. CBSA ATI # A-2017-20,562 and CBSA ATI # A-2019-00049. My emphasis on *suspicion*. The category 'status check' has been replaced in 2019 by 'status determination.' After using this language for 4 years, the new version reads 'Law Enforcement Officers may call to determine the status of an individual they have in custody or who is under criminal investigation or subject to an enforcement proceeding. They may also call to obtain validation of Immigration documents or foreign travel documents' – CBSA ATI # A-2020-02055.
8. While CPIC includes only criminal information such as records and warrants, the Police Records Information Management Environment (PRIME-BC) is a broader police database that includes police information about anyone who has been in contact with police in British Columbia.
9. Ministry of Public Safety and Solicitor General Coroner's Inquest in the Matter of the Inquest into the Death of Lucia Dominga Vega Jimenez – Proceedings at Inquest, Burnaby, B.C., 29 September 2014, p. 18–19. Document with the author.
10. Choosing which collective to cite after each idea would thus prove difficult. For lists of groups offering similar ideas in various contexts, see Rose (2018) or TRIP! Project (2018).
11. Many collectives have developed or gathered tools. See, for instance, resources developed by *INCITE! Women of Color Against Violence* or *Philly Stands Up* to address gender-based and sexual violence in a spirit of community accountability.

Disclosure statement

No potential conflict of interest was reported by the author.

ORCID

David Moffette http://orcid.org/0000-0002-4131-2671

References

Abji, S. 2018. "Postnational Acts of Citizenship: How an Anti-Border Politics Is Shaping Feminist Spaces of Service Provision in Toronto." *International Feminist Journal of Politics* 20 (4): 501–523. doi:10.1080/14616742.2018.1480901.

Alexander, M. 2012. *The New Jim Crow: Mass Incarceration in the Age of Colorblindness.* New York: New Press.

Armenta, A. 2017. *Protect, Serve, and Deport: The Rise of Policing as Immigration Enforcement.* Oakland, CA: University of California Press.

Berinstein, C., J. McDonald, P. Nyers, C. Wright, and S. S. Zerehi. 2006. *"Access Not Fear": Non-Status Immigrants and City Services.* Toronto: Preliminary Report.

Blomely, N. 2014. "Distangling Law: The Practice of Bracketing." *Annual Review of Law and Social Science* 10 (1): 133–148. doi:10.1146/annurev-lawsocsci-110413-030719.

Bowling, B. 2013. "The Borders of Punishment: Towards a Criminology of Mobility." In *The Borders of Punishment: Migration, Citizenship, and Social Exclusion*, edited by F. K. Aas and M. Bosworth, 291–306. Oxford: Oxford University Press.

Boyle, P., and T. Dafnos. 2019. "Infrastructures of Pacification: Vital Points, Critical Infrastructure, and Police Power in Canada." *Canadian Journal of Law and Society* 34 (1): 79–98. doi:10.1017/cls.2019.5.

Bruckert, C., and S. Hannem. 2013. "To Serve and Protect? Structural Stigma, Social Profiling, and the Abuse of Police Power in Canada." In *Selling Sex: Experience, Advocacy, and Research on Sex Work in Canada*, edited by E. van der Meulen, E. Durisin, and V. Love, 297–313. Vancouver: UBC Press.

Camp, J. T., and C. Heatherton, eds. 2016. *Policing the Planet: Why the Policing Crisis Led to Black Lives Matter.* Brooklyn: Verso.

Canada Border Services Agency. 2010. "CBSA Detentions and Removal Programs - Evaluation Study." November 2010. Online: www.cbsa-asfc.gc.ca/agency-agence/reports-rapports/ae-ve/2010/dr-rd-eng.html

Carrier, N., J. Piché, and K. Walby. 2019. "Abolitionism and Decarceration." In *The Handbook of Social Control*, edited by M. Deflem, 319–332. Hoboken, NJ: Wiley-Blackwell.

Carrier, N., and J. Piché. 2015. "The State of Abolitionism." *Champ penal/Penal Field* xii. doi:10.4000/champpenal.9164.

Chan, J. 2011. "Racial Profiling and Police Subculture." *Canadian Journal of Criminology and Criminal Justice* 53 (1): 75–78. doi:10.3138/cjccj.53.1.75.

Chase, R. T., ed. 2019. *Caging Borders and Carceral States: Incarceration, Immigration Detentions, and Resistance.* Chapel Hill, NC: University of North Carolina Press.

Childs, D. 2009. "'You Ain't Seen Nothin' Yet': *Beloved*, the American Chain Gang, and the Middle Passage Remix." *American Quarterly* 61 (2): 271–297. doi:10.1353/aq.0.0075.

Childs, D. 2015. *Slaves of the State: Black Incarceration from the Chain Gang to the Penitentiary.* Minneapolis: University of Minnesota Press.

Christie, N. 1982. *Limits to Pain.* Oxford: Martin Robertson.

Cleveland, J., and C. Rousseau. 2013. "Psychiatric Symptoms Associated with Brief Detention of Adult Asylum Seekers in Canada." *Canadian Journal of Psychiatry* 58 (7): 409–416. doi:10.1177/070674371305800706.

Correia, D., and T. Wall. 2017. *Police: A Field Guide.* Brooklyn: Verso.

Dafnos, T. 2012. "Beyond the Blue Line: Researching the Policing of Aboriginal Activism Using Access to Information." In *Brokering Access: Politics, Power and Freedom of Information Processes in Canada*, edited by M. Larsen and K. Walby, 209–233. Vancouver: UBC Press.

Davis, A. 2003. *Are Prisons Obsolete?* New York: Seven Stories Press.

Davis, A. 2016. "Political Prisoners, Prisons and Black Liberation." In *If They Come in the Morning … Voices of Resistance*, edited by A. Y. Davis, 49–86. London: Verso.

Davis, A., and G. Dent. 2001. "Prison as Border: A Conversation on Gender, Globalization, and Punishment." *Signs* 26 (4): 1235–1241. doi:10.1086/495654.

Deshman, A. 2009. "To Serve Some and Protect Fewer: The Toronto Police Services' Policy on Non-Status Victims and Witnesses of Crimes." *Journal of Law and Social Policy* 22: 209–235.

Dhillon, J. K. 2015. "Indigenous Girls and the Violence of Settler Colonial Policing." *Decolonization: Indigeneity, Education and Society* 4 (2): 1–31.

Diverlus, R., S. Hudson, and S. M. Ware, eds. 2020. *Until We are Free: Reflections on Black Lives Matter in Canada*. Regina: University of Regina Press.

Durkheim, É. 1973. "[1900]. "Two Laws of Penal Evolution."." *Economy and Society* 2 (3): 285–308. doi:10.1080/03085147300000014.

Escobar, M. 2008. "No One Is Criminal." *Abolition Now! Ten Years of Strategy and Struggle against the Prison Industrial Complex*, edited by The CR10 Publications Collective, 57–69. Oakland, CA: UK Press.

Feeley, M. M. 1979. *The Process Is the Punishment: Handling Cases in a Lower Criminal Court*. New York: Russell Sage Foundation.

Fortier, C. 2013. "No One Is Illegal Movements in Canada and the Negotiation of Counter-National and Anti-Colonial Struggles within the Nation-State." In *Negotiating Non-Citizenship: Precarious Legal Status in Canada*, edited by L. Goldring and P. Landolt, 274–290. Toronto: University of Toronto Press.

Foucault, M. 1995 [1977]. *Discipline and Punish: The Birth of the Prison*. New York: Vintage Books.

García Hernández, C. C. 2017. "Abolishing Immigration Prisons." *Boston University Law Review* 97(1): 245–300.

Gardner, K. 2017. "What's Happening to Sanctuary?" *Briarpatch*, May-June. Online: https://briarpatchmagazine.com/articles/view/whats-happening-to-sanctuary

Gill, N., D. Conlon, D. Moran, and A. Burridge. 2018. "Carceral Circuitry: New Directions in Carceral Geography." *Progress in Human Geography* 42 (2): 183–204. doi:10.1177/0309132516671823.

Gilmore, R. W. 2007. *Golden Gulag: Prisons, Surplus, Crisis, and Opposition in Globalizing California*. California: University of California Press.

Global Detention Project. 2018. *Country Report - Immigration Detention in Canada: Important Reforms, Ongoing Concerns*, Geneva.

Goldring, L., and P. Landolt, eds. 2013. *Producing and Negotiating Non-Citizenship: Precarious Legal Status in Canada*. Toronto: University of Toronto Press.

Gros, H. 2017. *Invisible Citizens: Canadian Children in Immigration Detention*. Toronto: International Human Rights Program, Faculty of Law, University of Toronto.

Gros, H., and P. van Groll. 2015. *"We Have No Rights": Arbitrary Imprisonment and Cruel Treatment of Migrants with Mental Health Issues in Canada*. Toronto: International Human Rights Program, Faculty of Law, University of Toronto.

Gusterson, H. 1997. "Studying Up Revisited." *PoLAR* 20 (1): 114–119. doi:10.1525/pol.1997.20.1.114.

Hale, C. R. 2001. "What Is Activist Research?" *Items* 2 (1–2): 13–15.

Herzing, R. 2016. "Black Liberation and the Abolition of the Prison Industrial Complex: An Interview with Rachel Herzing." *True Leap Press*. Online: https://trueleappress.com/2016/08/30/black-liberation-and-the-abolition-of-the-prison-industrial-complex-an-interview-with-rachel-herzing/

Hewitt, S. 2002. *Spying 101: The RCMP's Secret Activities at Canadian Universities, 1917-1997*. Toronto: University of Toronto Press.

Howe, M., and J. Monaghan. 2018. "Strategic Incapacitation of Indigenous Dissent: Crowd Theories, and Settler Colonial Policing." *Canadian Journal of Sociology* 43 (4): 325–348. doi:10.29173/cjs29397.

Hudson, G., I. Atak, M. Manocchi, and C.-A. Hannan. 2017. "(No) Access T.O.: A Pilot Study on Sanctuary City Policy in Toronto, Canada." *RCIS Working Paper* 2017/1. Toronto: RCIS.

Hussan, S. 2014. *Indefinite, Arbitrary and Unfair: The Truth about Immigration Detention in Canada*. Toronto: End Immigration Detention Network.

Immigration Legal Committee. 2008. *Police Services: Safe Access for All: Legal Arguments for a Complete "Don't Ask, Don't Tell" Policy*. Report Presented to the Toronto Police Services Board, May 2008.

INCITE! Women of Color Against Violence. 2012. *Law Enforcement Violence against Women of Color & Trans People of Color: A Critical Intersection of Gender Violence & State Violence (An Organizer's Resource and Tool Kit)*. Redmond, WA: INCITE!.

Kazansky, B., G. Torres, L. van der Velden, K. Wissenbach, and S. Milan. 2019. "Data for the Social Good: Toward a Data-Activist Research Agenda." In *Good Data*, edited by A. Daly, S. K. Devitt, and M. Mann, 244–259. Amsterdam: Institute of Network Cultures.

Kinsman, G., and P. Gentile. 2009. *The Canadian War on Queers: National Security as Sexual Regulation*. Vancouver: UBC Press.

Kronick, R., C. Rousseau, and J. Cleveland. 2018. "Refugee Children's Sandplay Narratives in Immigration Detention in Canada." *European Child & Adolescent Psychiatry* 27 (4): 423–437. doi:10.1007/s00787-017-1012-0.

Lagrange, S., and V. Ridde. 2018. "Comment améliorer l'accès et l'utilisation des services pour les résidents sans statut d'immigration à Montréal?" Report produced by Chaire REALISME for the City of Montreal. Obtained through FOI (54-2018-0029).

Lam, E. 2018. *Behind the Rescue: How Anti-Trafficking Investigations and Policies Harm Migrant Sex Workers.* Toronto: Butterfly – Asian and Migrant Sex Workers Support Network.

Larsen, M., and K. Walby, eds. 2012. *Brokering Access: Power, Politics and Freedom of Information Process in Canada.* Vancouver: UBC Press.

Larsen, M., and J. Piché. 2009. "Exceptional State, Pragmatic Bureaucracy, and Indefinite Detention: The Case of the Kingston Immigration Holding Centre." *Canadian Journal of Law and Society* 24 (2): 203–229. doi:10.1017/S0829320100009911.

Lippert, R. K., and K. Walby. 2019. *A Criminology of Policing and Security Frontiers.* Bristol: Bristol University Press.

Loyd, J., A. Burridge, and M. Mitchelson. 2009/2010. "Thinking (And Moving) beyond Walls and Cages: Bridging Immigrant Justice and Anti-Prison Organizing in the United States." *Social Justice* 36 (2): 85–103.

Loyd, J. M. 2019. "Prison Abolitionist Perspective on No Borders." In *Open Borders: In Defense of Free Movement*, edited by N. Heynen and R. Jones, 89–109. Athens: University of Georgia Press.

Lytle Hernández, K. 2011. "Amnesty or Abolition? Felons, Illegals, and the Case for a New Abolition Movement." *Boom: A Journal of California* 1(4): 54–68. doi:10.1525/boom.2011.1.4.54

Madan, G. R. 2019. "'I'm Just Your Friend Now': Community Policing in Toronto Schools." In *Critical Schooling*, edited by F. Villegas and J. Brady, 21–45. Cham: Palgrave MacMillan.

Maillet, P., A. Mountz, and K. Williams. 2017. "Researching Migration and Enforcement in Obscured Places: Practical, Ethical and Methodological Challenges to Fieldwork." *Social and Cultural Geography* 18 (7): 927–950. doi:10.1080/14649365.2016.1197963.

Martin, L. 2019. "Carceral Mobility and Flexible Territoriality in Immigration Enforcement." In *Handbook on Critical Geographies of Migration*, edited by K. Mitchell, R. Jones, and J. L. Fluri, 244–254. Cheltenham, UK: Edward Elgar.

Marx, G. 1984. "Notes on the Discovery, Collection, and Assessment of Hidden and Dirty Data." In *Studies in the Sociology of Social Problems*, edited by J. Schneider and J. Kitsuse, 78–113. Norwood, NJ: Ablex.

Maynard, R. 2017. *Policing Black Lives: State Violence in Canada from Slavery to the Present.* Winnipeg: Fernwood Publishing.

M'charek, A., K. Schramm, and D. Skinner. 2014. "Topologies of Race: Doing Territory, Population and Identity in Europe." *Science, Technology & Human Values* 39 (4): 468–487. doi:10.1177/0162243913509493.

Millar, P., and A. Owusu-Bempah. 2011. "Whitewashing Criminal Justice in Canada: Preventing Research through Data Suppression." *Canadian Journal of Law and Society* 26 (3): 653–661. doi:10.3138/cjls.26.3.653.

Moffette, D., and K. Gardner. 2015. *Often Asking, Always Telling: The Toronto Police Service and the Sanctuary City Policy.* Toronto: No One Is Illegal-Toronto and Law Union of Ontario.

Moffette, D. 2018. *Governing Irregular Migration: Bordering Culture, Labour and Security in Spain.* Vancouver: UBC Press

Moffette, D., and J. Ridgley. 2018. "Sanctuary City Organizing in Canada: From Hospitality to Solidarity." *Migration and Society* 1(1): 147–155.

Moffette, D., and A. Pratt. 2020. "Beyond Criminal Law and Methodological Nationalism: Borderlands, Jurisdictional Games, and Legal Intersections." In *Contemporary Criminological Issues: Moving Beyond Insecurity and Exclusion*, edited by C. Côté-Lussier, D. Moffette, and J. Piché, 15–39. Ottawa: University of Ottawa Press.

Monaghan, J., and K. Walby. 2017. "Surveillance of Environment Movements in Canada: Critical Infrastructure Protection and the Petro-Security Apparatus." *Contemporary Justice Review* 20 (1): 51–70. doi:10.1080/10282580.2016.1262770.
Monchalin, L. 2016. *The Colonial Problem: An Indigenous Perspective on Crime and Injustice in Canada*. Toronto: University of Toronto Press.
Mongia, R. 2018. *Indian Migration and Empire: A Colonial Genealogy of the Modern State*. Durham, NC: Duke University Press.
Moran, D., J. Turner, and A. K. Schliehe. 2018. "Conceptualizing the Carceral in Carceral Geography." *Progress in Human Geography* 42 (5): 666–686. doi:10.1177/0309132517710352.
Mountz, A. 2011. "The Enforcement Archipelago: Detention, Haunting, and Asylum on Islands." *Political Geography* 30 (3): 118–128. doi:10.1016/j.polgeo.2011.01.005.
Nail, T., F. Kamal, and S. Hussan. 2010. "Building a Sanctuary City: No One Is Illegal-Toronto on Non-Status Migrant Justice." *Upping the Anti* 11: 147–160.
Nakache, D. 2013. "Détention des demandeurs d'asile au Canada: Des logiques pénales et administratives convergentes." *Criminologie* 46 (1): 83–105. doi:10.7202/1015294ar.
Nichols, R. 2017. "The Colonialism of Incarceration." In *Legal Violence and the Limits of the Law*, edited by A. Swiffen and J. Nickols, 49–67. London: Routledge.
Nyers, P. 2010. "No One Is Illegal between City and Nation." *Studies in Social Justice* 4 (2): 127–143. doi:10.26522/ssj.v4i2.998.
Piché, J., and M. Larsen. 2010. "The Moving Targets of Penal Abolitionism: ICOPA, Past, Present and Future." *Contemporary Justice Review* 13 (4): 391–410. doi:10.1080/10282580.2010.517964.
Pires, A. 2001. "La rationalité pénale moderne, la société du risque et la judiciarisation de l'opinion publique." *Sociologie et sociétés* 33 (1): 179–204. doi:10.7202/001562ar.
Pires, A. 2007. "Une 'utopie juridique' et politique pour le droit criminel moderne?" *Criminologie* 40 (2): 9–18. doi:10.7202/016849ar.
Pratt, A. 2005. *Securing Borders: Detention and Deportation in Canada*. Vancouver: UBC Press.
Pratt, A., and S. K. Thompson. 2008. "Chivalry, 'Race' and Discretion at the Canadian Border." *British Journal of Criminology* 48 (5): 620–640. doi:10.1093/bjc/azn048.
Provine, D. M., M. W. Varsanyi, P. G. Lewis, and S. H. Decker. 2016. *Policing Immigrants: Local Enforcement on the Front Lines*. Chicago: University of Chicago Press.
Richmond, A. 1994. *Global Apartheid: Refugees, Racism and the New World Order*. Oxford: Oxford University Press.
Ridgley, J. 2008. "Cities of Refuge: Immigration Enforcement, Police and the Insurgent Genealogies of Citizenship in U.S. Sanctuary Cities." *Urban Geography* 28 (1): 53–77. doi:10.2747/0272-3638.29.1.53.
Rigakos, G. S., and S. R. Worth. 2011. "Access to Information (ATI) as a Double-Edged Sword for Critical Policing Research." *Canadian Journal of Law and Society* 26 (3): 645–652. doi:10.3138/cjls.26.3.645.
Ritchie, A. 2017. *Invisible No More: Police Violence against Black Women and Women of Color*. Boston: Beacon Press.
Robichaud, O. 2018. "Le SPVM ne sait pas pourquoi ses communications avec les services frontaliers ont augmenté." *Huffpost Québec*. 03 April 2018. Online: https://quebec.huffingtonpost.ca/2018/04/03/le-spvm-ne-sait-pas-pourquoi-ses-communications-avec-les-services-frontaliers-ont-augmente_a_23402208/
Rose, A. 2018. "What to Do Instead of Calling the Police." Blog. Online: http://www.aaronxrose.com/blog/alternatives-to-police
Ruggiero, V. 2010. *Penal Abolitionism*. Oxford: Oxford University Press.
Saleh-Hanna, V. 2015. "Black Feminist Hauntology: Rememory the Ghosts of Abolition?" *Champ pénal/Penal Field XII*. doi:10.4000/champpenal.9168.
Schenwar, M., J. Macaré, and A. Y.-L. Price, eds. 2016. *Who Do You Serve, Who Do You Protect? Police Violence and Resistance in the United States (A Thruthout Collection)*. Chicago: Haymarket Books.
Sharma, N. 2006. *Home Economics: Nationalism and the Making of "Migrant Workers" in Canada*. Toronto: University of Toronto Press.

Sharma, N. 2007. "Global Apartheid and Nation-Statehood: Instituting Border Regimes."." In *Nationalism and Globalism*, edited by J. Goodman and P. James, 71–90. New York: Routledge.
Silverman, S. J., and P. Molnar. 2016. ""Everyday Injustices: Barriers to Access to Justice for Immigration Detainees in Canada." *Refugee Survey Quarterly* 35 (1): 109–127. doi:10.1093/rsq/hdv016.
Solidarity Across Borders. 2017. "Solidarity across Borders Demands that the City of Montreal Implement Tangible and Meaningful Measures for a 'Sanctuary City'; No More SPVM Collaboration with CBSA." Press Release 18 February 2017. Online: http://www.solidarityacrossborders.org/en/solidarity-across-borders-demands-that-the-city-of-montreal-implement-tangible-and-meaningful-measures-for-a-sanctuary-city-no-more-spvm-collaboration-with-cbsa
Speed, S. 2006. "At the Crossroads of Human Rights and Anthropology: Toward a Critically Engaged Activist Research." *American Anthropologist* 108 (1): 66–76. doi:10.1525/aa.2006.108.1.66.
Spivakovsky, C. 2011. "The Need for Flexible and Adaptive Research in an Environment of Diverse Barriers to Accessing Data." *Canadian Journal of Law and Society* 26(3): 607–612
Stumpf, J. 2013. "The Process Is the Punishment in Crimmigration Law." In *The Borders of Punishment: Migration, Citizenship, and Social Exclusion*, edited by K. Franko Aas and M. Bosworth, 58–75. Oxford: Oxford University Press.
Sudbury, J. 2008. "Rethinking Global Justice: Black Women Resist the Transnational Prison-Industrial Complex." *Souls* 10 (4): 344–360. doi:10.1080/10999940802523885.
Sudbury, J. 2009. "Maroon Abolitionists: Black Gender-oppressed Activists in the Anti-Prison Movement in the U.S. and Canada." *Meridians* 9 (1): 1–29. doi:10.2979/MER.2008.9.1.1.
Toronto Police Service. 2008. "Victims and Witnesses without Legal Status". Online: http://www.torontopolice.on.ca/publications/files/victims_and_witnesses_wthout_legal_status.pdf
TRIP! Project. 2018. "What to Do Instead of Calling the Police – Some Options." TRIP! Project website. Online: http://tripproject.ca/what-to-do-instead-of-calling-the-police-some-options/
Valverde, M. 2016. "What Counts as Theory, Today? A Post-Philosophical Framework for Socio-Legal Empirical Research." *Brazilian Journal of Empirical Legal Studies* 3 (1): 172–181.
Varsanyi, M. W. 2008. "Immigration Policing through the Backdoor: City Ordinances, the 'Right to the City,' and the Exclusion of Undocumented Day Laborers." *Urban Geography* 91 (1): 29–52. doi:10.2747/0272-3638.29.1.29.
Varsanyi, M. W., Ed. 2010. *Taking Local Control: Immigration Policy Activism in U.S. Cities and States*. Stanford, CA: Stanford University Press.
Velloso, J. G. V. 2013. "Beyond Criminocentric Dogmatism: Mapping Institutional Forms of Punishment in Contemporary Societies." *Punishment & Society* 15 (2): 166–186. doi:10.1177/1462474513477979.
Villegas, P. E. 2015. "Fishing for Precarious Status Migrants: Surveillant Assemblages of Migrant Illegalization in Toronto, Canada." *Journal of Law and Society* 42 (2): 230–252. doi:10.1111/j.1467-6478.2015.00706.x.
Vitale, A. S. 2017. *The End of Policing*. London: Verso.
Walby, K. 2009. "'He Asked Me If I Was Looking For Fags … ' Ottawa's National Capital Commission Conservation Officers and the Policing of Public Park Sex." *Surveillance & Society* 6 (4): 367–379. doi:10.24908/ss.v6i4.3268.
Walby, K., and M. Larsen. 2011. "Access to Information and Freedom of Information Requests: Neglected Means of Data Production in the Social Sciences." *Qualitative Inquiry* 18 (1): 31–42. doi:10.1177/1077800411427844.
Walia, H. 2013. *Undoing Border Imperialism*. Oakland, CA: AK Press/Institute for Anarchist Studies.
Walia, H. 2014. "Sanctuary City from Below: Dismantling the City of Vancouver." *The Mainlander*, 2 June. Online: http://themainlander.com/2014/06/02/sanctuary-city-from-below-dismantling-the-city-of-vancouver/
Weber, L. 2013. *Policing Non-Citizens*. London: Routledge.

Wortley, S., and A. Owusu-Bempah. 2011. "The Usual Suspects: Police Stop and Search Practices in Canada." *Policing and Society* 21 (4): 395–407. doi:10.1080/10439463.2011.610198.

Statutes and Cases

Immigration and Refugee Protection Act, S.C. 2001, c. 27.

Immigration and Refugee Protection Regulations, SOR/2002-227.

Ministry of Public Safety and Solicitor General Coroner's Inquest in the Matter of the Inquest into the Death of Lucia Dominga Vega Jimenez - Proceedings at Inquest. Burnaby, B.C., 29 September 2014, p. 18-19.

Curated hostilities and the story of Abdoul Abdi: relational securitization in the settler colonial racial state

Nisha Nath

ABSTRACT

This paper offers the framework of relational securitization to understand the publicly documented story of Abdoul Abdi, a former child refugee from Somalia who spent the majority of his life in government care, and, at the age of 24, faced deportation because the state failed to secure his citizenship. Drawing from a reading of the Federal Court of Canada's 2018 ruling in *Abdoulkader Abdi v The Minister of Public Safety and Emergency Preparedness*, I argue that we can understand Abdoul's story as part of an organized logic, wherein the state regulates and securitizes marginalized subjects in *reliant* ways. Put differently, the intersecting and interacting custodial institutions of child welfare, policing, and borders and detention reveal how systemic anti-Blackness and settler colonialism are not separate enactments of the white supremacist settler colonial state but enactments that need and rely on each other; they are relational.

Introduction

In January 2018, during a town hall in Sackville, Nova Scotia, Canadian Prime Minister Justin Trudeau made this relatively unremarkable statement:

> ... we have something extraordinarily precious ... a population ... that is positively inclined towards immigration and welcoming refugees.... we know that immigration and diversity is an incredible source of strength, of growth for our communities, opportunities for us all.... But the way we continue to believe in our immigration system is to know that our immigration system is strong and rigorous and fairly applied.... we have a system that is based on rules and principles, but that also is compassionate and reflects on the individual cases.... We will do what Canada always does. Try to do the right thing based on rules and compassion....

While this statement was unremarkable in its articulation of familiar national narratives, what was remarkable about the comments was what incited them. Fatouma Abdi, who came to Canada as a child refugee from Somalia, had stood up and pointedly asked: 'Why are you deporting my brother? How come you're not stopping it?'

In this paper, I consider the publicly documented story of Fatouma's brother, Abdoul Abdi – a man who also came to Canada as a child refugee from Somalia and, at the age of 24, faced deportation. Fatouma's questions and Abdoul's story are significant because they lay bare a series of disjunctures between national narratives and the conditions that would make Abdoul's trajectory possible.

From the outset, there are four things to note about Abdoul's case. First, if deported, Abdoul would be sent to Somalia, a country he had never lived in. Though Abdoul came to Canada as a refugee and has lived here since 2000, his deportation was possible because Nova Scotia's Department of Community Services (DCS) did not secure his citizenship while he was in their care. Having been convicted of a criminal offense carrying a custodial sentence of more than six months, as a permanent resident, Abdoul could be deported under the *Faster Removal of Foreign Criminals Act* [2013], an amendment to the *Immigration and Refugee Protection Act* (IRPA) [2001].

Second, Abdoul's story occurs within a context where systemic anti-Black racism underwrites child welfare services in Nova Scotia and beyond, as well as underscoring Canadian border, detention and deportation policies, and law enforcement and policing. While this latter intersection of 'crimmigration' has been more readily confronted by researchers (Stumpf 2006; Aiken, Lyon and Thorburn 2014; Molnar and Silverman 2016), others demonstrate the intractability of this larger network of carceral spaces, including child welfare, that is evident through Abdoul's story (See Maynard 2017).

Third, as a site policed by the state, the infrastructure of child welfare is rooted in sustaining and reproducing settler colonialism and racialized hierarchies. Similarly, the infrastructure of immigration and detention has been animated to secure white settler colonial futurities, and the same relationship with whiteness and settler colonialism can be identified vis-à-vis policing (Crosby and Monaghan 2018, 13). Given this, one might read Abdoul's pathway to deportation as either an 'accumulation of governmental historical, social and moral failures' (Nethery and Silverman 2018), or instead as 'successes' of these institutions.

Finally, there is deep complexity to Abdoul's story, where intersecting and functionally interacting institutions (child welfare, policing, and immigration) and structures of power (anti-Blackness, border imperialism, and settler colonialism) work together to curate the hostilities marking his publicly documented life. Even a cursory examination of the lineage of state infrastructure demonstrates this link, starting with Canada's original department of citizenship and immigration: The Department of Immigration and Colonization. In 1936, the extractive nature of immigration, citizenship and settler colonialism would be laid bare as the Department of Mines and Resources became responsible for immigration. In subsequent years, this intertwining of citizenship, multiculturalism, immigration, security, racial capitalist extraction and settler colonialism would be repackaged and reconfigured in new language and shifting portfolio bundles.

Considering these observations, this paper offers the framework of relational securitization to understand and map these complexities. The state's focus on securing the border, on 'managing diversity', and on securing its governance over Indigenous People and their territories represent not simply *different* regulatory strategies for *differently* marginalized people; rather these relationships of governance are intrinsic to each other and to the regulatory apparatus of the white supremacist settler colonial state (Nath 2018). In contrast to comparativism, relational accounts signal how '... state formations or histories, logics of oppression and exploitation are linked, whether causally or symbolically, ideationally or semantically' (Goldberg 2009, 1275). The state's need to '... constitute, maneuver, and govern Othering in diverse but interconnected ways' reflects the state's need to '... constitute and reconstitute *itself* as if it were a legitimate and ordered authority' (Dhamoon 2019, 6 – emphasis added). As carefully detailed by Dhamoon (2019), there is a growing body of significant multidisciplinary work that attends to this relationality by exploring histories of 'Indigenous dispossession, anti-Black racism and displacement, and Asian immigration and settlement', along with the centrality of Indigeneity in studies of migration, the co-implication of people of colour in anti-Black racism and colonial domination, and the potential and limits of ethics of solidarity and alliance amongst Black people, Indigenous Peoples and people of colour (BIPOC) (2).

Here, I contribute to this broader conversation and argue that the state is invested in particular kinds of connections *and* disconnections amongst BIPOC, meaning that the state regulates and securitizes these subjects in profoundly reliant and relational ways. Relational securitization not only helps us understand Abdoul's story, but this relational dynamic is illuminated through Abdoul's story, wherein we see how the convergence and mutuality amongst institutions of child welfare, policing and border security work to actively secure white settler colonial futurities. Part of securing this futurity includes the structuring of the relative positionality of BIPOC. In this way, securing decolonial, anti-racist and decarceral futurities requires a different kind of convergence and mutuality amongst BIPOC. In that spirit, I take up Abdoul's story as a way to understand the organizing logic of the white settler colonial state, wherein the context of anti-Blackness that produces the Nova Scotia Home for Colored Children, is one where the state has a reliant interest in settler colonialism, and where securing the borders and asserting state sovereignty reinscribe the same. These processes are not separate enactments of the state, but enactments that need and rely on each other; they are relational.

After outlining the theoretical framework for relational securitization, I provide an overview of the anti-Black and settler colonial imperatives of child welfare in the Canadian context, as a means to draw out specific connections to the other custodial institutions (borders and detention, policing) at play in the securitization of Abdoul. Drawing from a reading of the Federal Court of Canada's ruling in *Abdoulkader Abdi v The Minister of Public Safety and Emergency Preparedness*, 2018 [hereafter Abdi], I then examine two modalities of relational securitization: 1) rightlessness and 'little banishments'; and, 2) foreignness and goodness.

Through the public record: Abdoul Abdi's story

At the age of 6, Abdoul Abdi came to Canada as a child refugee, after his mother had died in a Djibouti United Nations refugee camp. He would be raised by his Aunt Asha and Aunt Hawa who, in his words 'saved him' (Barton 2018, 00, 59). Within a year of arriving, he and his sister were apprehended into government care in Nova Scotia. It is unclear why.

After being placed into care, Abdoul would ultimately become a permanent ward of the state by the age of 9. He was never adopted, and over the following 11 years, was placed in 31 different 'care arrangements'. This would include permanent and temporary foster homes, halfway houses, hospitals, wards, etc. (Nethery and Silverman 2018), one of which he describes as physically and emotionally abusive (Khandaker 2018). His sister would be removed from this home after stating that she had been sexually assaulted (Khandaker 2018).

While in care, several things would (and would not) happen. Abdoul would 'age out' and the highest level of education he received was Grade 6 (Federal Court of Canada 2018, at para 12). In his early teens, Abdoul would start to have conflicts with the law, accumulating a youth criminal record, and living an incredibly precarious life, at one point being homeless (Federal Court of Canada 2018, at para 13). Despite multiple attempts by his Aunt to resolve his citizenship status, the state would never make his application for citizenship. In 2005, DCS actively prevented Asha from making a citizenship application on his behalf, stating that she did not have guardianship (Federal Court of Canada 2018, para. 13). Three years later, Asha would attempt to gain custody of Abdoul but was unsuccessful. In her application, she noted she was concerned about Abdoul's static permanent resident status (Federal Court of Canada 2018, para 13). By the age of 19, thirteen years after first entering into care, Abdoul would be advised that he was ineligible for citizenship because of his criminal record (Federal Court of Canada 2018, at para 16).

Upon being incarcerated in 2014 for aggravated assault and other crimes, this lack of citizenship status would prove critical. These charges and his permanent resident status would give rise to the inadmissibility proceedings under the IRPA. Pursuant to s. 44(1) of the IRPA, the Minister's Delegate (MD) made a finding that there were reasonable grounds to believe that Abdoul was inadmissible to Canada on the grounds of 'serious criminality', hence should be deported.

This would incite a series of Federal court rulings, which in 2018, landed on Abdoul's side. The court found that the MD had erred by failing to properly weigh Abdoul's rights under the *Canadian Charter of Rights and Freedoms* [hereafter *the Charter*] in her determination, and in this, failed to demonstrate 'justification, transparency, and intelligibility' (Federal Court of Canada 2018, at para 5). One day later, Ralph Goodale, the Minister of Public Safety and Emergency Preparedness, would tweet: 'The Government of Canada respects the decision filed on July 13 by the Federal Court concerning Abdoul Abdi. The Government will not pursue deportation for Mr. Abdi.'

Relational securitization within a settler colonial racial state

Abdoul's positioning within the carceral network of policing and prisons, and border imperialism (including detention, deportation, immigration and citizenship) lends itself to an analysis attentive to securitization, wherein Abdoul is produced as a 'risky' subject, and in that gesture, a range of interventions and intrusions into his life are authorized. Critically, the elasticity of the concept of security and the process of securitization are also fitting to examine a third carceral space implicated here: child welfare.

In thinking about security, there are five analytic insights that are helpful. First, national security has been deployed to regulate citizens and non-citizens labelled dissident or subversive (Kinsman, Buse, and Steedman 2000, 278), as well as those whose mere presence threatens to unravel the power structures underscoring status quo social relations and state policy in the white supremacist settler state (Nath 2016, 42).

Second, the state's deployment of security has consistently been repressive, with its contours and boundaries hardening and sharpening during periods of perceived and actual crisis (Macklin 2006, 48). This rigidifying and honing of boundaries is augmented by the perception of *chronic crisis* seen to be posed by multiculturalism and Indigenous self-determination (Macklin 2006, 68).

Third, national security positions the state as under threat. Within this configuration, the state is treated as the benign guarantor of security, despite the reality that the state is in many respects the *guarantor of insecurity* for BIPOC.

Fourth, that the state is seemingly founded on the promise to secure its members against each other, belies the fact that what is being secured through the presumed social contract is access to Indigenous land, through the '*transfer of* property' and the '*transformation into* property' (Nichols 2018, 14 – emphasis in original). In considering anti-Blackness, it is not merely land but people who are also transformed into 'things' and 'currency'.

Fifth, security discourses are both externally and internally focused. Border imperialism is internalized, while white supremacy, capitalism and settler colonialism are externalized in migration and security policy; this is relational.

Certainly, there are some temporal tensions in thinking through the lens of security and in deploying the language of securitization. Some scholars critical of securitization approaches note '... a temporal move from some supposed pre- or non-security time, towards the (exceptional) violence of security. This is linked to White nostalgia for a better, more innocent time: a time which does not exist for those who have been subject to colonialism or the racial contract on scales from the local to the global, that is to say, the majority of the world's people' (Howell and Richter-Montpetit 2019, 18). Others point to the evolution of securitization over time, in particular to changes in the post-9/11 context (Neocleous 2006). In deploying relational securitization as a framework, the intention here is to be tethered neither to coherence nor disjuncture (See for example Abu-Laban and Bakan 2020, 82), and instead to draw focus to sets of structured relationships that have been consistently treated as either distinctive from each other, or as one and the same. Put differently, the white settler colonial state has always been a security state, and it continues to be one even in an age of reconciliation, or what Joyce Green (2020) has described as 'wreckonciliation'.

This is consequential for citizenship. The structures of settler colonialism, racial capitalism, and imperialism, along with the targeted Subjects – Indigenous people, Black people and other people of colour – are fundamentally intertwined. Thobani (2007) reminds us that capitalist, Orientalist, colonial and imperialist projects shape how racialized migrants become subject(ed) to the institution of white supremacy and white settler citizenship (71–74). With this gesture, the white supremacist settler colonial state becomes a nation of immigrants, and citizenship becomes a promise, not peril. Thobani continues: 'The category citizen, born from the genocidal violence of colonization, exists in a dialectical relation with its Other, the Indian, for whom *the emergence of this citizenship was deadly, not emancipatory*' (2007, 74 – emphasis added). Yet, as pathways to citizenship become more elusive, for racialized migrants' citizenship is never only or simply a promise. Rather, the currency here for the state is precariousness and what precariousness enables the state to do. Inseparable from 'the forced internal migrations of Aboriginal peoples onto reserves and the destruction of their communities as sovereign entities', the institution of Canadian citizenship bundles together settler-colonialism, nation-building, economic development, settlement, white supremacy and security (Thobani 2007, 74).

The emergence of the racial capitalist settler state is grounded in the simultaneity of settler colonialism, imperialism, slavery and anti-Blackness; the genocide of Indigenous people is fundamentally related to Black life and death, of Columbus the murderer *and* Columbus the enslaver (Lethabo-King 2016). As Leroy (2016) notes, the common thread between settler colonialism and slavery are 'justifications for extermination – of bodies, of sovereignty, of self-possession'. These 'unique global levels of devastation', continue to shape the lives of Indigenous and Black people today (Amadahy and Lawrence 2009, 106). Indigenous people are 'targeted for physical and cultural destruction', and characterized as unviable nations, and Black diasporic people are 'uniquely racialized' by a discourse created through slavery and hinging on 'degrees of phenotypic blackness' that map onto entire black-led nations (Amadahy and Lawrence 2009, 106). Variably criminalized, surveilled, exploited, and entrapped by, through and within borders, these unique and interacting legacies of hostility – of Indigenous genocide and black dehumanization – present themselves in the child welfare context as well.

The point here being that binary and dichotomous analyses of Indigenous/settler can obscure as much as they reveal (Johnston 2015, 23). As Lethabo-King (2016) argues, a singular focus on *terra nullius* or settler's relation to land '... disappears the settler's relationship to violence and the intricate and violent processes of the human's self-making'. Put differently, a binary focus displaces *how* the settler becomes the agent of conquest/the conquistador(a)/human through *both* Indigenous genocide and Black dehumanization (Lethabo-King 2016).

The framework of relational securitization adds to a broader conversation that foregrounds that the relational dimension is not simply between White settlers and the Other, but rather a relational securitization amongst Others in ways that variably support dominant power structures and relations. These tensions have been taken up by several scholars, who describe not only the fundamental overlap between immigration, settlement and colonialism, but how the

> '... separation of Indigenous sovereignty and migration issues is ... productive....It is economically productive in that it helps mask the ways in which the generation of wealth is premised on the perpetuation of colonial inequality.... Furthermore, the discourses and imagined geographies of the settler state (like liberal multiculturalism) whose agency derives from certain representations of settler society undermines both struggles for Indigenous self-determination and the recognition of colonial domination by fixing Indigenous peoples as a minority group and their rights within the rubric of groups rights descendent from political arrangement with a benevolent, (neo)liberal state' (Stanley et al. 2014).

Critically, this does not mean that there are inherent alliances between BIPOC, nor does it mean that we trace complicity '... along the same coordinates as white people's complicity' (Patel et al. 2015, 9). State policing of the border and of Black and racialized communities buttresses the regulatory apparatus of the white supremacist settler colonial state with its continuing preoccupation with Indigenous mobility and sovereignty (Smith 2014, x–xi). In this sense, the positioning of racialized immigrants/settlers/arrivants vis-à-vis Indigenous people – relational securitization – is specifically relational *as a strategy of the state*. Historically, this has included measures to maintain a spatial separation between racialized immigrant communities and Indigenous communities, with Indigenous people excluded from settler cities (Johnston 2015, 127–128). Or, as noted above, the state's strategic adoption of the language of 'cultural diversity' to position Indigenous people as 'one of many' (Johnston 2015, 128).

Whether described as a 'triangulated formation' (Thobani 2007), a 'triad of relationships' (Tuck and Gaztambide-Fernández 2013), or as three pillars of white supremacy (Morgensen 2014; Smith 2006), the point here is that while these struggles are not equivalent, they are reliant. White supremacist settler governmentality *needs* immigrants of colour and racialized labourers in service of the liberal multicultural state's assertion of sovereignty and in service of securing ongoing capitalist economic exploitation. This manifests in policing, border and detention policies and child welfare.

Circling back, the intention here is to draw connections between this framework of relational securitization and the curated hostilities marking Abdoul's trajectory. The remainder of this paper explores these dynamics, first by tracing out a partial context of white settler colonial securitization through child welfare in Canada, and second by highlighting two modalities of relational securitization – rightlessness and 'little banishments' and, foreigness and goodness – that manifest in various aspects of Abdoul's story.

What does child welfare secure?

In the Nova Scotia *Children and Family Services Act* [1990], child welfare is described as '[protecting] children from harm, [promoting] the integrity of the family and [assuring] the best interests of children'. On the ground, the clarity of these principles is debateable. Cindy Blackstock (2009) writes:

> I have practiced child welfare for over 20 years and I am still not sure what it does. I cannot understand why there are so many poor children in child welfare care. I cannot understand the difference between social disadvantage and child maltreatment and I cannot understand why a system faced with such overwhelming overrepresentation of First Nations children in care is not marshalling all of its resources to deal with the problem (202).

Commenting specifically on Abdoul's case, Julia Huys from Justice for Children and Youth remarks on the disjuncture: 'The way it's all set up doesn't make sense – you have young people in care from the state, then that same state tries to remove them once they become adults' (Massa 2018).

I have practiced child welfare for over 20 years and I am still not sure what it does. I cannot understand why there are so many poor children in child welfare care. I cannot understand the difference between social disadvantage and child maltreatment and I cannot understand why a system faced with such overwhelming overrepresentation of First Nations children in care is not marshalling all of its resources to deal with the problem (202).

Commenting specifically on Abdoul's case, Julia Huys from Justice for Children and Youth remarks on the disjuncture: 'The way it's all set up doesn't make sense – you have young people in care from the state, then that same state tries to remove them once they become adults' (Massa 2018).

The disjuncture between stated policy goals and the experiences of those within the system are not unique to the child welfare context. As noted in the introduction to this special issue, the stated policy goals underlying detention also fail to be supported by evidence. Just as we might query, who or what does detention secure, we can similarly ask, who or what does child welfare secure? Further, these sites of state policing, one supposedly guided by an ethic of care and the other an ethic of security, are related in more fundamental ways. The lineages of the infrastructures of immigration and detention, policing *and* child welfare reveal how they work to secure white settler colonial futurities. This raises important questions of how they work *together* to produce subjects as variably risky, therein providing rationalizations for the extraction of subjects from their families, communities and nations, and ultimately curating a broader set of organized hostilities. Within this, child welfare is not only treated as external or separate from immigration detention, but child welfare is understudied as a reliant and reinforcing site of pacification, extractivism and securitization.

That child welfare agencies emerged within the context of white supremacy, patriarchy, colonialism and anti-Black racism offers some clarity in responding to the question, what does child welfare secure? Social work and social welfare were not singularly a response to the poverty that settlers and Indigenous people experienced (Fortier and Wong 2018, 2). Rather, these policies developed specifically to entrench settler colonialism (Maynard 2017, 191). Animated by an impetus to Christianize and 'civilize' the Other, paternalistic and patriarchal social welfare provisions offered support in exchange for submission (Fortier and Wong 2018, 2). As opposed to responding to the catastrophic impact of settler colonialism, social welfare acted as regulators of 'gendered and racialized systems of morality and social control' (Srivastava 2005, 30 as cited in Badwall 2015, 5), and attempted to make Indigenous people more 'industrious', hence easing their 'burden' on the state (Fortier and Wong 2018, 3).

The administrators/enunciators of these gendered and racialized narratives of civility, responsibility and pathology were Christian missionaries granted control over the education of Indigenous children, and Indian agents as social service providers, settling disputes, enforcing provincial laws, administering funds, keeping financial records, and dispensing social welfare to those whose "' … neck was within the noose woven by foreign laws"' (Manuel and Posluns 1974, 54 as cited in Fortier and Wong 2018, 3–4). By the late 19th century, children's aid societies would be established explicitly in child welfare legislation, through which white, middle-class women would make their 'friendly visits' (Maynard 2017, 187).

Upper-class British European morality was positioned as a virtue, simultaneously casting poor and racialized women (and their families) as immoral (Maynard 2017, 187). This relational dimension was key not simply because it sanctified white children and denigrated Black children, but it justified segregation and separation, and turned on discourses of security and safety (Maynard 2017, 187). Landertinger (2017) describes how child welfare emerged as an imperial project that was premised on the assertion that it could '… save the damaged but salvageable white settler child' (11). In contrast, during the late 19th and early 20th century, orphanages in Nova Scotia were reluctant to accept Black children, with some rejecting them outright (Maynard 2017, 188). The Black community mobilized to create a special home to protect Black children (Taylor 2015, 30), a project the state was eager to support because it kept supposedly dangerous, less evolved, and unsalvageable Black children away (Maynard 2017, 188). Thus, The Nova Scotia Home for Colored Children was born, an inequitably funded space that ultimately reinforced the systemic racism of a system that kept Black children 'outside of the protection of society at large', and ultimately did nothing to protect these children from rampant abuse, exploitation, overcrowding and the denial of the fundamentals of education, hygiene and care (Maynard 2017, 189).

Returning to the broader point, the subjects of peril were not the Black children in care – rather, white children, property and social stability were all positioned as being in jeopardy (Schumaker 2012, 34). Clearly, this insecurity was gendered and racialized. As Maynard (2017) traces, in 1920, the federal government created a federal child welfare branch headed by Helen MacMurchy, a prominent eugenicist (187). MacMurchy worked specifically with the Women's branch of the Immigration and Colonization Department in order to carefully monitor and surveil the racialized population (Maynard 2017, 187). At this juncture, we can see how these imperatives fed a justification of racialized social surveillance, policing, and the regulation of racialized immigrants, with white women social workers on the frontlines.

In the post-war welfare state, a few dynamics are worth noting. First, the 1951 amendments to the Indian Act which divested the social welfare functions of the Indian agent would position social workers officially as primary agents within the shifting settler colonial context (Fortier and Wong 2018, 5). This would help to recode and legitimate the political intent of the state 'under the guise of a more humane and professional provision of social welfare to Indigenous communities' (Fortier and Wong 2018, 5).

Second, in the post-war state, this deep intimacy between white supremacy and settler colonialism manifest in what Thobani (2007) describes as the exaltation of white, middle class, heteronormative people as national subjects who are not simply entitled but *entitled to entitlements* through citizenship (Doret and Pon 2018, 86). BIPOC would be characterized as (potentially) unworthy and undeserving (Doret and Pon 2018, 86), entrenching a long-standing dynamic in which citizenship – as a site of regulated inclusion (See Dhamoon 2013) – is itself positioned on a precipice of penalty and privilege.

Third, the expansion of the post-war welfare state had a gendered impact on white women's economic advancement and employment opportunities, imprinting upon these exalted national subjects the 'nation-state's values of compassion, benevolence, and care.' (Doret and Pon 2018, 87). This exaltation of white femininity as compassionate, innocent and courageous trades on its inverse, where Black and Indigenous mothers were (and are) pathologized, marginalized and humiliated through state-sanctioned surveillance and intrusions. It remains worth nothing that in 2008, 82% of the child welfare workface was white, with 85% being women (Doret and Pon 2018, 87).

These histories map onto the contemporary context. While there has been limited published research on the experiences of Black families and communities in the context of child welfare, what has been published points to the 'systemic nature of surveillance, discipline, punishment and humiliation experienced by Black families' (Doret and Pon 2018, 96). Child welfare represents a critical site through which Black life is policed, resulting in catastrophic rates of removal (Maynard 2017, 186). In Toronto, 40.8% of children in care are Black children, even though they represent 8.6% of the population (Mochama 2017). Black children in Toronto are 28% more likely to be placed in care than

White children whose families are investigated (Ontario Human Rights Commission 2018, 21). Moreover, children in Black-led families are in care longer than children with white parents or other differently racialized groups (Ontario Human Rights Commission 2018, 22).

Indigenous children and youth represent 5% of the population and make up 30–40% of all children in care, and up to a staggering 80% of youth in the care system in Manitoba (Maynard 2017, 191). According to a 2016–17 provincial government report, of the 11,000 children and youth in care in Manitoba, nearly 10,000 are Indigenous and nearly 6,000 are permanent wards of the province (Edwards n.d.). As Blackstock (2011) has noted, there are more Indigenous youth in state care today than ever before, and that number continues to increase. Critically, for Indigenous children, they are over-represented at *all* junctures in child welfare decision-making (Ontario Human Rights Commission 2018, 17).

The purpose in offering this partial history is decidedly *not* to compare the experiences of Black and Indigenous children, nor is it to collapse their experiences onto the other. Rather, the purpose here is twofold: 1) to consider how and why the experience of Abdoul represents a *systemic* set of organized encounters as opposed to an individual one; and, 2) to reflect on the lineages of hostility – Indigenous genocide and slavery/anti-Blackness – their temporal and institutional co-implication, and their ongoing entrenchment. In response to the question, 'What does child welfare secure?', we can reasonably infer what it *should* secure. However, in response to the question, 'What does child welfare secure systemically?', four points stands out.

First, with social workers acting in many respects as 'petty sovereigns' (Butler 2006, 56), social work and child welfare enables the state to regulate at a distance (Doret and Pon 2018, 96), but with a level of staggering intrusive intimacy. Second, vis-à-vis Indigenous and Black people, we see how the management of childhood is a central concern in creating a racially structured settler society, even if the specific management of childhood is underwritten by different logics (Landertinger 2017, ii; Badwall 2015, 4). Third, the provision and denial of social welfare has been a 'core technology of the settler apparatus', which also includes policing and surveillance, genocidal legislation that facilitates ongoing dispossession, the geographical and physical containment of Indigenous people, the targeting of culture and language, and the removal of children from communities (Fortier and Wong 2018, 3–4). For both Indigenous Peoples and Black people, white supremacy has and continues to support the separation of Black and Indigenous mothers from their babies. For Indigenous women, this ongoing attempt to extract them from their communities – through extraordinary levels of violence and dehumanization (Simpson 2016), as well as the designation of and erasure of Indian status (Napoleon 2001) – has been intrinsic to settler colonialism's drive to erase Indigenous People. There is also a marked specificity to the violence and invisibility of Black women's experiences captured in the term 'misogynoir' (Maynard 2017, 130). Here, the intersection of racism, anti Blackness and misogyny imprint in particularly heightened ways on Black woman cast as 'deviant', for example, those who are single mothers, require social assistance, face challenges related to mental health, or engage in sex work (Maynard 2017, 130).

Fourth, racialized populations have been targeted in parallel ways, particularly through the weaponization of capitalist discourses of industriousness and self-reliance, often through the twinning of 'charity' with 'settlement' (Fortier and Wong 2018, 4). This is invariably accompanied by social policy goals that create dependence and trade on precariousness amongst Indigenous and racialized people (Pasternak 2015, 326). This too reproduces the settler state by securing access and legitimizing the quest for access to 'mis-managed' Indigenous territories, by subduing Black and Brown people into a pool of compliant labour, and through legitimation and the creation of a 'buffer zone'. Here social welfare and social workers alleviate *some* of the suffering from racial capitalism, settler colonialism, and heteropatriarchy, but simultaneously delegitimize solutions put forward by communities that signal assertions of sovereignty or autonomy (Fortier and Wong 2018, 10).

Curated hostilities

All of these dynamics bear down on Abdoul, and in examining his case, relational securitization brings forward two modalities through which the state's imperative to secure the settler racial state is enacted through these interacting custodial spaces. While Indigenous and Black children are positioned according to different logics, these modalities – rightlessness and little banishments, and foreignness and goodness – illustrate the intersecting discourses and infrastructures of state securitization and regulation.

Rightlessness and 'Little Banishments'

Law functions centrally in securitization processes wherein only some groups seem to reside within an ambiguous state of rightlessness that is, in fact, replete with law. Historically, the state's position has been to deny non-citizens involved in immigration proceedings the legal protections afforded to defendants in the criminal justice system. This has been done by adopting a stance where deportation has been positioned as a 'regular act of sovereignty' (Nyers 2019, 4), immigration is framed as a privilege and not a right, and deportation and removal are characterized as qualitatively different from criminal punishment (Nath 2018, 13). Clearly the difference between deportation and criminal punishment is not merely qualitative given that non-citizens can be doubly punished. Permanent residents convicted of a criminal offense can 'do their time', and then still be detained and deported. For those with Canadian citizenship, the trajectory is at least *potentially* different, including access to the status 'rehabilitated' and to the possibilities of being able to return to a home and/or community.

Abdoul's status is fully precarious – as a profiled Black Somali child/boy/man, a permanent resident, and a ward of the state whose home with his Aunt has been denied. Yet, Abdoul's experience is not unique. Nyers (2019) writes of a 'global deportspora', an 'underclass of global travellers – rejected asylum seekers, irregular migrants, deportees – that make up an ever-increasing share of global population movements' but that also includes a class of 'irregular citizens' (4). Bashi (2004) characterizes Western immigration law, policy and practice as a form of globalized anti-Blackness manifest specifically through detention and deportation, where '... Black life ... is marked by vulnerability to being placed into cages and banished by criminal justice and immigration systems' (Maynard 2017, 158).

A precarious citizenship status becomes a gateway to a range of traumatic vulnerabilities that are systemic in nature; these are experienced disproportionality and specifically by poor and racialized people. Since the passage of the *Faster Removal of Foreign Criminals Act* [2013] the charge of 'serious criminality' has become even more flexible, given that small scale offenses with 6-month custodial sentences are increasingly deportable (Maynard 2017, 173). The power here being that the nexus of security and immigration penalty is normalized as race-neutral, just and reasonable (Maynard 2017, 159).

While deportation constitutes an intrinsic deprivation of liberty that is about the security of the person, non-citizens who face deportation are positioned in the first order as threats, not as rights bearers; their subject position cannot sustain both dimensions (Nath 2016, 428). The series of losses facing Abdoul are incredibly violent – the loss of home, the loss of one's state's protection, or in Arendtian terms, the loss of belonging to any community (Oriola 2009, 266). These losses are recognized minimally. In the state's submission to the court, all *Charter* and international human rights arguments are described as 'speculative and premature', leading one commentator to write: 'Our government argues that the rights of children are so irrelevant that they should not even be spoken about' (Jones 2018). Justice McDonald of the Federal Court does rule that the MD erred by not weighing the statutory objectives of the IRPA with the values of the *Charter*, yet the court provides no guidance here. Moreover, Justice McDonald notes that since the judicial review is allowed on the grounds of an administrative error, 'there is no need to address the larger constitutional issues posed by Mr. Abdi' (Federal Court of Canada 2018, at para 99).

The court also declines submission of affidavits from two experts: Rebecca Bromwich of the Ontario Youth Justice Advisory Panel, and Kiaras Gharabaghi, the Director of the School of Child and Youth Care and an Associate Professor in Immigration and Settlement Studies at Ryerson University (Federal Court of Canada 2018, at para 42). Both affidavits discussed children in care who cross over to the criminal justice system, as well as the vulnerability of youth in care (Federal Court of Canada 2018, at para 42). For the court, the state's argument that the affidavits 'do not meet the tests of reliability and necessity' was compelling and the court declined to receive them into evidence (Federal Court of Canada 2018, at para 44).

While there is clarity in the law with respect to the court's constrained handling of Abdoul's case, it is worth pausing to consider what can be evacuated from the law. Which incursions and losses are recognizable, and who is most likely to experience these losses? What does this suggest about status, and at whose discretion is this recognition?

Without guidance, how an MD weighs *Charter* considerations involves significant discretion. As David Matas has stated, 'We do not need racist laws to have racial discrimination in immigration; all we need is unlimited discretion.' (People's Commission 2007, 16). This matters because the violence of deportation is directly tethered to a lack of status. If involved with law enforcement officials, '... the bureaucratic difference between holding permanent resident status and full citizenship status creates a staggering divergence in one's life trajectory' (Maynard 2017, 175). Abdoul's lawyer, Benjamin Perryman, echoes this by maintaining that 'The biggest thing a non Canadian child in care needs is citizenship – it gives the right to have rights' (Williams 2018).

Building from a framework of relational securitization, we may be well served to think more broadly about deportation and the hostilities here. Nyers (2019) writes that *abandonment* functions as a *de facto* deportation (6), and then draws more broadly from Sassen (2014) who writes on expulsions and 'little banishments'. Expulsions in the contemporary era involve the '... multiple little banishments that happen *inside* our countries and that often entail a move into systemic invisibility – the loss of rights as an event that produces its own partial, or specialised, erasure' (Sassen 2014, 45 as cited by Nyers 2019, 6 – emphasis added).

This seems fitting to think through Abdoul's story given the context of a settler colonial racial state that enacts 'little banishments' daily. It is no small matter that Abdoul's Aunt repeatedly and actively seeks to resolve his citizenship status, and that DCS repeatedly prevents her. The reticence of Nova Scotia government officials is telling; from their perspective, citizenship is not something that the state can 'foist' upon a child in its care, and in the words of Nova Scotia Premier Stephen McNeil, '... it is up to those children as they grow into teenage years to decide whether or not they take advantage of those options' (Williams 2018). Recall here that Abdoul, under the care of the state, has achieved only a grade 6 level education, has been shuttled 31 times from home to home, and is in a precarious position with the law. We can reflect here too on the Minister's argument that the DM is not a lawyer or a judge, hence *cannot be expected* to understand *Charter* rights, and apply them (Jones 2018).

Systemically, Abdoul's story reads as an *organized banishment and abandonment* – through law, through policing, through child welfare, through borders – that is familiar in the Canadian context. Consider how settler governmentality organizes the expulsion of Indigenous people, through internal forced migrations and displacement, legal subjectivity and status, land theft, and community dislocation.

In fact, it is precisely the intrusiveness of the settler colonial racial state, and the subsequent entanglement with multiple systems and bureaucracies that seems to overwhelm, subdue and negate the right to have rights. Within the context of the white supremacist settler colonial state, the insulating strength of citizenship is tenuous given that we know that the state has and continues to authorize itself to carry out a range of oppressive hostilities and banishments of Indigenous People and racialized settlers/arrivants precisely *through* citizenship. This weaponization of citizenship trades in a currency of precariousness, meaning that unravelling these hostilities also requires thinking outside of the state sanctioned borders that reify citizenship. These banishments and hostilities lay bare the violence of this paternalistic state which Abdoul is supposed to be cared for by, an ethos of care where Abdoul, as a child of the state, becomes potentially expendable or disposable through organized abandonment.

Foreigness and Goodness

The project of settler colonial nation building suppresses and contains difference to cultivate the 'right' national identity. This is accomplished through intellectual work (e.g. the doctrine of discovery and *terra nullius*), physical and material work (e.g. incarceration, suppression of dissent, removal), and emotional and symbolic work (e.g. the portrayal of Indigenous people as entitled, alcoholic, etc. ... and the settler population as righteous, benevolent and deserving) (Fortier and Wong 2018, 8). Social work contributes to this, wherein supports are provided in ways that elevate the white settler population at the expense of Indigenous people, Black people and other people of colour (Fortier and Wong 2018, 8).

While *en masse* the poor are targeted and surveilled through the allocation of social services, the specificity here is that social work and child welfare are steeped in racialized, gendered and heteronormative taxonomies of difference and civility (Badwall 2015, 4). In security contexts, some are marked as having an inherent capacity for violence, meaning that race becomes crucial to pre-emptive punishment and detention (Razack 2007, 6; Duffy and Provost 2009, 549). Part of the work race does more broadly is to signify difference and enable the sorting of subjects into categories of worthiness ('good') and unworthiness ('bad') (Monaghan 2013, 488). The need to secure the 'rightful citizen of the nation' functions alongside the dispensation of 'care', meaning that the regulation of childhood is critical.

Securitization is not often deployed as a framework to examine child welfare, yet the intersection of security, national belonging and child welfare is powerful because the mantra of security ('we must keep children safe' and 'we must keep our nation safe') depoliticizes and forecloses contestation. In the name of security and/or kin, the state can justify increasing investment in surveillance infrastructure, exempting itself from having to explain why it does what it does. This racial governmentality that intersects care, security and race can '... at times give rise to the exoneration of dehumanizing practices of quarantining and population management (i.e. racial profiling, imprisonment, deportation, police brutality, and targeted killing)' (Moffette and Vadasaria 2016, 295).

Building from here, notions of foreigness and goodness intersect as enabling conditions. Consider the specificity of Somali experiences in Canada, particularly in the early 1990s when there was a massive influx of Somali asylum seekers fleeing the civil war (Maynard 2017, 160). Estimates hold that between 1988 and 1996, 55 000– 70,000 Somalis arrived in Canada (Ontario Council of Agencies Services Immigrants (OCASI) 2016, 1). As compared to other groups of refugees, Somali refugees have not been 'accorded the same welcome and resettlement support' (Ontario Council of Agencies Services Immigrants (OCASI) 2016, 1). In addition to facing unique and disproportionately negative challenges with presenting adequate documentation, Somali refugees have also existed in legal limbo with the introduction of the Undocumented Convention Refugees in Canada Class, which mandated a five-year wait before being eligible to apply for permanent residency (Ontario Council of Agencies Services Immigrants (OCASI) 2016, 2). This meant that by the late 1990s, an estimated 13,000 Somali asylum seekers did not have the full protections of Canadian citizenship, nor could they sponsor family members from whom they were separated (Maynard 2017, 160; Canadian Council for Refugees (CCR) 2015). Adding to this, in both the pre- and post-9/11 period, Somali refugees have been characterized as economic burdens and security threats (Ontario Council of Agencies Services Immigrants (OCASI) 2016, 2–3), with Somali refugee women being a particularly pointed site of hostility and social panic (Maynard 2017, 133–134). Black motherhood has been depicted as void of caring, protection, and nurturing, hence replete with neglect (Doret and Pon 2018, 92). This also reflects a broader dynamic where Black, Indigenous and other women of colour are criminalized for the structural conditions of their own poverty (Maynard 2017, 133–134).

Lying '... at the intersection of anti-Blackness and Islamophobia' has meant significant barriers for those with ties to Somalia (Maynard 2017, 160). Consider that the Government of Canada continues to advise that all travel to Somalia be avoided, describing conditions where the 'rule of law is virtually non-existent', suicide bombings, violent attacks and demonstration and military activity 'occur regularly', 'anti-Western sentiment' can be strong, and there is a 'very high risk of kidnapping, murder and arrest without notice or apparent cause' (Government of Canada 2019). In this context, acceptance rate of Somali claimants has declined dramatically from 90% between 1990 and 1993 to 57% in 2015 (Ontario Council of Agencies Services Immigrants (OCASI) 2016, 1).

Yet, Abdoul's deportation to Somalia – a country considered so dangerous that Canadian officials are banned from accompanying deportees there, and a country in which he has never lived – becomes thinkable because of his 'foreignness' (Maynard 2017, 178; Zilio 2013). In contrast, in her opening argument to the Federal Court, the lawyer for the Minister states that the theme of the argument would be "brought to you today by the letter 'P', which includes the 'p'rivilege of immigration, the 'p'rematurity of the applicant's arguments based on 'hypothetical' harm, and the reality that the MD is just a 'person', not a lawyer, presumably someone in the system just doing their best (Jones 2018).

Access to the status that one is just a 'good' person 'doing their best' is foreclosed for supposedly 'foreign children', but also for Indigenous children, in part through a particular kind of invisibility and hypervisibility that marks a range of profiling practices that target BIPOC. Consider that in 2016, the Children's Aid Society of Toronto found that Indigenous and Black children are far more likely to be investigated and taken into care than white children (Cotenta, Monsebraaten, and Rankin 2016). Aboriginal children – to use the language of the report – are 130% more likely to be investigated as possible victims of child abuse or neglect than white children, 15% more likely to have maltreatment confirmed, and 168% more likely to be taken from their homes and placed into care (Contenta, Monsebratten, and Rankin 2016). Studies indicate that 'neglect' is the main reason that Indigenous children enter into the child welfare system, with the rate of 'neglect only' investigations 6 times higher for First Nations children than for non-Aboriginal children (Ontario Human Rights Commission 2018, 18). Neglect here is associated with 'risk factors that stem from chronic family concerns, such as poverty, poor and unsafe housing, substance use, mental health issues, and social isolation.' (Ontario Human Rights Commission 2018, 18).

Black children are 40% more likely to be investigated for abuse of neglect, 18% more likely to have maltreatment confirmed, and 13% more likely to be taken from their homes and placed with foster parents or in group homes (Cotenta, Monsebraaten, and Rankin 2016). As with Indigenous children, most child removals in Black families (70%) fall under the category 'neglect' (Maynard 2017, 196). Abdoul himself would remark: 'A lot of kids that get taken and put in DCS, it's because of neglect from their parents. So how are you going to take children for neglect from their families, never see their families again, and then neglect them yourselves? It just – it doesn't make sense.' (Barton 2018).

Far from racially neutrally, the category of 'neglect', while deployed under different logics, operates in similar ways when used against Black and Indigenous children. 'Neglect' is an individualizing narrative that locates problems within the family, therein *invisibilizing* systemic discrimination and the conditions arising from poverty (i.e. high rates of substandard and dilapidated housing for migrant communities, and the massive underfunding of on-reserve schools, housing and child welfare).

Racial extractivism – where processes of racialization and dispossession underwrite neoliberal extractivist projects – is at play with Indigenous and Black children. Vis-à-vis Indigenous children, the state's interest in removing and containing children is 'annihilative and carceral' (Landertinger 2017, iii), and vis-à-vis Black children, and particularly Black immigrant families, the state's interest also includes the incorporation and management of pliable labour. Social workers, for example, delegitimize Indigenous care practices that are not in keeping with a capitalist economic context, offering to help those who '... bear the brunt of the social consequences of increasing industrial development in their communities' under '... the guise of a human and benevolent activity' (Fortier and Wong 2018, 7).

Mindful of the extractive logic that underscores notions of foreigness and goodness, consider the harrowing experience that Abdoul's Aunt describes in her 6 December 2017 affidavit to the court:

> Upon our arrival in Canada, we were settled in Cape Breton, Nova Scotia, where we lived for nine months. The children experienced difficulties in adjusting.... We came to believe that Abdoul and Fatouma experienced a severe assault at school. My sister and I struggled to managed [sic] the situation because of the language barrier. As a result, the Department of Immigration, Refugees and Citizenship Canada requested that we move to Halifax. It was my understanding that there would be more services available to support us there. Unfortunately, our struggles were not mitigated in Halifax. Shortly after our move, we realized that Abdoul and Fatouma were not recovering from the assault they suffered in Cape Breton, so we took them to the hospital. My sister and I were terrified that the children were hurt, and we struggled to understand what was happening. We could not communicate effectively with the hospital staff. We later found out that [they] had called the Department of Community Services....On December 3 2001, just 17 months after arriving in Canada, DCS apprehended Abdoul and Fatouma. I was absolutely shocked and horrified to be separated from my children. The police forced them out of our home.

Asha's account illuminates not only how categories like 'neglect' can authorize the violent removal of children from families who are experiencing structured precariousness but also the double movement of visibility and invisibility in which infrastructures developed to monitor and track *external* security threats have historically also been turned inwards (Nath 2018). Abdoul is clearly lodged within systems of surveillance that come to 'know him'; he is profiled as a Black man and monitored by borders as a Black Muslim non-citizen. His potentiality for deportation relies on explicit communication and coordination amongst these carceral spaces. Monaghan (2013) explains how securitization in the white supremacist settler colonial state is also premised on the need to 'know' Indigenous Peoples and their territories (488). This need to 'know' is accompanied by identification, categorization and enumeration, with reserves having been a primary tool of surveillance allowing for a broad network of state agents to keep track of, systemically report on, and create a body of knowledge '... about Indigenous peoples, their use of land and resources, the way they provided for themselves and their families, their way of life, and a myriad of less significant details' (Smith 2009, 18; Monaghan 2013, 488).

Yet, there are some things the state *does not* want to know or to make visible. In Abdoul's case, DCS's approach to immigrant children is entirely ad hoc, with no official policy or data collection specifically tracking immigrant children who are moving through care (Leavitt 2018; Mochama 2017). Without this data, it becomes impossible to accurately capture racial disparities in referrals, in decisions to open investigation cases and in admissions into care (Ontario Human Rights Commission 2018, 34). Moreover, it becomes impossible to develop a policy for those children in care with unresolved citizenship status. This is reflected in the fact that before 2017, Immigration, Refugees and Citizenship Canada did not accept children's aid societies as parents/guardians on citizenship applications for children in care (Massa 2018).

This aversion to keep comprehensive data on racialized immigrant children in care enables the perpetuation of the mythology that racism is not a problem in Canada, an approach that eerily echoes earlier immigration policies that prevented the immigration of Black people in order to avoid problematic 'race relations'. Erasure and exclusion functions in other ways too. In the hearings before the Federal Court, lawyers for the government rejected affidavits from Bromwich and Gharabaghi that drew from social science research to demonstrate that children in care, in particular migrant and racialized children, face unique vulnerabilities, including over-incarceration, marginal educational attainment and employment, instability and trauma (Jones 2018). The Minister's lawyers dismissed the affidavits because they do not provide 'legislative facts' and are 'wholly irrelevant' (Respondent's Further Memorandum of Argument 2018 at para 33 and 34). Here, the profound invisibility of not counting Black children and families positions the Canadian Border Services Agency, police and child welfare workers as the experts on the 'best interests' for Black families (Jones 2018).

This raises different implications for Indigenous people. Simpson (2015) has written about colonialism's logic of elimination and the 'fear of disappearance – a basic, terrifying, omnipresent reality of being Indigenous and particularly of being an Indigenous woman or queer person and occupied by Canada'. Dafnos (2013) adds to this complexity, by noting that within liberal democratic society, the repertoire of 'legitimate' political engagement includes the electoral process, the enforcement of the rule of law and rights through judicial procedures, but also 'participating in acts of political dissent in public spaces' (60). Public dissent brings Indigenous people into contact with institutions of law enforcement and policing (Dafnos 2013, 60). In this way, to be counted and tracked by the colonial state, in fact to be 'recognized' by the colonial state, carries unique and substantive risks for Indigenous people.

In both contexts, however, we see similar strategic moves by the state that work to censure Black and Indigenous children, their families and communities as pathological. When deficits lie within children, families and communities, interventions become mandated to enable them to be 'self-regulated' and contribute to a 'healthy and prosperous society' (Doret and Pon 2018, 94). Yet, in the context of the nation-building imperatives of social work and child welfare, pathological deficits mean that the process of integration is never fully realizable (Fortier and Wong 2018, 9). If rehabilitation is *never* possible, Lethabo-King's (2016) assertion that blackness has become apposite to humanity brings deep resonance.

Thinking back to when he first found out about his deportation order, Abdoul stated, 'Honestly, I had a breakdown. I don't remember my language, I don't remember nothing, you know. I know nobody there' (Barton 2018). His sister echoes this: 'I don't even know my culture no more.... They stripped me from my culture. They put me in group homes where I wasn't allowed to speak my language. I can't speak two sentences to you in my language' (Khandaker 2018). Fatouma further explained that the reason that Abdoul and she do not speak Somali is because when they would speak to each other in their language, they would be put on a 'time out', isolated in their rooms, and accused of plotting to escape (Jones 2018). Fatouma described this as 'solidarity confinement' (Khandaker 2018). As Nethery and Silverman (2018) write, 'By attempting to deport Abdi, the Canadian government has indicated an adherence to biological determinism: The view that Abdi's "nurture" – his social ties, relationships and mutually reinforcing personal and communities histories – matters less than his "nature" as a perpetual foreigner'. The complexity here becomes that Abdoul's 'nurture' has been within the arms of the state.

Conclusion

In a 2018 interview Abdoul states:

I guarantee if I just get swept under the rug, that there will be another child in the same position as I am because Criminal law and kids in care are hand in hand. Every kid in the group homes, if they misbehave even slightly there's the police called on them. (Barton 2018).

Abdoul's reflection is telling in that he names the conditions of possibility for his story – interacting institutions and structures of power such as policing, child welfare and immigration that organize abandonment as they pivot on foreigness and goodness. Moreover, Abdoul specifically notes that his story is not unique. Indeed it is not. In 2010, the University of Toronto's International Human Rights Program clinic students filed a complaint to the UN Human rights committee on the case of Jama Warsame. Jama and his family had fled Somalia, and he had arrived in Canada as a young child (Boulanger and Hakak 2018). After living in Canada for 20 years, a deportation order was issued for Jama because of his criminal record (Boulanger and Hakak 2018). While the UN Human Rights Committee determined that deporting to Somalia would violate Canada's human rights obligations under the International Covenant on Civil and Political Rights, in 2012, Jama would be deported (Boulanger and Hakak 2018).

Or, there is Kiwayne Jones. After spending approximately 10 years in foster homes as a ward of the state, Kiwayne Jones would age out of the system as a permanent resident in Canada. Kiwayne Jones is the representative plaintiff in a reported 200 USD million class-action lawsuit against the Ontario government, brought forward by non-citizen children who were Crown wards (Gallant 2018). The suit states that '... 'the Crown' breached its fiduciary, statutory and common law duties to the plaintiff and the class members through its failure to take all reasonable steps to maintain permanent residency status and pursue and obtain Canadian citizenship for the non-citizen Crown Wards in its care.'

And then most recently is the case of Abdilahi Elmi, a former Somali refugee and foster child who became a ward of the province of Ontario who also failed in their duty to secure citizenship. As with Abdoul, Abdilahi would face deportation to Somalia, a deportation that was suspended because the United Nations Human Rights Committee asked for a delay so they could review the case.

In my consideration of Abdoul's case, I explored two broad questions that can help to contextualize cases like his. What makes Abdoul's story possible, and what is the relationship to settler colonialism? The purpose of this article was to foreground how, as a political strategy and technology of racialized subjectivity, white settler colonial governmentality needs immigrants of colour and racialized labourers in service of the liberal multicultural state's assertion of sovereignty and in service of ongoing capitalist economic exploitation. This is not a tidy process. Rather, not only is white supremacy a foci but also the more complex ways that non-white people '... become sutured, even necessary, in racist and colonizing hegemonies' (Dhamoon 2019, 5). In this instantiation, the imprints of these dynamics can be read in the broader logics structuring Abdoul's trajectory. The multiple lineages of Abdoul's story converge in ways that defy siloed analyses of his subjectivity or of the multiple custodial spaces in which he was ensnared. Relational securitization as a strategy of the state means that rightlessness and 'little banishments', and foreignness and goodness adhere to racialized settlers/arrivants and Indigenous people in distinct but profoundly reliant ways.

This paper also reflects the taking up of a particular kind of accountability that Abdoul invites from us when he cautions that his story not be 'swept under the rug'. Being confronted with a two-foot stack of papers representing Abdoul's publicly documented story raised many ethical questions as I considered how to take up his story as a researcher and community member. As a non-Black woman of colour with secure citizenship status, I was particularly mindful of Tuck's (2009) critical intervention that researchers stop reinscribing one-dimensional damage-centred research, wherein BIPOC are invited to speak only '... from that space in the margin that is a sign of deprivation, a wound, an unfulfilled longing' (hooks 1990, 152). To that end, the intention here has been to signal how Abdoul's story is bigger than himself in that it is structured in and through these interacting custodial spaces. In the same breath, his story is indicative of how scholars, activists, community members, families and individuals might betray these organizing logics through defining their own ethics of relationality. This is not a novel intervention in that for years BIPOC grassroots organizers have been confronted by and organizing against the complexities of what Harsha Wahlia (2013) has described as the 'violence of border imperialism' (16). Consequently, this article is an invitation to researchers to think beyond the sometimes comforting clarity of a white-Other binary.

By centering this focus on relationality, scholars within the field of immigration detention can consider the interconnecting systems and histories that make detention possible, particularly those systems that are presumed to be driven by logics other than security. In this we can remember that detention and deportation within a white settler colonial state are never simply questions of immigration, meaning that how we trace the pathways of detention and deportation must be more expansive. The white racial state and the settler colonial state are fundamentally intractable. While in many different states, detention and deportation target racialized communities, the ongoing imperatives of securing white settler futurities in Canada mean that detention and deportation *here* are underwritten by logics of expropriation, erasure, displacement and evasion, as well as logics of expulsion and extraction. By considering child welfare as a site of securitization that is part of a broader carceral network, it becomes possible to understand how child welfare is deployed in systemic ways to extract compliance, organize abandonment and curate hostilities in a settler colonial and racial state. Put differently, the lens of security and surveillance turns both inwards and outwards as the white settler colonial state structures relationships among BIPOC in ways that reinforce the state narrative articulated by the Prime Minister at the outset of this paper. Consequently, the framework of relational securitization will illuminate different inflections across different racial states. For scholars and community organizers contemplating precariousness in the context of immigration detention in white settler colonial states, Abdoul's struggles raise important questions of how, and indeed whether citizenship provides a firm grounding for decolonial and decarceral futurities. Critically, for those of us who are non-Black people of colour, Abdoul's voice invites us to step into our accountabilities by subverting the state's interest in structuring our relationality with each other.

Acknowledgement

I'd like to thank the anonymous referees for their careful consideration of this work. Much thanks also goes to the editors of this special collection, Stephanie Silverman and Sharry Aiken, who modelled the best qualities in steering this to completion. While all mistakes are my own, I'm indebted to Rita Dhamoon who saw the earliest versions of this work and helped me see (and name) both the forest and the trees.

Disclosure statement

No potential conflict of interest was reported by the author.

ORCID

Nisha Nath http://orcid.org/0000-0002-3227-6998

References

Abu-Laban, Y., and A. B. Bakan. 2020. *Israel, Palestine and the Politics of Race.* London and New York: I.B. Tauris.

Aiken, S. J., D. Lyon, and M. Thorburn. 2014. "Introduction: 'Crimmigration, Surveillance and Security Threats': A Multidisciplinary Dialogue." *Queen's Law Journal* 40: 1.

Amadahy, Z., and B. Lawrence. 2009. "Indigenous Peoples and Black People in Canada: Settler or Allies?" In *Breaching the Colonial Contract: Anti-Colonialism in the US and Canada,* edited by A. Kempf, 105–136. New York: Spring Publishing.

Badwall, H. 2015. "Colonial Encounters: Racialized Social Workers Negotiating Professional Scripts of Whiteness." *Intersectionalities: A Global Journal of Social Work Analysis, Research, Polity and Practice* 3: 1–22.

Barton, R. 2018. "Abdoul Abdi Talks to the National's co-Host Rosemary Barton". *CBC News*, January 26. Retrieved from https://www.cbc.ca/news/abdoul-abdi-talks-to-the-national-s-co-host-rosemary-barton-1.4504839.

Bashi, V. 2004. "Globalized Anti-blackness: Transnationalizing Western Immigration Law, Policy and Practice." *Ethnic and Racial Studies* 27 (4): 584–606. doi:10.1080/0141987042000216726.

Blackstock, C. 2009. "When Everything Matters: Comparing the Experiences of First Nations and non-Aboriginal Children Removed from Their Families in Nova Scotia from 2003 to 2005." PhD thesis, University of Toronto.

Boulanger, A.-R., and T. Hakak. 2018. "Canada's Failed Commitment to International Human Rights Law in the Abdoul Abdi Case". *The Toronto Star*, May 28. Retrieved from https://www.thestar.com/opinion/contributors/2018/05/28/canadas-failed-commitment-to-international-human-rights-law-in-the-abdoul-abdi-case.html.

Butler, J. 2006. *Precarious Life: The Powers of Mourning and Violence*. London: Verso.

Canadian Council for Refugees (CCR). February 2015. "Somalis and Canadian Immigration Policy". Retrieved from https://ccrweb.ca/sites/ccrweb.ca/files/somali_issues_in_canadian_immigration-2016.pdf.

Cotenta, S., L. Monsebraaten, and J. Rankin. 2016. "CAS Study Reveals Stark Racial Disparities for Blacks, Aboriginals". *The Toronto Star*, June 23. Retrieved from https://www.thestar.com/news/canada/2016/06/23/cas-study-reveals-stark-racial-disparities-for-blacks-aboriginals.html.

Crosby, A., and J. Monaghan. 2018. *Policing Indigenous Movements: Dissent and the Security State*. LOCATION: Fernwood Publishing.

Dafnos, T. 2013. "Pacification and Indigenous Struggles in Canada." *Socialist Studies* 9 (2): 57–77.

Dhamoon, R. 2013. "Exclusion and Regulated Inclusion: The Case of Sikh Kirpan in Canada." *Sikh Formations* 9 (1): 7–28. doi:10.1080/17448727.2013.774709.

Dhamoon, R. K. 2019. "Relational Othering: Critiquing Dominance, Critiquing the Margins." *Politics, Groups, and Identities*. doi:10.1080/21565503.2019.1691023.

Doret, P., and G. Pon. 2018. "Anti-Black Racism, Bio-Power, and Governmentality: Deconstructing the Suffering of Black Families Involved with Child Welfare." *Journal of Law and Social Policy* 28: 81–100.

Duffy, M. T., and R. Provost. 2009. "Constitutional Canaries and the Elusive Quest to Legitimize Security Detentions in Canada." *Case Western Reserve Journal of International Law* 40: 531–560.

Edwards, K. n.d. "Fighting Foster Care: The Stunning Number of First Nations Kids in Care Is a New Touchstone for Activists – And for Rebel Parents". *Macleans*. Retrieved from https://www.macleans.ca/first-nations-fighting-foster-care/

Federal Court of Canada. 2018. *Abdi v The Minister of Public Safety and Emergency Preparedness*, [2018] F.C. 733.

Fortier, C., and H.-S. Wong. 2018. "The Settler Colonialism of Social Work and the Social Work of Settler Colonialism." *Settler Colonial Studies* doi:10.1080/2201473X.2018.1519962

Gallant, J. 2018. "Lawsuit Accuses Ontario Government of Leaving Foreign-born Crown Wards in the Lurch". *The Toronto Star*, March 9. Retrieved from https://www.utoronto.ca/news/why-try-deport-man-canada-childhood-u-t-expert-looks-case-abdoul-abdi.

Goldberg, D. T. 2009. "Debate: Racial Comparisons, Relational Racisms: Some Thoughts on Method." *Ethic and Racial Studies* 32 (7): 1271–1282. doi:10.1080/01419870902999233.

Government of Canada. 2019. Somalia Travel Advisory. Retrieved from https://travel.gc.ca/destinations/somalia.

Green, J. 2020. "Opinion: Wreckonciliation for Wet'suwet'en". *Saskatoon Star Phoenix*, February 18 https://thestarphoenix.com/opinion/letters/opinion-wreckonciliation-for-wetsuweten.

hooks, B. 1990. *Yearning*. Boston: South End Press.

Howell, A., and M. Richter-Montpetit. 2019. "Racism in Foucauldian Security Studies: Biopolitics, Liberal War, and the Whitewashing of Colonial and Racial Violence.„ *International Political Sociology* 1 (13): 2–19.

Johnston, K. R. 2015. "Unsettling Citizenship: Movements for Indigenous Sovereignty and Migrant Justice in a Settler City". PhD thesis, York University.

Jones, E. 2018. "Abdoul Abdi Hearing Speaks Volumes About How Canada Treats Child Refugees". *ByBlacks*, June 20. Retrieved from https://byblacks.com/main-menu-mobile/opinion-mobile/item/1932-abdoul-abdi-hearing-speaks-volumes-about-how-canada-treats-child-refugees.

Khandaker, T. 2018. "Foster Care System 'Failed' Child Refugee". *Vice News*, January 11. Retrieved from https://news.vice.com/en_ca/article/qvweqm/nova-scotias-foster-care-system-failed-child-refugee-facing-deportation-to-somalia.

Kinsman, G., D. K. Buse, and M. Steedman. 2000. "How the Centre Holds: National Security as an Ideological Practice." In *Whose National Security? Canadian State Surveillance and the Creation of Enemies*, edited by G. Kinsman, D. K. Buse, and M. Steedman, 278–285. Toronto: Between the Lines.

Landertinger, L. 2017. "Child Welfare and the Imperial Management of Childhood in Settler Colonial Canada, 1880s-2000s." PhD thesis, University of Toronto.

Leavitt, K. 2018. "Abdoul Abdi and the Nova Scotia Home for Colored Children". *The Coast*, January 25. Retrieved from https://www.thecoast.ca/halifax/abdoul-abdi-and-the-nova-scotia-home-for-colored-children/Content?oid=12258639.

Leroy, J. 2016. "Black History in Occupied Territory: On the Entanglements of Slavery and Settler Colonialism." *Theory and Event* 19 (4). Retrieved from https://muse.jhu.edu/article/633276

Lethabo-King, T. 2016. "New World Grammars: The 'Unthought' Black Discourses of Conquest". *Theory and Event*, 19:4. Retrieved from https://muse.jhu.edu/article/633275.

Macklin, A. 2006. "Exile on Main Street: Popular Discourse and Legal Manoeuvres around Citizenship." In *Law and Citizenship*, edited by Law Commission of Canada, 22–54. Vancouver, Toronto: UBC Press.

Manuel, G., and M. Posluns. 1974. *The Fourth World: An Indian Reality*. Toronto: Collier-Macmillan.

Massa, G. 2018. "Lawyer Says System Puts Some Canadian Foster Kids at Risk of Deportation". *CityNews*, January 10. Retrieved from https://toronto.citynews.ca/2018/01/09/some-canadian-foster-kids-at-risk-of-deportation/.

Maynard, R. 2017. *Policing Black Laves: State Violence in Canada from Slavery to the Present*. Winnipeg: Fernwood Publishing.

Mochama, V. 2017. "Deportation of Refugee One More Hostility Inflicted by Canada". *The Star*, December 7. Retrieved from https://www.thestar.com/opinion/star-columnists/2017/12/07/deportation-of-refugee-one-more-hostility-inflicted-by-canada.html.

Moffette, D., and S. Vadasaria. 2016. "Uninhibited Violence: Race and the Securitization of Immigration." *Critical Studies on Security* 4 (3): 305–391. doi:10.1080/21624887.2016.1256365.

Molnar, P., and S. Silverman. 2016. "Cracks Where the Light Gets In: Recent Breakthroughs in Detention and Crimmigration in Canada." *Metropolitics.eu*. Retrieved from https://metropolitics.org/IMG/pdf/met-molnar-silverman.pdf

Monaghan, J. 2013. "Settler Governmentality and Racializing Surveillance in Canada's North-West." *Canadian Journal of Sociology* 38 (4): 487–508. doi:10.29173/cjs21195.

Morgensen, S. L. 2014. "White Settlers and Indigenous Solidarity: Confronting White Supremacy, Answering Decolonial Alliances". *Decolonization: Indigineity, Education and Society* 26 May 2014. https://decolonization.wordpress.com/2014/05/26/white-settlers-and-indigenous-solidarity-confronting-white-supremacy-answering-decolonial-alliances/.

Napoleon, V. 2001. "Extinction by Number: Colonialism Made Easy." *Canadian Journal of Law & Society/La Revue Canadienne Droit Et Société* 16 (1): 113–145. doi:10.1017/S0829320100006608.

Nath, N. 2016. "Far from Belonging: Race, Security, Dissent and the Canadian Citizenship Story after 9/11." PhD thesis, University of Alberta.

Nath, N. 2018. "Missing Dissident Citizens: The Securitization of Resistance." Paper presented at the Annual Meetings of the Canadian Political Science Association. University of Regina, Regina, Saskatchewan.

Neocleous, N. 2006. "The Problem with Normality: Taking Exception to 'Permanent Emergency." *Alternatives: Global, Local, Political* 31 (2): 191–213. doi:10.1177/030437540603100204.

Nethery, A., and S. J. Silverman. 2018. “Why Try to Deport a Man in Canada since Childhood? U of T Expert Looks at the Case of Abdoul Abdi”. *UofT News*, March 14. Retrieved from https://www.utoronto.ca/news/why-try-deport-man-canada-childhood-u-t-expert-looks-case-abdoul-abdi.

Nichols, R. 2018. “Theft Is Property! the Recursive Logic of Dispossession.” *Political Theory* 46 (1): 3–28. doi:10.1177/0090591717701709.

Nyers, P. 2019. *Irregular Citizenship, Immigration, and Deportation*. London and New York: Routledge.

Ontario Council of Agencies Services Immigrants (OCASI). 2016. “Somali Refugee Resettlement in Canada.” Paper presented at the Metropolis Conference in Toronto. Retrieved from http://ocasi.org/sites/default/files/OCASI_Presentation_Somali_Resettlement_Metropolis_2016.pdf.

Ontario Human Rights Commission. 2018. *Interrupted Childhoods: Over-representation of Indigenous and Black Children in Ontario Child Welfare*. Retrieved from http://www3.ohrc.on.ca/sites/default/files/Interrupted%20childhoods_Over-representation%20of%20Indigenous%20and%20Black%20children%20in%20Ontario%20child%20welfare_accessible.pdf

Oriola, T. 2009. “Counter-terrorism and Alien Justice: The Case of Security Certificates in Canada.” *Critical Studies on Terrorism* 2 (2): 257–274. doi:10.1080/17539150903010764.

Pasternak, S. 2015. “The Fiscal Body of Sovereignty: To ‘Make Live’ in Indian Country.” *Settler Colonial Studies* 6 (4): 317–338. doi:10.1080/2201473X.2015.1090525.

Patel, S., G. Moussa, and N. Upadhyay. 2015. “Complicities, Connections, & Struggles: Critical Transnational Feminist Analysis of Settler Colonialism.„ *Feral Feminisms* 4: 5–19.

Razack, S. H. 2007. “‘Your Client Has a Profile’: Race and National Security after 9/11.” *Studies in Law, Politics, and Society* 40: 3–40.

Sassen, S. 2014. *Expulsions: Brutality and Complexity in the Global Economy*. Cambridge, MA: Harvard University Press.

Schumaker, K. 2012. “An Exploration of the Relationship between Poverty and Child Neglect in Canadian Child Welfare.” PhD thesis, University of Toronto.

Simpson, A. 2016. “The State Is a Man: Theresa Spence, Loretta Saunders and the Gender of Settler Sovereignty.” *Theory & Event 19* (4).

Simpson, B., Leanne. 2015. “The Mistery of Settler Colonialism: Roundtable on Glen Coulthard’s Red Skin, White Masks and Audra Simpson’s Mohawk Interruptus”. October 8. Retrieved from https://www.leannesimpson.ca/writings/the-misery-of-settler-colonialism-roundtable-on-glen-coulthards-red-skin-white-masks-and-audra-simpsons-mohawk-interruptus.

Smith, A. 2006. “Heteropatriarchy and the Three Pillars of White Supremacy: Rethinking Women of Color Organizing.” In *Color of violence: the INCITE! Anthology*, edited by INCITE! Women of Color Against Violences, 66-73. Cambridge, MA: South End Press.

Smith, A. 2014. “Foreward.” In *Undoing Border Imperialism. By Harsha Walia*, ix–ixxx. Oakland: AK Press/Institute for Anarchist Studies.

Smith, K. D. 2009. *Liberalism, Surveillance and Resistance: Indigenous Communities in Western Canada, 1877-1927*. Edmonton: AU Press.

Srivastava, S. 2005. “‘You’re Calling Me a Racist?’ the Moral and Emotional Regulation of Antiracism and Feminism.” *Signs* 31 (1): 29–62. doi:10.1086/432738.

Stanley, A., S. Arat-Koç, L. K. Bertram, and H. King. 2014. “Intervention–‘Addressing the Indigenous-immigration “Parallax Gap”’.” *Antipode Foundation*. Retrieved from https://antipodeonline.org/2014/06/18/addressing-the-indigenous-immigration-parallax-gap/

Stumpf, J. 2006. “The Crimmigration Crisis: Immigrants, Crime, and Sovereign Power.” *Am. UL Rev* 56: 367.

Taylor, W. 2015. *Nova Scotia Home for Colored Children: The Hurt, the Hope and the Healing*. Halifax: Nimbus Publishing.

Thobani, S. 2007. *Exalted Subjects: Studies in the Making of Race and Nation in Canada*. Toronto: University of Toronto Press.

Tuck, E. 2009. “Suspending Damage: A Letter to Communities.” *Harvard Education Review* 79 (3): 409–427. doi:10.17763/haer.79.3.n0016675661t3n15.

Tuck, E., and R. A. Gaztambide-Fernámdez. 2013. "Curriculum, Replacement, and Settler Futurity." *Journal of Curriculum Theorizing* 29 (1): 72–89.
Williams, M. 2018. "How Canada's Child Welfare System Fails Refugees like Abdoul Abid". *Maclean's*, July 17. Retrieved from https://www.macleans.ca/opinion/how-canadas-child-welfare-system-fails-refugees-like-abdoul-abdi/.
Zilio, M. 2013. "Deportee Says He Was Smuggled in Disguise through Mogadishu Airport". *iPolitics*, January 18. Retrieved from https://ipolitics.ca/2013/01/18/deportee-says-he-was-smuggled-in-disguisethrough-mogadishu-airport/.

Index

For Product Safety Concerns and Information please contact our EU
representative GPSR@taylorandfrancis.com
Taylor & Francis Verlag GmbH, Kaufingerstraße 24, 80331 München, Germany

www.ingramcontent.com/pod-product-compliance
Ingram Content Group UK Ltd.
Pitfield, Milton Keynes, MK11 3LW, UK
UKHW050054200926
475702UK00019B/2836
* 9 7 8 1 0 3 2 1 9 7 9 0 6 *